THE QUEEN AND I

Peter

me ke aloha

THE QUEEN AND I

A STORY OF DISPOSSESSIONS
AND RECONNECTIONS IN HAWAI'I

Sydney Lehua Iaukea

UNIVERSITY OF CALIFORNIA PRESS

Berkeley   Los Angeles   London

University of California Press, one of the most distinguished
university presses in the United States, enriches lives around
the world by advancing scholarship in the humanities, social
sciences, and natural sciences. Its activities are supported by
the UC Press Foundation and by philanthropic contributions
from individuals and institutions. For more information, visit
www.ucpress.edu.

University of California Press
Berkeley and Los Angeles, California

University of California Press, Ltd.
London, England

Library of Congress Cataloging-in-Publication Data

Iaukea, Sydney L. (Sydney Lehua), 1969-.
    The queen and I / Sydney L. Iaukea.
        p.   cm.
Includes extensive passages from an unpublished work
by Curtis Piʻehu ʻIaukea.
    Includes bibliographical references and index.
        ISBN 978-0-520-27066-4 (cloth : alk. paper)
        ISBN 978-0-520-27204-0 (pbk. : alk. paper)
    1. Hawaii—History—1900–1949.   2. Hawaii—
History—1893–1900.   3. Hawaii—Annexation to the
United States.   4. Hawaiians—Government relations.
5. Hawaiians—Land tenure.   6. ʻIaukea, Curtis Piʻehu,
1855–1940.   7. Liliʻuokalani, Queen of Hawaiʻi, 1838–1917—
Friends and associates.   I. ʻIaukea, Curtis Piʻehu, 1855–
1940.   II. Title.
DU627.5.I38   2012
996.9'02092-dc22   2011001970
[B]

Manufactured in the United States of America

20   19   18   17   16   15   14   13   12   11
10   9   8   7   6   5   4   3   2   1

In keeping with its commitment to support environmentally
responsible and sustainable printing practices, UC Press has
printed this book on 50# Enterprise, a 30% post consumer
waste, recycled, de-inked fiber and processed chlorine free. It
is acid-free, and meets all ANSI/NISO (z 39.48) requirements.

For my mother and sister,
Liâne Patricia Carmen Iaukea and Lesley Kehaunani Iaukea

CONTENTS

ILLUSTRATIONS

ACKNOWLEDGMENTS

This book is dedicated to my mother, Liâne P. C. Iaukea, and to my sister, Lesley Iaukea. We embarked on this journey through our family history together, and we've come out of it with a greater appreciation of our own resilience, amidst forces that would see us as smaller than we really are.

This book is written in honor of my *kūpuna, 'aumakua, akua, a me nā Ali'i. Mahalo nui* for leading me back and for allowing me to tell your stories. I honor your *mana* and stand in awe of the grand experiences and the depths of character that your narratives reveal.

I want to acknowledge my dissertation committee: Chair Michael J. Shapiro, Phyllis Turnbull, Kanalu Young, Kathy Ferguson, and Brian Murton—mentors who allowed me to write the dissertation that I wanted to. I acknowledge the financial support I received as a longtime scholarship recipient of The Kamehameha Schools, as an 'Ōiwi Dissertation Fellow, and as a Mellon-Hawai'i Postdoctoral Fellow; and I wish to acknowledge Matt Hamabata, the staff, and the Advisory Council at The Kohala Center; The Kahiau Foundation; The Andrew W. Mellon Foundation; and the Hawai'i Council for the Humanities.

Thank you to Niels Hooper, editor at the University of California Press, for your support of this project. I am also appreciative of Cindy Fulton and Marian Rogers of the University of California Press. *Mahalo nui* to Craig Howes for the careful editing of this manuscript and the moral support given throughout the book-writing process; to Luella Kurkjian at the Hawai'i State Archives for helping me uncover my ancestor's documents; and to Ted Wong at the Bureau of Conveyances for his patient support during the research stage. A special heartfelt thank you to Team Sydney—those individuals who emotionally and energetically support and sustain me. Other important individuals to me are Geoff Alm, Chris Angell, Kim Kiʻili, Leslie Kuloloio, Eddie Rothman, Jon Osorio, and Michael Jay Green.

To my surfing and paddling communities, the Suis and Silvas morning crews, and other lifelong friends—I am appreciative of the deep friendships, the laugh-out-loud camaraderie, and the untold amount of love and support shared over the years. Finally, along with Suis and Silvas, *mahalo* to the places where I feel at home and where I find connections to myself: Haapiti, Pavones, Rice Bowls, Velzyland, Black Point, and Hoʻokipa.

Introduction

Insanity runs through my family—insanity driven by the manipulation and control of private property, as family members work against one another. Insidious in its influence, private property shadows and shapes my family's history and contemporary existence. The hiding of land goes back generations. Among many other things, this is a story of that manipulation through my eyes. I embody all that went before, and I bring forth that narrative here. But this is not the entire story, because private property is not the definer of a genealogy that goes back to the beginning.

For Hawaiians, land, identity, and *moʻo kūʻauhau* (genealogy) were all impacted by the illegal overthrow of the Hawaiian Kingdom in 1893 and the subsequent occupation of Hawaiʻi by the United States. Shifting sociopolitical structures and combative personal relationships one hundred years ago affected how *ka ʻāina* (the land—literally, "that which feeds") was understood and how private property was divided. How *nā kūpuna* (our ancestors) navigated their political and emotional terrains still influences both our connection and disconnection with this place today, because their memory echoes in our actions. Here then is a story of the consequences of this influence, based on archival research and as relayed directly by my great-great-grandfather, Curtis Piehu Iaukea, who lived through the upheavals and now bridges the gaps of understanding by bringing the story of *nā aliʻi* (kings, queens, chiefs) to the forefront.

The necessary but brief historical highlights are as follows. On January 17, 1893, a group of members of the white business elite, many of whom also served in the legislature, overthrew the Hawaiian Kingdom government and its

FIGURE 1. Queen Liliʻuokalani, 1880s. Hawaiʻi State Archives.

reigning sovereign, Queen Liliʻuokalani (figs. 1 and 2). This illegal overthrow was led by attorney Lorrin A. Thurston; more importantly, it was made possible by the support of U.S. foreign minister John L. Stevens and the U.S. Marines aboard the USS *Boston*. Once in power, a Committee of Public Safety renamed the government the Republic of Hawaiʻi and set about trying to annex Hawaiʻi to the United States as a territory to assure the continued flow of Hawaiʻi's sugar to the United States tariff free. A treaty of annexation never

FIGURE 2. Queen Lili'uokalani, 1890s. Hawai'i State Archives.

passed. Instead, in 1898 President McKinley signed into law a joint resolution, passed only as an internal bill in both houses of the U.S. Congress, and not voted on in Hawai'i, which was already internationally recognized as a sovereign and independent state. This joint resolution made Hawai'i a territorial outpost of the United States, which occupied it as a staging ground for U.S. troops fighting the Spanish-American War in the Philippines.

The official rhetoric of this time, which can still be heard today, was that although the illegal overthrow was (perhaps) an unfortunate event, the political status of Hawai'i changed seamlessly from monarchy to republic to territory to state of the United States. But this smooth metamorphosis never occurred except in the fantasies of certain government officials. In fact, for the first half of the twentieth century, an oligarchy sat in power over every aspect of the political, economic, and social life in Hawai'i, and firmly ruled the territorial government. As part of their mission of remaking Hawaiian Kingdom subjects into U.S. citizens, they followed agendas that rewrote the *ali'i* national terrain, with the geography undergoing further massive changes that mirrored the desired status quo. The era of the Territory of Hawai'i (1900–1959) was also marked by a historical silencing. Outside of an allegiance to the occupying government, the collective memory of this era has been suppressed.

Queen Lili'uokalani was the physical and spiritual link for the Hawaiian people to an entire Hawaiian epistemology. Portions of Queen Lili'uokalani's life and legacy are documented here, and especially the unending attacks against her personhood, her kingdom, and her personal properties in her later years, which did not end with her death in 1917. Inseparable from her struggle, and from Hawai'i's struggle one hundred years ago, were often violent reorientations of various public and private spaces. How was this transition envisioned, articulated, and enacted? Who were the various actors responsible? And how do we still simultaneously struggle and coexist as both subjects and subjugated in these spaces? Or more generally, how have resistance, complicity, and desire shaped and reshaped our history and society?

Eight years ago I wanted to know something about my genealogy, so I began a search through the written records. Curtis Piehu Iaukea, my great-great-grandfather (fig. 3), was an internationally known, locally celebrated, and very active official in the Hawaiian Kingdom and in the territorial government. In his lifetime, he held over forty political positions. As Hawai'i's foreign diplomat in search of sugar plantation laborers in the 1880s, he was the second Hawaiian official to circumnavigate the globe, and he represented Hawai'i at some historically celebrated moments, such as the coronation of Czar Alexander III in Russia in 1881 and Queen Victoria's Golden Jubilee in England in 1887.

At home, he was the commissioner of Crown Lands, subagent of "Public Lands," Queen Lili'uokalani's business agent, and one of the first trustees of her estate. In the territorial government, he was appointed the secretary of

FIGURE 3. Curtis P. Iaukea in dress uniform, 1880s. Hawaiʻi State Archives.

Hawai'i by U.S. president Woodrow Wilson, he was the acting governor at one point, and he was a leader in Hawai'i's emerging Democratic Party.[1] Upon his death in 1940, American flags at the federal buildings and courts in Hawai'i flew at half-mast in his honor, and he was given a funeral procession that rivaled that of any political leader in any state. He lived an unprecedented, historically vibrant, and very active life.

It was also a life about which I knew virtually nothing before beginning my research. I have lived most of my life without knowing about this Curtis P. Iaukea, and therefore, without ever really knowing my mo'o kū'auhau. Besides the résumé then, just who was Curtis P. Iaukea? And how does he relate to who I am today? I am also descended from ship's pilot James (Jemmy) Darrell, my great-great-great-great-grandfather on my mother's side, who is recognized as the first black freed slave in Bermuda to own private property. My great-great-grandmother's father was Fred L. Hanks, a sailor in the Pacific who recorded some of the important early state relations between Japan and the United States in the 1840s, and who also came from the same family as Nancy Hanks, mother of Abraham Lincoln. And both my paternal lineages track my genealogy back over sixty generations to Papa and Wākea (Earth Mother and Sky Father) from the Kumulipo, the famous Hawaiian creation chant. In a document housed at the Hawai'i State Archives, a handwritten account of the sixty generations of names exists, both the maternal and paternal paired names of those who preceded Curtis P. Iaukea, back to the source. I am a product of all of these lineages and hereditary connections, but again this is all relatively new to me, since neither our history books nor exchanges among members of my family provide much information on any of these connections.

I therefore came to know Curtis P. Iaukea through my research. The branch chief for historical records recognized my last name as indicating Curtis P. Iaukea's direct descendant, and told me about the boxes and boxes of unpublished and unprocessed Iaukea material that was sitting in the basement of the Hawai'i State Archives. Here my great-great-grandfather's story, the story of my family and therefore myself, and the historical narrative of Hawai'i as he understood it, are laid bare. As I was recovering my own ancestral memory, I realized Curtis P. Iaukea had preserved a larger memory that he obviously wanted to be made public. His documents include chapters for a book, diaries, letters, and official correspondence—much of which was put in the archives by himself when he was a board member, but has been waiting for discovery for nearly three-quarters of a century.

Curtis P. Iaukea provides a view into Hawaiʻi that is all but nonexistent in history books and in collective Hawaiian memory, because he writes from his personal experience of the time, the place, and the key personal relationships that affected so much in this era. He writes intimately about such land legislation as the Hawaiian Homes Commission Act (1921) and the Waikīkī Reclamation Project (1928). He also documents the Crown Lands congressional fight between Queen Liliʻuokalani and the U.S. government (1909), the formation of Queen Liliʻuokalani's trust deed (1909), and the bill of complaint (1915) filed by Prince Kūhiō, which charged the Queen with mental incompetence because he wanted two sections of her private property in fee simple. Enormous in scope and significance, this last case had personal and public implications for Curtis P. Iaukea because of his intimate involvement, as he willingly recorded the personal aftermath of the illegal overthrow for prominent Hawaiians.

I begin every chapter with a substantial portion of Curtis P. Iaukea's unpublished chapters, and I also include long portions of the primary documents so that the actors present at the time can have their voices heard. My task of remembering and filling in the gaps of the historical narrative can be carried out only with the aid of their writings, and for this reason each chapter foregrounds these primary sources. They document aggressive and often violent attacks upon Hawaiian notions of ʻāina and ʻohana (family) as part of a strategy to impose capitalist, race-based principles on the population. But Curtis P. Iaukea's writings also display Hawaiian political agency and legal acumen. Hawaiians had an effect on territorial land laws and ordinances because our kūpuna (ancestors) were often active participants in the legal and socioeconomic discourses of the time. Curtis P. Iaukea and many other Hawaiian writers and government officials did not simply accept complete subjugation to U.S. political dominance in Hawaiʻi, nor did they view themselves in passive terms, even when the territorial government sought to dominate both the people and the place, further complicating Hawaiian agency. A reading of the harsh but navigable political realities that our kūpuna encountered complicates the historical narrative in Hawaiʻi.

I also at various times include my own moʻolelo (story), because to a native researcher, history and land here are personal. As Hawaiians, our identity and sense of knowing come directly from relating to ka ʻāina (the land) and ke kai (the sea). A hundred years ago and today, we are connected to land and deeply affected by its loss, because ka ʻāina is our older sibling, part of our genealogical makeup, and the entity that connects us to all that is—including *nā akua* (gods, goddesses), *aliʻi,* and one another. Since we cannot be separated from this entity, this *ʻāina,* in our very being, we experience an acute sense of loss of ourselves when we are separated from this entity in our day-to-day lives. To recognize the loss of land as the loss of self is an enormous and very personal endeavor, one that makes historical occurrences very real.

What happens when the continuity is broken because of family alliances and/or geopolitical events? We are currently engaged in yet more legal battles as we search to reconnect ourselves epistemologically and ontologically to *ka ʻāina,* and try to understand our own genealogy in the process. Land embodies larger social and political orders, because our personal histories and awareness of personal identities come from our sense of place. The heartache of the separation that has resulted from land displacement over the last one hundred years is understandable and resonates in the texts presented here. But it is also important to understand that a total severing is impossible—as impossible as severing ourselves from our genetic makeup.

Not surprisingly, growing up without private property made me question my own connection to *ka ʻāina.* I grew up on Maui in the projects—dispossessed, disconnected, and displaced. This is my Hawaiʻi, and this is also my family history. Coming from a well-known family in Hawaiʻi silenced me. If I speak the truth, what will others think? My father, Curtis P. Iaukea III, was a former professional wrestler and a local celebrity in Hawaiʻi and elsewhere. Many still remember his wrestling matches, and the showmanship and wrestling character he embodied. He also left us without monetary or familial support, but I was left speechless because of the larger-than-life image my father so masterfully displayed. Though I mention him here, people looking for a book about his wrestling career or his public persona will not find it. This is instead a narrative about how I have been affected by being born into this genealogy.

Among other things, the first Curtis P. Iaukea therefore is also the starting point for this study. I discovered that in 1904 my great-great-grandfather owned approximately 500 acres of land on the island of Oʻahu. King Kalākaua deeded him 455 acres of this land in Kamanaiki Valley, Kalihi, but this portion left Curtis P. Iaukea's possession in the early 1900s. I have yet to find the land deed that transferred this title. A much smaller piece of property, the Lele of Hamohamo, almost eight acres of land in Waikīkī that Queen Liliʻuokalani left to my *kupuna,* provided the key to much greater understandings. In researching this land, I learned that my great-great-grandmother, Charlotte

FIGURE 4. Charlotte Kahaloipua Hanks Iaukea. Hawaiʻi State Archives.

Kahaloipua Hanks Iaukea (fig. 4), owned over seventeen acres of the properties adjoining the Lele of Hamohamo, called Hooulu and Lei Hooulu.

The Lele of Hamohamo was promptly condemned by the territorial government after the title was transferred to Curtis P. Iaukea, and sections of these
other properties were also condemned for the building of the Ala Wai Canal.
But a large amount of this land was known in the 1940s and 1950s as the Iaukea
Estate Land, and was sold off by the benefactors of Charlotte Iaukea's trust

deed. This area today includes the subdivison of Date Street between Kapa-hulu Avenue and Kaimukī High School, just *mauka* (toward the mountains) of Waikīkī. This is where other members of my family have profited greatly. Over the years, very little of the land that remained passed from one genera-tion to the next, and whatever property did pass through the line of successors is kept secret, while still more land was purchased with these proceeds, and is hidden from family members by other family members today. What remains is therefore scarred by recriminations concerning an open secret.

My story is part of the larger story of land and dispossession in Hawaiʻi. I will argue here that the personal, everyday, and ordinary are inextricably linked to the larger social, political, and geographic realms, and therefore a reading and understanding of one is a reading and understanding of the other. There is no separation, and so no need for silence. The unarticulated and perplexing pain in my family's life is, I surmise, present in the lives of many other Hawai-ian families. Fighting over land is not uncommon for us. What is uncommon is the willingness to talk about it. And I have found that the more I uncover, the more I can understand and express my emotions, the closer I return to my own *moʻo kūʻauhau,* and the more appreciation and compassion I surprisingly feel for my own family today. All were influenced by what came before us.

I tell these personal and collective narratives knowing it is my *kuleana* (responsibility) to do so, and also knowing that when I need assistance, all I have to do is ask. We are never so far distant from our *moʻo kūʻauhau* as we have been led to believe, for that space is always available to us. For me, that place is in the ocean. When I'm happy and everything makes sense, I go to the ocean. When I'm upset and things seem insurmountable, I go to the ocean. So it's no wonder that much of this book took its shape as my self and being were captured in those precious moments, hours, days, and years spent surf-ing and reflecting, surfing and being, surfing and enjoying, and sometimes just surfing—connecting with the extension of land to the sea in personal ways.

Here is the story of my great-great-grandfather's documents. In 1937, Cur-tis P. Iaukea commissioned Jeanne Hobbs, a writer and researcher, to help him write his book. The trail of correspondence shows that he was not happy with her "breaching of (her) contract and not completing his memoirs," and his attorneys took her to court to have his personal papers returned.[2] He died in 1940, with Jeanne Hobbs still in possession of these papers and refusing to return them.

In 1941, Curtis P. Iaukea's daughter, Lorna Kahilipuaokalani Iaukea Watson,

FIGURE 5. Curtis P. Iaukea in Hawaiian Kingdom dress uniform, 1930s. Hawaiʻi State Archives.

my great-aunt, had a dream.[3] In her dream, Lorna walked into her father's study, where he was standing on a stepladder in front of shelves of books with arms stretched upward. When he saw her, he exclaimed, "Oh, I'm so glad you've come—I can't hold up these books any longer!" Lorna had also worked with her father to complete his memoirs, and after this dream she knew that

FIGURE 6. Curtis P. Iaukea with his ceremonial horn, 1930s. Hawai'i State Archives.

she should try to retrieve her father's missing papers from Jeanne Hobbs. She fought for their return, and in 1953, after Hobbs died, the lawyers finally consented. Lorna then prepared for publication parts of her father's collection dealing with his childhood and early adulthood memories in the book *By Royal Command*.[4]

I have felt similarly guided and compelled to research and make public his writings as my great-aunt did, knowing that my responsibility lies in presenting these papers as my *kupuna* would have wanted. The words of Curtis P. Iaukea that are shared here are from the later years of his life (see figs. 5 and 6), and I share only diary notes that were also accompanied by his chapters. I can only hope that my great-great-grandfather feels even more relief as more of his words are shared with the larger community. I also hope his words and those of others aid in the general healing of the collective, because the knowing of such truths could allow for more understanding and more compassion, both for the individuals involved and for the complicated societal landscapes we have inherited.

CHAPTER I

Family Secrets and Cartographic Silences

Chatty Maps and Memory

For memory to function well, it needs constant practice.

—Milan Kundera

Land, body, and memory all inform one another. The land, extending out and into the ocean, holds the practical and epistemological memories of encounters. The body is the agent, the participant in the environment, and the container of memories. For Hawaiians in the past, vital information was relayed through the environment, and this memory of *ka ʻāina* (the land; that which feeds) affected close interpersonal relationships and societal structures. Vestiges of that connection to *ka ʻāina* still exist in places and still hold valuable information about who we are. The dynamics and evolution of land, body, and memory can be glimpsed in the land tenure documents and in the personal stories that accompanied the exchanges of private property. I search and wonder at the connections, then and now, of land and ocean, body, and memory.

I found the following narrative about the Lele of Hamohamo at the Hawaiʻi State Archives eight years ago. I was there researching my last name, and when I found this handwritten chapter by my great-great-grandfather, Curtis Piehu Iaukea, I had only a glimmer of a clue as to what he was talking about. I had only just recently found the map to this property at the Bureau of Conveyances in Honolulu, but had not yet uncovered the Kalanianaʻole suit he refers to from the Circuit Court (Oʻahu First Circuit). This narrative and others like it helped me piece together and gain insight into the larger story of the political transfer of land in general from Hawaiian Kingdom sovereign territory to the Territory of Hawaiʻi, the story of Curtis Piehu Iaukea, and finally my own personal narrative. The three stories collide but intimately inform one another, and they do so because of my great-great-grandfather's recorded memory of land—how it was transferred, who transferred it, and what the continuing consequences of these transactions are a century later. Memory fills in the *moʻo kūʻauhau* (genealogy) in practical and more fundamental ways. The Lele of Hamohamo starts and ends this book because it is a microcosm of how I have come to understand myself, my *kūpuna* (ancestors), and my community.

The "Lele of Hamohamo" and the Attempt to Deprive Of It
Whilst the Kalanianaole suit was still pending and to my surprise and astonish-
ment, Mr. W.O. Smith showed me a letter which the Queen had sent him a day or
two before. The letter was dated February 13, 1912, and read as follows:
"I find I have devised to Mr. C.P. Iaukea a certain lot in Hamohamo, to his
heirs and assigns forever. It was not my intention that he should have the benefit of
it forever, and as you know I have devised my other beneficiaries their portions for
their life and their heirs, failing which the property should revert back to my trust-
ees. It is now my purpose to revoke that and revert the property back to the trust."
Having all the earmarks of one whom I had good reason to believe had written
the letter, whose name I'd rather not mention, I had no hesitation in saying so, when
asked by my colleagues on the board of trustees what I thought of the Queen's propo-
sition. Convinced as I was that it was not the Queen's wish, I said to them that if they
wanted to consent to the request by an amendment to the deed of trust, they could do
so, but that I would not be a party to it. It would be a sign of weakness, I said, and
might affect our side of the case when the Kalanianaole suit comes up for trial, as
showing that the Queen was mentally unsound at the time she signed the deed of trust.
I further called Mr. Smith and Mr. Damon's attention to the fact that, on the
two occasions when the draft of the trust deed and the deed itself were read to the
Queen, the difference in tenure between the other beneficiaries and mine was referred
to; the Queen distinctly saying in the presence of those who were then there with her
at the time, myself included, "I wish it so; Mr. Iaukea has done a great deal for me."
What I said impressed them. I heard nothing further in the matter until a day or
two later when Mr. Smith reported that, he had interviewed the Queen on two sepa-
rate occasions; when the Queen said to him, "We will consider it further; put it off."
And on the next visit, "Oh, let that go, We won't follow that any further." Mr. Smith
leaving her with the impression that she wished nothing further done about the matter.

Closing another chapter of the many intricacies and machinations that surround court life which I have experienced in the course of a lifetime, Liliuokalani's being no exception to the rule.

Speaking of the tract of land in question, Queen Liliuokalani devised to me, known as the "Lele of Hamohamo," situate at Waikiki waena, a quarter of a mile away from the main tract known as the "Ili of Hamohamo," it contained some seven acres, a little more or less. Rice land, and under lease at $200 a year rental. I did not come into possession of the land until eight years had passed with the Queen's death in September of 1917 and when I did it was encumbered by a lease to a Mr. H.A. Heen for some years to run at the same rental of $200 per annum, the prevailing rental for rice lands in those days, of between $25.00 and $30.00 per acre. So that, it wasn't the magnificent gift as many have erroneously claimed, when the services I had rendered the grantor is taken into consideration. It wasn't very long after I had obtained the fee to the land under the provisions of the trust deed, when I turned the whole tract over to my wife, who owned in her own right some fifteen acres adjoining the "Lele of Hamohamo" on the Diamond Head side and next the Fair Grounds.[1]

The Lele of Hamohamo. *Lele* translates as "jump" in Hawaiian land tenure discourse. It is a section of land in a different part of the *ahupua'a* (land division with districts running from the mountains to the sea) that contains either taro or forestland for that *ahupua'a*.[2] As for the phrase "the Attempt to Deprive of It" in the title, it strongly resonated with me. I readied myself for the story about to unfold.

I know that name Lele—it's what I once called my sister when we were younger, because "Lesley" was too hard to say. I may have always known that Lele was part and parcel of my family, of our interfamilial interactions, and of our larger social histories. I was impressed when I first saw the map of this property. Almost eight acres, and in such a prominent location: right there in the middle of what was once the larger Waikīkī area, surrounded by and containing duck ponds, *lo'i* (taro) and rice fields. Lēʻahi (Diamond Head) stood on one side, and the ocean was off to the other. Two rivers ran alongside, and two *ahupua'a* converge in that place. So much history here. So much *mana* (power) in the landscape.

The *mana* remains but is buried under schools, homes, and parking lots and is layered over with multiple social articulations—the result of the last one hundred years of history in Hawai'i. Pulling away some of these layers uncovers parts of my family's history and reveals the larger consequences of capitalism, land dispossession, secrecy, and manipulation both then and now.

My great-great-grandfather describes a contest over this property early on in our family's and Hawai'i's modern history. But no one ever told me about the Lele of Hamohamo. The intrigue surrounding the title to this property first appeared to me in the unpublished chapters of my great-great-grandfather's writings, which I read with curiosity driven by some deep, personal anxiety. Other family members know about this property, and the connecting property Hooulu, intimately. Some in the family are completely aware of these properties—in fact, they have profited greatly from this land, providing themselves with house lots, mansions, and private-school educations. But how much do they really know? And how much did they really profit? I was about to learn more.

I needed to pinpoint exactly where the Lele of Hamohamo was located. Then would come the more difficult tasks of deciphering how this specific land deed figured in the larger mystery of the Queen Lili'uokalani's deed of trust proceedings in 1909, of understanding the suit brought against her in 1915 by Prince Kūhiō with the "insanity trials," and of tracking the government's condemnation of this property into the 1930s. My *kupuna* (ancestor) wrote about all of these land deals. His memory reveals how private property law in Hawai'i was used to disenfranchise and disassociate us individually and collectively from land, from our *mo'o kū'auhau* (genealogy), and from our *'ohana* (family). Territorial land laws in Hawai'i a century ago privileged and disempowered practical land ownership. They also undermined native connectivity through *'āina, mo'o kū'auhau,* and *'ohana.* We live with the consequences of these legal maneuverings today.

Searching through these documents took me on a journey into a mystery. I pulled on the threads of entanglements that never seemed to loosen. I looked for the virtual keys to this property, but each new discovery led me to more locked doors that needed to be opened. Along the way, familial and political relationships, some Machiavellian, were revealed to me. But at first, simply the land ownership itself sparked my interest and fed my desire to know. Who owned it? Who sold it? How did a Waikīkī fortune, if only a small piece of it, slip away from my mother, my little sister, and me?

I grew up on Maui without property. After my parents divorced, my father sold our farm in upcountry Maui. Most of our share of the proceeds, along with any child and spousal support, never materialized, and so my mother always worked a minimum of three jobs to provide for our survival. For the three of us, something in the social system became unhinged, and we lived landless. Growing up without legal title to land not only disconnected us from *ka ʻāina*, but also forced us into the low-income housing apartments in central Maui known as Harbor Lights. We lived in marginal and unsafe surroundings. I both questioned the fairness of this social reality, and later wondered about my own identity as a Hawaiian.

If as Hawaiians we know ourselves through our connection to *ka ʻāina*, what happens when this connection is broken, and never allowed to flourish? Who am I without this? How did this dispossession not only affect my practical needs, but also alienate me from deeper understandings of self, genealogy, and community? And finally, once this loss of self, experienced as loss of land, is recognized, how do I fill the void? Luckily *ke kai*, the ocean, was close by and free. We spent most of our lives swimming, paddling canoe, and surfing, and this welcoming expanse still provides me with a constant means of escape and a source of solace.

The severing of immediate family connections also served to disassociate me from my larger *ʻohana* and its narratives. I didn't know who the first Curtis Piehu Iaukea was. Our only glimpse of family history came from periodic ventures to Waikīkī on the island of Oʻahu, where we would look at the giant oil painting of Colonel Curtis Piehu Iaukea next to the escalators on the second floor at the Queen Kapiʻolani Hotel. We decided he must have done something important to deserve a full-size portrait of himself in a hotel in Waikīkī, but we didn't know what. Some years later, at the University of Hawaiʻi, I enrolled in a class on nineteenth-century Hawaiian history. The assigned reading included two books by and about Curtis P. Iaukea. Now my interest was piqued, because what I knew about both the man and the era amounted to almost nothing. Information about my father's side of the family had been nonexistent. Or had it been withheld?

Someone suggested that I research my last name. This intrigued me because I had thought that I knew all I needed to know about my family. For me, family consisted solely of my small nuclear family. The larger Iaukea family wasn't encountered or discussed much except when the holidays rolled around, and we were painfully reminded of them by their silent absence.

So I started by researching my last name at the Bureau of Conveyances—where the land tenure records of Hawaiʻi are kept. Within a very short time, what my research uncovered truly shocked me. My great-great-grandfather came to life—instead of simply appearing in an oil painting on a hotel wall, he appeared before me as a foreign diplomat of both the Hawaiian Kingdom and the Territory of Hawaiʻi, as an integral member of Hawaiian governance for more than seventy years, and as a property owner on almost every main island in the Hawaiian archipelago.

Questions of native subjectivity, especially with regard to land and private property, soon were driving my academic work, because the history of dispossession and social dislocation in Hawaiʻi is my own immediate family's history. I grew up landless, marginalized, and without a place or a voice in the contemporary world, but my great-great-grandfather held over forty appointed and elected positions during his career as a public servant in Hawaiʻi in the late 1800s and early 1900s.

He also clearly wanted the history of his times preserved. Toward the end of his life, Curtis P. Iaukea was a member of the Hawaiʻi State Archives Commission and a founding member of the Hawaiian Historical Society. The territorial government commissioned him as the "chief historian" of the islands, and in 1939 he wrote weekly columns for the *Honolulu Advertiser* about everything from his memories of growing up on Hawaiʻi Island and being called to Oʻahu to serve *Nā Aliʻi* to his official trips abroad as the representative of the Hawaiian Kingdom. Throughout his career, he was both a repository for and creator of state discourse, representing Hawaiʻi internationally, and later preserving Hawaiian memory after the islands had become socially and politically occupied and reconfigured as a territory of the United States.

My great-great-grandmother, Charlotte Kahaloipua Hanks Iaukea, was an *akamai* (knowledgeable) landowner and prominent social figure in her own right. From her ancestral line of Kahaloipua and Hanks, she inherited most of what is today Date Street, located off of Kapahulu Avenue in Waikīkī. Her paternal line through Frederick Leslie Hanks links her to the same family as Abraham Lincoln's mother, Nancy Hanks. Her maternal line, Kahaloipua, stems from Kekualaula and Keawaaua, high chiefs on the islands of Hawaiʻi and Oʻahu. Akini Wahinekapuokaahumanu was her mother. Charlotte also served as a lady-in-waiting, commissioned as a Knight Companion of the Royal Order of Kapiʻolani, to Queen Kapiʻolani and was a friend of Queen Liliʻuokalani.

This was all new to me, and this Curtis P. Iaukea seemed to be a strong, enigmatic, worldly, and all-knowing figure. But so many questions still came to mind, and I had my doubts about his integrity. My experience with others of his name did much to instill trepidation and caution, since these descendants are now living on acreages or benefiting from trusts passed down from

Curtis and Charlotte Iaukea, and have also knowingly cut us out of the familial loop, because my mother divorced my father due to his infidelity with someone who later became his fourth wife, one who could never bear to see us communicating in any sort of way with our father, and who would ultimately make sure that we were not allowed to attend his funeral. The interfamilial dynamics are still full of strife and emotional pain. The management of inheritance, land titles, and wealth is hidden. Knowledge is jealously guarded.

Private property continues to be a cause for division among family members today. My mother, my sister, and I were not invited to my grandfather's funeral, for what we can only guess had to do with the hiding of his assets. And make no mistake about it—attendance at a family funeral is by invitation only. My grandfather's wife, whom he married after my grandmother died and whom I have never met, kept the location of his funeral services a secret from us. The mortuary told us that we must check with the "family" to find out when the services would occur, but my grandfather's wife never returned our calls. My father and uncles also kept the location of the services secret. They inherited and now with my half brother closely control most of the remaining property that passed down from Charlotte and Curtis P. Iaukea.

The death of my father proved even more emotionally violent. My stepmother filed court papers to forbid my mother, my sister, and me from seeing our father on his deathbed. We fought these papers in court and won. However, by the time the court issues were settled, my father had died, which we found out about with everyone else on the evening news. My stepmother then hastily held my father's funeral service in private. We were deprived of saying our last good-byes, as were the legions of friends and wrestling fans who wanted to grieve this loss. Only a few family members were present, including a couple of half sisters, a half brother, along with a few stepmothers. How they justify their actions to themselves is a mystery to me, but ultimately, all that mattered is that we were on good terms with my father just before his death— regardless of the shadow that private property had cast over his life, and the chaotic relations that ran rampant up until his death.

This paranoia regarding geography continues to splinter my own genealogy by disrupting its continuity. Such a separation—driven by western notions of property and inheritance—is nonsensical in Hawaiian epistemology. This is a form of insanity, is it not? *Kānaka maoli* (Hawaiian people) are directly descended from *ka ʻāina*, and so forced separation from this entity represents a level of cultural violence that is unrecognizable within Hawaiian thought practices. Becoming cut off from *ka ʻāina* is more then a physical separation. Layers of connectivity are severed.

On the island of Oʻahu, Curtis and Charlotte Iaukea owned land in Waikīkī, Kalihi Valley, Waialua, and Nuʻuanu, totaling more than five hundred acres. By 1900, over four hundred acres of this land in Kamanaiki Valley, Kalihi, had simply disappeared from the land title books. Even though a Royal Patent in 1887 gave Curtis P. Iaukea fee-simple ownership to this land, nothing in his reminiscences even hints at his ownership. The transfer of title from his name does not appear in the official ledgers, and the land title folders that would hold such information are literally empty. This is one cartographic silence that remains in that empty folder. What I did find, however, was a large number of papers documenting the social relationships that affected the land held in fee simple by Curtis and Charlotte Iaukea in Waikīkī. And in this process, their agency as landowners became apparent.

By 1920, Curtis, with my great-great-grandmother Charlotte, owned over twenty-three acres in Waikīkī, including those eight acres referred to as the Lele of Hamohamo. Written in 1909 and upheld through court proceedings in 1915 and 1918, Queen Liliʻuokalani's trust deed speaks of this land as follows:

> Upon the death of the Grantor, the Trustees shall make, execute and deliver to Curtis P. Iaukea, of Honolulu, a deed conveying to him, absolutely and forever, (subject only to said mortgage if the same be not then discharged with respect thereto) all of the land and improvements thereon known as the *Lele of Hamohamo*, at Waikiki, adjoining his wife's land at Kaluaolohe, containing eight acres a little more or less.[3]

The map of the Lele of Hamohamo shows how this property was connected to Hooulu. Also known as Kaluaolohe, it is recorded as Land Grant 2615 and was owned by my great-great-grandmother, Charlotte K. Iaukea.[4] Another two-acre parcel, known as Lei Hooulu and granted to Akini, Charlotte Iaukea's mother, was also granted to Charlotte Iaukea and sits below Hooulu.

In the 1930s and 1940s, large portions of this area, once known as the Iaukea Estate Land and containing more than fifteen acres at the time of Charlotte Iaukea's death, were rapidly sold off by her trust company, the Bishop Trust Co. Some of the acreage was also condemned in accordance with the Waikīkī Reclamation Act for the building of the Ala Wai Canal. The Lele of Hamohamo was condemned in its entirety by the territorial government, resold, and became known as the Hamohamo Tract. In addition to this land condemnation, the beneficiaries of the Charlotte Kahaloipua Iaukea trust; Lorna, her

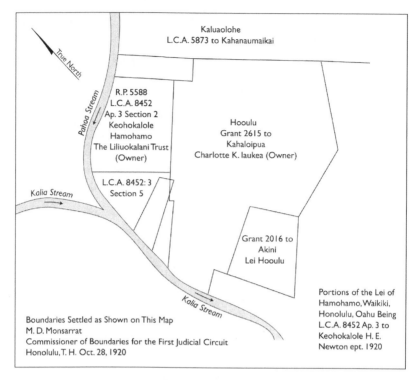

Kaluaolohe
L.C.A. 5873 to Kahanaumaikai

Pahoa Stream

R.P. 5588
L.C.A. 8452
Ap. 3 Section 2
Keohokalole
Hamohamo
The Liliuokalani Trust
(Owner)

Hooulu
Grant 2615 to
Kahaloipua
Charlotte K. Iaukea (Owner)

L.C.A. 8452: 3
Section 5

Kalia Stream

Grant 2016 to
Akini
Lei Hooulu

Kalia Stream

Boundaries Settled as Shown on This Map
M. D. Monsarrat
Commissioner of Boundaries for the First Judicial Circuit
Honolulu, T. H. Oct. 28, 1920

Portions of the Lei of
Hamohamo, Waikiki,
Honolulu, Oahu Being
L.C.A. 8452 Ap. 3 to
Keohokalole H. E.
Newton ept. 1920

True North

Lele of Hamohamo, Hooulu, and Lei Hooulu, October 1920.

daughter; and my grandfather Curtis P. Iaukea II and his brother Frederick were the benefactors of numerous land deeds and became the landlords of the remainder of the land not sold. My father, his son, and my father's brothers then sold and bought more land and today hold title to property across the state. As a descendant, I am both saddened by the condemnation, and overwhelmed that members of my own family would sell virtually an entire subdivision, while still keeping secret both the ownership of this land and all of the monetary proceeds. Upon this land today sit low-rise apartment buildings, schools, and more people crammed into these spaces than imaginable.

None of the architectural and personal intricacies appear on the map. This map, and others like it, represent and track the contractual arrangements of land title transfers. They do not record the *reasons* for property exchanges and ownerships, for geographic gains and losses, or for the actions of people involved in the legal transfers of land. These deeper readings are beyond the scope of the map, and therefore are systematically silent and even silenced by these maps.

A search of the handwritten and typed land title entries at the Bureau of Conveyances in Honolulu documents the transfer of the Lele of Hamohamo to other grantor books. One entry records that almost immediately after he received title, Curtis P. Iaukea transferred this land out of his name to someone named William Woon for $1. Woon then immediately transferred this title to my great-great-grandmother, Charlotte Iaukea, for $1.

Ah, this looks familiar! He's hiding the title to the land under his wife's name. My family still does this today; so now I know this trick goes back a few generations. But why would my great-great-grandfather want to hide this property? The subtext to these maps remained silent, not about to give anything away. I then discovered that this property was sanctioned for "eminent domain" and condemned by the territorial government almost immediately after these quick transfers of title. Now I was truly confused, because Curtis P. Iaukea worked for the territorial government.

Soon after leaving the Bureau of Conveyances in downtown Honolulu, I took my thoughts to the ocean. Surfing—my sanctuary, my escape. Luckily, I had the waves just off Diamond Head all to myself that day. I remember catching wave after wave while wondering not only about the Lele of Hamohamo, but also the Iaukea Estate Land, and the whopping four hundred plus acres of land titled to Curtis Piehu Iaukea before 1900.

As I sat waiting for waves, I began a conversation out loud with my *kupuna* (great-great-grandfather): "What is going on here? I don't understand what the land title sheets are saying. What happened to our ownership of Kamanaiki Valley? Why did the territorial government condemn the Waikīkī land when you worked for the territory? How much of this land is still in the family? What is going on?" And finally, "If you want me to do this work, then you are going to have to HELP ME." I was sitting in the ocean, shedding tears of frustration and completely confused. Pleading for clarity.

Three or four days later, my mother called and told me that she had just found boxes and boxes of information in an "Iaukea Collection" at the Hawai'i State Archives. She was helping me research. The breadth and depth to be discovered was too much for just one person, so we worked as a team, trying to unearth as much as we could about the family history. It was there in the archives that the maps began to speak, that memories began to inform the landscape. The stories documented throughout this book share what the maps alone simply cannot.

Stories of people and communities are largely absent from the land tenure documents, because bureaucratic ledgers were deliberately employed to replace detailed social interactions, as part of the homogenization of people and place in Hawai'i. The result was a giant matrix of land title transfers that performs admirably for the purposes of state bureaucracy but reveals little of the social and personal relationships that condition land as site, land as private property, and land as capitalist, race-based social currency in Hawai'i.

This is not to say that Hawaiians never striated space prior to the introduction of textual maps. According to George Kanahele, Hawaiians had a "deep-seated feeling of Territoriality." Every part of the 'āina had a name and function, and in addition to constructing detailed descriptions of space to connote place, Hawaiians also had what Kanahele calls a "vertical perception" of space, as exemplified in the *mauka* and *makai* orientation to spatial understanding.[5] Directions are all given upward "to the mountain" or downward "to the sea."

Understanding Hawaiian geography requires repositioning the physical and mental landscape along vertical lines of knowledge, because the terrain is literally alive and dynamic with its forests, hillsides, beaches, land, and sea that reach up, out, and down. The stories and experiences of the people in these places also enliven the land, making the place itself recognizable as an important extension of community.[6] Mary Pukui and Samuel Elbert point out that "Hawaiians named taro patches, rocks and trees that represented deities and ancestors, sites of houses and *heiau* (sacred site), canoe landings, fishing stations in the sea, resting places in the forests, and the tiniest spots where miraculous or interesting events are believed to have taken place."[7] This dynamism is squashed down in contemporary maps.

The *ahupua'a* system of viewing and employing the land recognized this flow between geographic features that created both natural and social boundaries in the process. The *ahupua'a* was a land division that contained within it various boundaries in its stretch from the mountains down to the sea. Approximately six hundred years ago, the people divided Hawaiian land into *palena* (boundaries) that included *moku* (district) and *ahupua'a* (subdivision).[8] Each island was divided into several *moku*. The *konohiki* (land agent) then collected land taxes for the *Mō'ī* (king) from the people living in the various *ahupua'a* within a *moku*. Or as the surveyor general described it in 1882, "The typical *Ahupua'a* is a long narrow strip, extending from the sea to the mountain, so that its chief may have his share of all the various products of the *uka* or mountain region, the cultivated land, and the *kai* or sea."[9]

This dynamic understanding of land cannot be accurately represented on western maps. Property, landscaping, and surveying are all western products that take into account the purely visual aspects of space, the production of that space with regard to capital gains, and the need for cartographic representation of that space to set boundaries and borders for the contemporary nation-state.[10] Within this epistemology, property is that which can be mapped, and the map itself serves as a general history of communication about space, and in these contexts, about capital.

Not only visual representations of epistemology, western maps also served as expressions of secular power, dividing space into finite jurisdictions—that is, townships, states, territories, and properties—as early as the 1600s.[11] This conceptual leap from land to demarcated property also nurtured a spatial understanding of land as capital. "The classical view of property is premised on the notion that property rights identify a private owner who has title to a set of valued resources with a presumption of full power over those resources," Joseph Singer writes. "The image underlying ownership is absolute power of the owner within rigidly defined spatial boundaries."[12]

In Hawai'i, Kamehameha I first divided conquered lands when he was a paramount chief in 1782, after the battle of Moku'ōhai.[13] He divided the remainder of the archipelago except for Kaua'i after 1795, when he conquered O'ahu. These lands were divided out to the chiefs, who divided the lands again and again. Kamehameha I also kept a portion of the lands for himself. The land taxes collected from them were "rent" and "went to the King as his private income or revenue."[14]

The notion of the contemporary nation-state entered Hawai'i's consciousness early and became codified in the first Hawaiian Kingdom Constitution of 1840. Thereafter, failure to pay taxes resulted in a forfeiture of lands to the Mō'ī. The Legislative Council approved the "Principles adopted by the Board of Commissioners to quiet land titles" on October 26, 1846.[15] This act set out the mechanisms confirming the land titles as personal property to native tenants, which made the subsequent Māhele (land division) in 1848 possible. The Māhele ultimately "allowed for large-scale privatization of lands in the Hawaiian Kingdom."[16]

Land mapping occurs early in Hawai'i's national history. Kamanamaikalani Beamer and Kaeo Duarte have recognized and evaluated the native agency involved in Hawai'i's first maps. In the early 1800s, the maps produced by Hawaiians represented the traditional land boundaries. For example, the surveyor Kalama's Hawaii nei map of 1839 shows the moku divisions and ahupua'a in color codes. Not only did it reproduce native land epistemology in a western medium, but it also alerted other nation-states to Hawaiian Kingdom sovereign territory. Or as Beamer and Duarte put it,

> Kalama seems to have adapted the Western mode of mapping to create a product that reflects a distinctively ʻŌiwi (native) approach or view of place and boundaries. Effectively this conveyed the message that the Hawaiian Kingdom was not empty of inhabitants who have claim to the land, and that the land was, in fact, ordered under a complex Hawaiian system of knowledge.[17]

But even then, a western *regime of truth* forces maps into well-placed silences.[18] In Hawaiʻi, as land transitioned from *ʻāina* to private property, the map itself enacted a parallel recasting of geography and citizenry. Even the early native maps demanded erasures in the landscape. There was simply no space, no language, no preserving the personal relationships and the social persona of the community as a whole. These, like the land, became sharply divided. And yet, though unintelligible at first as a social index, when read in conjunction with other documents, codes to the maps can be broken. When reunited with the voices of their various actors, maps speak volumes.

Stories and personal agendas suffuse the transfers of land title in Hawaiʻi. As Curtis P. Iaukea's personal and professional papers demonstrate, a lot happened in the private realm that directly affected land ownership. After I read his manuscript chapters, the once-silent maps suddenly became very chatty, as the community of actors involved at the time came into clearer focus. It's like the Balinese "metaphysical shadow line" that bars outsiders from ways of knowing. Once admitted into the *insider* culture in Hawaiʻi, "you are at least regarded as a human being rather than a cloud or a gust of wind."[19] Admittance here is gained by recognizing and affiliating yourself with stories about family and community. Or put more methodologically, the researcher must analyze the discourse surrounding property in order to understand how property is viewed not just *by* this discourse, but *because of* it.

From my genealogically and temporally distant, yet exceedingly close personal observation point of my ancestors through maps and land title abstracts, I can conclude that my ancestors managed to make the epistemic leap from *ʻāina* to private property quite well. In both their political and their personal capacities, each understood and participated knowingly in western landscaping and mapping agendas. Their names are consistently displayed through the grantor/ grantee books of a century ago to be found at the Bureau of Conveyances in Honolulu. As far as mapping property was concerned, my *kūpuna* (great-great-grandparents) definitely understood both the meta- and mininarratives of the state. Curtis and Charlotte Iaukea, like many other Hawaiian Kingdom subjects, kept clear in their minds the distinctions between ʻāina, land, and landscape and were not confused about the legal titling of these entities.

But when and how did the passing down of family history and land, also known broadly as genealogy, get stuck? Who did the sticking, and why? All meetings and departures between our larger and smaller histories are completely interconnected, and the consequences of what happened then still affect how we relate to one another as family and how we participate, or don't participate, in these contractual exchanges today. For me, the titling of land is very personal.

For Jamaica Kincaid, these particular questions and circumstances are not really that surprising. Such dislocations from the familial, the political, and the geographic can generally be expected for *those people* caught in the imperial agendas of nation-states.[20] In *The Autobiography of My Mother*, Kincaid points out that drawing distinctions between "man" and "people" is important, because the particular and different realities of each can be predetermined by their pasts: "For one of them came off the boat as part of a horde, already demonized, mind blank to everything but human suffering, each face the same as the one next to it; the other came off the boat of his own volition, seeking to fulfill a destiny, a vision of himself he carried in his mind's eye."[21]

But, *those people* in Hawaiʻi, including my own ancestors, did not undergo transport through slavery or suffer the usual colonial markings of modernity. Our ancestors were voyagers and by 1843, Hawaiʻi was recognized internationally as a sovereign state, and Hawaiians were regarded as an independent people well within the framework of the forthcoming family of nations. Throughout the nineteenth century, the *aliʻi* (kings and queens) made great strides in solidifying Hawaiʻi's sovereign status in the international arena. So something else, added, lost, or perhaps erased from our collective memories, occurred in Hawaiʻi that would manage to sustain colonial-like relations by constantly confusing Jamaica Kincaid's *those people* with "we the people" under a U.S. jurisprudence. The rewriting of our historical and physical landscape ultimately constructed a territorial citizen and landmass—both shaped by U.S. ideology.

Curtis P. Iaukea not only embodied these changes but was directly implicated in this process as a permanent figure in the government of both the Hawaiian Kingdom and the Territory of Hawaiʻi. Toward the end of his life, he was celebrated as one Hawaiian who made the leap to American citizenry successfully. His obituary in the March 7 issue of *Hawaii Hochi* draws the moral of his story:

He proved the possibility of perfect adaptation to historic changes and the progress of the times. Few men have been able to do that. Yet if a man can do it successfully it can be done by a race. The Hawaiians have been pitied as a dying race,
but they need not suffer extinction if they learn the lesson taught by the lives of
such members of their race as Col. Iaukea.[22]

Another newspaper article a few years before his death makes this transition
seamless:

A distinguished survivor of the monarchial era in Hawaii, Col. Iaukea for many
years was chamberlain of the royal Hawaiian household and special representative
of the kings and queens of Hawaii in all parts of the world.

For more than a score of years prior to the overthrow of the monarchy in 1893,
Colonel Iaukea served the royal families of Hawaii in various capacities, having
been chief secretary to the department of foreign affairs and special envoy of the
Hawaiian Monarchy at the coronation of the last Czar of Russia, in addition to
acting as chamberlain of the royal household. Following his visit to St. Petersburg
for the Russian coronation, Col. Iaukea visited all the royal courts of Europe on
behalf of the Hawaiian monarchy, subsequently going to Japan and India to negotiate labor treaties. His role resulted in the importation of the first Japanese
laborers to come to Hawaii.

In 1887, while chamberlain, Col. Iaukea had charge of arrangements for the
Hawaiian royal party that attended Queen Victoria's jubilee. The members in-
cluded Queen Kapiolani, Princess Liliuokalani, Governor Dominis and others.
En route to London the party visited President and Mrs. Cleveland at Washington.
In 1897 Col. Iaukea accompanied the embassy of the Republic of Hawaii to Lon-
don to the Diamond Jubilee of Queen Victoria. The next year he accompanied
President and Mrs. Dole to Washington as secretary and military attaché.[23]

These articles note that Curtis P. Iaukea served government to the best of his
ability. My great-aunt, Lorna K. Iaukea Watson, makes the same point about
her father:

My father lived long—he died at the age of eighty-four on March 5, 1940. Men
have lived longer and have seen extraordinary changes which are inevitable in such
a span, but few Hawaiians, if any, have had such dramatic and colorful experiences
as my father did, first, under a monarchy; second, under a provisional form of government; third, under a republic; and finally, under a territory governed by the
United States of America. And he was honored for public service in all four.[24]

Finally, a "Ripley's Believe It or Not" feature from the 1930s presented him to
the world as the remarkable "Secretary to 5 Kings of Hawai'i and to 2 Presi-
dents." It read:

Col. C. P. Iaukea, born in 1855, was taken from his parents and adopted by an uncle in accordance with a Hawaiian custom. He is now the most decorated citizen of Hawaii, having served in secretarial capacities to five royal rulers, Kamehameha IV, Kamehameha V, Lunalilo, Kalakaua and Queen Liliuokalani. After Hawaii became a republic, Mr. Iaukea continued as secretary to President Dole. Another President, Woodrow Wilson of the United States, appointed Mr. Iaukea as secretary of the U.S. territory of Hawaii.[25]

Curtis P. Iaukea was celebrated as a Hawaiian who *survived* the monarchy and lived to tell about it. He was also regarded as representing all that was apparently good about becoming American, even though until the end of his life the photos of my great-great-grandfather show him proudly wearing the uniforms and medals that accompanied his trips to faraway places as a diplomat for the Hawaiian Kingdom. He was never pictured wearing his uniforms, after the fact, for the Republic of Hawai'i as its official diplomat. Even so, the territorial government regularly drew on his memories to close the gap between the Hawaiian Kingdom and the territory and in order to legitimize its own existence in the process. It needed to insert its inevitability into the historical narrative, and used my great-great-grandfather's public memories to represent its "evidence of inheritance."[26] But I wonder if the transitions for him were as seamless as we are led to believe.

A search of my great-great-grandfather's recorded memories often uncovers unrecorded emotions. In the Hawaiian word *mo'olelo*, memory and history are interchangeable concepts. I explore the more private *mo'olelo* in later chapters. Here, though, is an example of the more public *mo'olelo*. In 1937, Colonel Iaukea was approached to give a live radio broadcast in Hawai'i and England after radio executives heard him speaking about "monarchical days in Hawai'i" at a luncheon of the Visitors' Club. This speech commemorated the fifty-year anniversary of Queen Victoria's Golden Jubilee.

E. W. Miller pitched the broadcast to John Balch, president of the Mutual Telephone Company, this way:

> The attention of the world has of late been focused on the British throne. King George will be coronated May 12th, exactly one hundred years later than the coronation of his grandmother Queen Victoria.
>
> In Hawaii today lives a man who was present in an official capacity at the Golden Jubilee of Queen Victoria in 1887 and also at her Diamond Jubilee in 1897. As King Kalakaua's Chamberlain, he acted as interpreter between Queen Kapiolani and Queen Victoria in London and met all the European ruling monarchs present at that time. At the 1897 Jubilee he was in London as an official of the

Republic of Hawaii.

A broadcast direct from the ONLY THRONE ROOM in the United States by Colonel Curtis P. Iaukea, who, with Queen Kapiolani and Liliuokalani (who later became Queen of Hawaii—the last one), was present at London fifty years ago on the occasion of the Golden Jubilee of Queen Victoria, with a description of the highlights of the celebration and mentioning the prominent people he came in contact with at the time, in his capacity of Chamberlain to Kalakaua (The Last King of Hawaii). The broadcast could end with the singing, by one of the better vocalists in the Islands (Mrs. A. G. M. Robertson for instance) of the songs composed in London by Liliuokalani at the time in honor of the occasion.[27]

The broadcast itself was as follows:

National Broadcast
May 7, 1937

As our announcer has told you, I promised to relate some of the colorful and interesting things about two jubilee celebrations of her Majesty, Queen Victoria, Great Grandmother of the Duke of York soon to be crowned King of England. I first had the honor of representing my country at the Court of St. James in 1883. Hawaii was an independent kingdom with its own sovereign, government and royal family, its own elaborate and ritualistic court life modeled after that of England. On the occasion of this visit, I had returned from the pleasant duty of representing Hawaii at the coronation of Czar Nicholas of Russia, father of the last royal ruler of that country. A delightful experience on this same mission was when an informal audience was granted me by the Prince of Wales, later King Edward and grandfather of the present king. I was received at Marlborough House, and there presented mementoes and gifts from my sovereign to members of the Royal family. The Prince of Wales graciously presented me with a diamond ring in remembrance of the visit and it is among my most cherished possessions.

My second visit to the Court of St. James was on the occasion of Queen Victoria's Golden Jubilee in 1887. I accompanied Queen Kapiolani, Consort of King Kalakaua, in the capacity of Court Chamberlain. Also in our party was the Princess Liliuokalani, then heir apparent and later Queen of Hawaii.

Enroute to England and via the United States we had many happy experiences. Among the most interesting was our reception and entertainment in Washington by President and Mrs. Cleveland. The official dinners and receptions were magnificent affairs.

Finally, the great objective of our journey was reached. London, historic old London. Here we were the guests of Her Majesty Queen Victoria at the old Alexandra Hotel. Our Fellow Guests were members of Royalty representing many countries. Among them, Prince Komatsu of Japan, the Prince of Siam and the Prince of Persia. It was indeed an awe inspiring and glittering aggregation of royal personages.

It was not until June 20 when Queen Victoria made her official entry into

London from Scotland where she had been resting, that the festivities really began. On that day our party was summoned to an audience in Buckingham Palace.

Her Majesty was seated on a sofa, this with two chairs comprised the only furniture in the room. In attendance on her Majesty were their Royal Highnesses the Duke of Connaught and the Prince and Princess of Battenberg. As the Hawaiian Queen entered the room Queen Victoria rose and graciously taking the visitor's hands in hers kissed her on both cheeks. The Princess Liliuokalani was greeted with affection, Her Majesty Victoria kissing her on the forehead. The conversation between the two queens was friendly and animated. I acted as interpreter for Kapiolani as she did not speak English. The visit of King Kalakaua to England some years previous was recalled with much pleasure by Queen Victoria, who spoke of him with warm friendliness. After some minutes of general conversation, we took our leave.

On the following day we attended the service at Westminster Abbey. We were accorded the unusual honor of an escort drawn from the famous Life Guards of Queen Victoria to accompany our carriage in the line of march. The carriage, by the way, was one of the Queen's personal conveyances.

Thru a cheering crowd said to number several millions, we passed in orderly array to be greeted at the door of the Abbey by Lord Lathom and Sir Henry Ponsonby and by them to be escorted to seats reserved for royalty. In the center of this great historic edifice a platform or dais had been placed.

Seated upon it were royal guests, the grandchildren of the Queen and members of the Royal Household. It was on this dais that Queen Kapiolani and Liliuokalani were presented. The focal point of all eyes was an elaborately carved arm chair standing in the exact center of the dais. In this chair have been crowned all the sovereigns of Britain, save two, since 1308. The Queen entered, dressed simply in black. She advanced and seated herself on this great chair. It will be in this same chair that King George will be crowned.

The Archbishop of Canterbury opened the ceremonies with prayer. Then followed the Te Deum, the great choir filled the lofty edifice with their anthems. When the ceremonies were concluded, the procession formed to leave the Abbey. We arrived at Buckingham Palace for luncheon, driving thru the streets where the crowds had waited the return procession. At the palace a great table had been spread the length of the main hall and it was assigned to the use of visiting kings and members of royalty.

In passing let me say that England's hospitality knew no bounds. In 1897 I again had the honor of visiting England, the occasion was Queen Victoria's Diamond Jubilee. I attended as Secretary and Aid to the Honorable S. M. Damon who was the Special Envoy from Hawaii. The ceremonies marking the 60th anniversary of the Good Queen's reign were even more elaborate than those of the Golden Jubilee.

We of Hawaii fell [sic] very close to the British people on this historic occasion for the friendship of the two people dates back to 1847 [sic] when England was the first world power to recognize Hawaii as a sister nation and to guarantee the independence of this island kingdom. And so, on behalf of the people of Hawaii I respectfully extend to Their Majestys King George and Queen Elizabeth hearty greetings and best wishes for a long peaceful reign. Long live the King.[28]

Recognizing the importance of dates, Curtis P. Iaukea sums up his experiences with a reference to Hawai'i's close relationship with England, and England's early recognition of Hawai'i as a sister nation. What neither he nor Miller supplies is any reference to the sequence of events that turned Hawai'i into an occupied U.S. outpost at the turn of the twentieth century. Also not mentioned are the sister nation privileges that made Hawai'i the first non-European state to be recognized as sovereign.

Milan Kundera once wrote: "Like blows from an ax, important dates cut deep gashes into Europe's twentieth century."[29] Replacing emotional impulses or responses, the historical date marks rites of passage for both states and individuals. The injunction to recall important dates reinforces specific historical interpretations that themselves help to legitimize the markers of the date as the true authors of historical realities. By dating events, placing them in sequence, we are assured of the state's continuity. We can have faith in a settled, given registered past, and stand in anticipation of an authorized future. Within this linear continuum of dates, the more anterior the date the better, because it not only extends the narrative of the community in question but affirms that community's unrevisable, "natural" continuity.

In this way, history and memory become divided and separate discursive entities; in fact, history seeks to eradicate memory.[30] In contrast, Pierre Nora recognizes *true memory* as genealogy, or as a force that "installs remembrance within the sacred."[31] Ingrained in natural cycles, and celebrating the larger patterns of existence, *true memory* involves many more actors, more agency, and more complications in its construction. Nonlinear and generational, this form of knowing the past demands that we track ourselves through the narrative itself as opposed to the representation of that narrative. This is a far more complicated and chaotic task, and history is a strategy for placing *true memory* into a grid of intelligibility authored and legitimated by the state. History is a *suggestion* of past experiences—a representation of occurrences and specific relationships.

How then might we know ourselves generationally, and through *true memories?* This is a frightful proposition—to seek to know myself as my mother knows herself, my father, grandfather, and grandmother knew themselves, and back to Curtis and Charlotte Iaukea and before. "Frightful," because to do this, I would have to accept that their *complete* stories make up who

I am. And I already know some of their stories are darker in composition than I would want to acknowledge—including generational alcoholism, drug abuse, infidelity, neglect, and violence, violence, violence—all on my paternal side in recent memory. It's all here—I know it's here in me. The emotions attached to past deeds and events are written into my hereditary code and resonate in my DNA, and I am often strongly drawn to people who remind me of these tendencies. The distance between "them" and myself closes through this genetic memory, and I want some of these memories to lose their subconscious power to manipulate and control.

And so I turned to the early diaries of Curtis P. Iaukea to make further sense of the darker sides as well. I looked for hints, for premonitions of what was to come politically and personally for him, but didn't see any. I still see someone intent on representing Hawai'i to the best of his abilities, and who was committed to preserving those interactions on paper. Later memories covered in other chapters undress the emotional aspects and point to some of the emotional difficulties he experienced. But these earlier recorded memories are straightforward and uncomplicated.

I read the diary my *kupuna* wrote in 1883 when he was circumnavigating the globe on official business, representing the Hawaiian Kingdom at some historical international events, such as the coronation of Czar Alexander III of Russia in 1883.[32] The diary begins on Monday, April 8, 1883: "Appointed H.H.M's Special Envoy to Russia, Spain, Servia. Bearer of dispatches to H.M. the Queen Great Britain and Ireland." On Tuesday, April 10, he "made formal calls on Royal Family and Friends," and on April 11, "left Honolulu for Australia at 12 o'clock noon. Friends went off to bid us God speed and return in the King's boat. Weather a little threatening—sea boisterous. Towards night very rough."[33]

And the voyage is begun. As I read, I could not believe that I held the personal record of my ancestor as he traveled through Australia, the United States, Russia, Budapest, Vienna, Paris, England, and Italy. Amazing. His attention to detail allows the reader to voyage with him, as I came to know very well.

Here, for example, is an entry on a dinner he attended with the king of Servia:

Thursday 28ᵗʰ June.

    Passed a splendid night. Woke at 10 AM breakfasted and dressed for Reception by the King. At 11:45 the State Carriage arrived with the King's Aide de Camp. I rode with him and Henry with our Attache in another carriage. A Marshal mounted, preceded us. On arrival at the Palace I was received at the entrance by the Court Marshal. Guard of honor, Salutings, and Band playing national anthem. In the corridor stood on each side the Kings Aids de camps, about 20 in number. At the entrance to the Reception room a guard. I was then ushered in the reception room where they Received me. The Emperor entered shortly after. I addressed his Majesty in Hawaiian. After addresses and presenting of decoration he invited me to a seat by him and conversed. Our conversation being interpreted by Foreign Office. After 15 minutes the Emperor retired to the Queen's reception room where I was then ushered by the Minister of Foreign Affairs. After presenting decoration she invited me to a seat and had a pleasant interview. After 15 minutes retired. A.M. reception throughout was of the most pleasant and friendly character. Both the Emperor and Empress were charming. The Empress spoke excellent English.

Another entry describes some of his activities while in Russia for the coronation of Alexander III:

Wednesday 30th June.

9AM Received notice from grand master Ceremonies regarding reception by Emperor & Empress. 10:30AM Went to the Palace and was received by the Emperor & Empress. Reception Room crowded with Ladies & Gentlemen of rank waiting to be presented. Returned to Hotel 11:30AM. Changed & went out to pay visits to the British Embassy, United States & Spanish. Left cards at the Embassies. Took dinner at the Slovensky Bar and returned to Hotel. 2PM called on Mr. Madrin. Found on return to hotel invitation cards from Master Ceremonies to the Emperors Theatre for tonight. No one admitted but invited guests. 7:30PM went to Theatre in uniform. Emperor & Empress Ihito arrived 8PM. Magnificent sight. The whole of the banquette was one mass of uniforms, all officers. The boxes were lined with Diplomatic officials & suites on each side of the Emperor's box. My box was the 2nd to the right of the Emperor's— about 20 feet off. The play was some ancient piece of Moscow artists. The performance lasted until 10:30PM. After the performance I went out with Madriz to the Yard to supper & returned 4AM.

In these records of daily experience, there is no great distance in the tone, precision, or content between the public events and the private recording. My own recorded memories are haphazard, seemingly more chaotic, and definitely not as well articulated. A look at my old diaries, if and when I ever wrote in anything resembling a diary, reveals nothing like the steadily unfolding and coherent narration that my great-great-grandfather recorded. Messy, both in content and in emotional response, is how I would describe my own intermittent recordings of the past.

As I read, I feel both connected to and disconnected from this illustrious life. Where's his pain, his grief, his confusion? This particular diary seems almost to expect to be read by someone else. Did he guess that portions of his diary would one day be made public? Or do these words of my great-great-grandfather in fact completely represent and gauge his exciting life and wondrous experiences? Perhaps because Curtis P. Iaukea frequently served as the official spokesperson for all things monarchial, maybe even his private thoughts came to be disciplined by his diplomatic correctness.

A later memory, however, immediately stands apart from the rest. After the illegal overthrow of the Hawaiian Kingdom, Queen Liliʻuokalani asked Curtis P. Iaukea to remain in office to "watch" the Crown Lands revenues. A page from Curtis P. Iaukea's unpublished chapter describes how Queen Liliʻuokalani set forth his *kuleana*:

> It is my belief that at this time those behind the Provisional Government expected immediate annexation by the United States for contained in the announcement of their seizure of power was this interesting sentence "to exist until terms of Union with the United States of America have been negotiated and agreed upon." But five long years, brought with bitterness and intrigue, were to pass before this ambition was realized.
>
> The next time I saw Queen Liliuokalani to speak to was on the morning of the day she was vacating the Palace after surrendering her authority to the Provisional Government, January 18, 1893 at 11am. She was seated at the breakfast table, just about finishing. I walked in to see if she had any request to make of me before going to take up her home at Washington Place.
>
> Sitting at table with her was Mrs. C. B. Wilson (the wife of the late Marshal of the Kingdom who had resisted surrendering the Police Station and arms under his control until compelled to do so by orders of the Queen's Cabinet) the Queen's most intimate friend and companion since early day, and two others of her personal retainers. I could see that they were all disheartened, almost overcome to see the Queen leaving the Palace. The Queen put her hands up to her forehead and leaned over for quite a little while without speaking to anyone, she was overcome with grief, which of course we could not relieve.
>
> On seeing me at the doorway the Queen said "mai." A familiar expression amongst Hawaiians bidding one to come and be welcome. As she gave me her hand when I reached the head of the table where she was sitting, I felt a slight tremor as I bent to kiss it. Her eyes were filled with tears. She motioned to me to sit beside her, which I did and it was as much as I could to restrain my own tears and emotion. All of us were feeling too depressed to speak or say much.
>
> My object in going to see the Queen before she left the Palace was, as I said, to offer my personal services to her as I felt it my duty, and to inform that the Provisional Government had asked me to remain in office as Crown Land Agent, an office that I had held under her brother Kalakaua and to which she had reappointed me when she came to the throne in 1891.
>
> After some intense moments of silence I told her what I had come for. She then said, "No, I'll not need your service as there will be nothing for you to do at Washington Place. Stay where you are until I come back. You will keep account of the Crown Land

revenues for they belong to the reigning sovereign. I know my rights as Queen and constitutional monarch of Hawaii which I have been wrongly deprived of through the connivance and perfidy of the United States Minister Resident in Hawaii, will be restored to me when the people and government of the United States have been fully informed as to the way the fall of the monarchy was accomplished."

Then recovering herself somewhat, she added, "Yes, come and see me sometimes and keep me informed of what is going with the Provisional Government."

Acting with her full knowledge and approval, I left the breakfast table after bidding the Queen and her company good-bye with the expression of hope that she would soon be restored to her own.[34]

I am proud of my *kupuna*, and I am relieved that Queen Liliʻuokalani was the one who asked him to stay in order to watch over the Crown Lands revenues. Like many Hawaiians who had served the Hawaiian Kingdom, Curtis P. Iaukea continued to work under the new regimes, to such an extent that the territorial government is often said to have consisted of white elites and Hawaiian *aliʻi.* The results of these relationships were varied, and often emotionally charged when they intertwined. Yet, even as the ongoing social construction that the territorial government had embarked upon occurred, nostalgia for the Hawaiian Kingdom was often a mainstay for the new wave of politics and politicians.

The files give more away. The key question is, How exactly did the public discourse change so rapidly in this era, so as to produce American citizenry and commodified space? The methods were numerous and occurred rapidly, and for territorial representatives, the chance to remake the past was often very welcome, because a re-represented past then becomes "true," since it's the only past being represented.

Incoming governments often legitimize themselves by incorporating themselves into the past. Memories are "purified," and the law itself is used to appropriate issues of inheritance and "rights" in a tumultuous political climate. Whether in the case of the American Indians, or in shaping the emerging American consciousness in Hawaiʻi, "Americans attempted to come to terms with the restless ghosts of the national past, the legacy of a history of conquest and revolution that threatened the moral foundations of nationhood."[35]

The insistent and ultimately violent political forces that sought to destroy Hawaiʻi's independent status not only produced social dislocation but also advocated a collective memory around safe ground. And yet, while such nostalgia might be offered more obviously for consumption by traveling and settled immigrants, and by those without a homeland, even though this social dislocation did not occur as a result of a complete geographic separation, for Hawaiians living in Hawai'i the need and desire to constantly evoke those memories proved just as pressing—and still continues to inform a limited historiography of place and space.

This, I believe, is why my great-great-grandfather publicly recalled his memories so often, and also why the public was interested. Memory itself is an important social organizer in Hawaiian epistemology. So why would either the public or my great-great-grandfather have wanted to forget? In the form of genealogy (*mo'o kū'auhau*), memory tells the Hawaiian population who we are, where we are, and why we are. It also provides the baseline for how place is understood by Hawaiians and by other native people.

In Hawai'i, a story of creation is told by the Kumulipo, a primary genealogy chant containing sixteen *wā* (eras) and two thousand lines. "Composed by the court historians of King Keaweike Kahialiiokamoku on the island of Hawai'i about 1700 in honor of his firstborn son, Kalaninni Iamamao,[36] "the Kumulipo belongs to a category of sacred chants known as *pule ho'ōla'a ali'i*, 'prayer to sanctify the chief,' which was recited to honor a new-born chief."[37] In addition to commemorating the birth of Kalaninuiiamamao, the Kumulipo traces the genealogical descent of both the *ali'i* and the *maka'āinana* (commoners) from the gods, and in particular Papahanaumoku and Wākea, who establish the direct genealogical connection of Hawaiians to the land, the ocean, and the sky.

In practical terms, "genealogy played a very important role in deciding precedence and rights to claims of senior and junior lines of families in Hawai'i,"[38] and this creation chant served as the social organizer of an entire population. It confirmed the right to exist individually and collectively in spatial and temporal reality. According to Roger T. Ames, the Kumulipo "combines both a linear sense of temporal development with the richness of one particular moment in time. It justifies the social and political organization of this particular moment against the background of the more universal natural order, and in so doing, naturalizes the prevailing social values."[39] The Kumulipo declares the power relations of every entity in the cosmos, and thereby explains the *mana* (power) of certain individuals over others. The result is a comprehensive and coherent understanding of the world: "The whole development of the Kumulipo is based upon the idea of blood descent from a single stock established from the beginning of the race and derived from primary gods."[40]

The Kumulipo is a remembrance text for native Hawaiians. Originally, a feat of memory was necessary to preserve this genealogy, since this *oli* (chant) was not written down. The Kumulipo was first translated into English and published in 1889 by Queen Liliʻuokalani, who among other things wanted to show both her and her brother Kalākaua's right to claim to be *Aliʻi Nui* (high chief), since they are descended from Keaweikei Kahialiiokamolu on their father's side of the genealogy and Keaweaheulu on their mother's (Keohokalole) side.[41]

At the Hawaiʻi State Archives, I found a book that lists my own *moʻo kū ʻauhau*. The book is handwritten and lists the names of ancestors in pairs; both *aliʻi* and *akua* (gods) are recorded. My own genealogy records that I am the sixty-fourth generation from Papanuihānaumoku and Wākea—Earth Mother and Sky Father. Piikea and Umi-a-Liloa are fifteen generations separated from myself. Kamehameha I's first wife, Kaneikopolei, had a daughter named Kahiwakaneikopolei. Iaukea is descended from her marriage to high chief Namiki of the Paʻao Order, their daughter Puahaunapuoko, and her daughter Hanamuahaleonaihe.[42] But Iaukea is also descended from Kamehameha I's mother, and Lapaha, Curtis P. Iaukea's mother, is the daughter of Nalanipo, a Big Island *Aliʻi*. It was because of this genealogy that my great-great-grandfather was taken at age six by his uncle Kaihupaʻa to "begin the task of becoming a *kahu* or retainer of royalty."[43] The Kumulipo is a primary source on my great-great-grandmother's side as well, and the Kahaloipua genealogy is also listed and referenced alongside the larger genealogy of the Hawaiian people. She had more *mana* than her husband because of her more direct genealogical link to *aliʻi* and *akua*.

I am overwhelmed when I read this genealogy, and I wonder if I will ever really understand the contents. However, I cannot read the lines and lines of ancestors without feeling my own senses awaken. I am they, and they are me. And even though this true memory was stricken from my own history, I nevertheless feel more connected to this large and unfolding past that celebrates connections to all that is and all that was. For me, this genealogy connects me to a memory impervious to my own immediate family's trials and tribulations. It echoes understandings of something more. Thanks to such longevity, I do not feel so alone. And I realize that I have never been alone.

In Hawaiʻi, *moʻo kūʻauhau* was, and to some extent still is, an important tool for knowing self, environment, and cosmology. Place is obviously important for social identity anywhere, but how we know ourselves as Hawaiians rests on how well we know both our geographic and our social place(s). So perhaps my great-great-grandfather, like Queen Liliʻuokalani, recalled his past through numerous forms of social media during his era, because it was simply his *kuleana* to do so. The profound shift from oral memory to memory in media might have informed his actions and others of his time. The key was to record and remember whatever possible.

As a Hawaiian navigating between many social dimensions, remembering the past for his contemporaries and for his *moʻopuna* (future generations) might have not only influenced which memories my great-great-grandfather recalled, but also caused his need to record these memories. My task now is to pull up some of his recorded memories that have thus far escaped public review, and also to determine the reasons for the apparent social amnesia. These submerged memories will also reveal the union of land/body/memory, and our individual place(s) within this historical context.

Returning to the narrative of my own family, I feel a sense of community and camaraderie with others who face similar challenges. The Lele of Hamohamo, and my great-great-grandfather's memory of it, have come to represent all of these complicated familial and contractual relationships for me. Private property contains emotional currency. It's a tool used to privilege and disenfranchise. It's the source of decades-long-and-beyond squabbles within and outside of the family unit. Many Hawaiians have encountered such turmoil. I speak from this perspective, knowing that it is important to uncover and declare whatever we can from our own narratives, not just so we may understand and participate in the geographic and legal realms, but so we can then collectively operate with a more complete understanding of self and community.

My family is not the only example of fighting provoked by rewritten codes of conduct, written in accordance with American capitalist interpretations of *ka ʻāina*. Land is a commonly contested arena for Hawaiians, and I know of other stories of dispossession that also include inheritance, secrecy, and the consumption of land for strictly material means. These intimate and combative experiences often remain untold and hidden, as if this will somehow negate the actual practical and painful ramifications. Experience tells us not to recognize and validate the darker sides of our personal and political histories.

When and how did this disconnect occur between land/body/memory for many Hawaiians?[44] When did it occur for my own family? Both occurred gradually over time, and today the connect and the disconnect are written into the same hereditary code.

CHAPTER 2

Land as the Vehicle

The Hawaiian Homes Commission Act (1921) and Defining Nativeness

With my genealogy reconfiguring in my mind, and the pull of generations past urging me to bring forth what was put in my path, getting from here to there in understanding is now the voyage. Land legislation was the vehicle for erasing emotional and epistemological ties to the Hawaiian Kingdom, and for rewriting the national fabric of the *ali'i* system and Hawaiian Kingdom national terrain. As the Crown Lands commissioner for many years, and then as the subagent of "Public Lands," Curtis P. Iaukea had primary responsibility for and a strong interest in land legislation. He wrote glowingly about Sanford B. Dole and the 1884 Homestead Law, "under the provision of which the man of small means may acquire a tract of government land upon which to build himself a home and settle." But in a public debate in 1922, his tone changed dramatically when he criticized the Hawaiian Homes Commission Act (HHCA), supposedly created to provide homesteading opportunities for native Hawaiians, as nothing but a tool for benefiting the sugar planters.

Even though he later served as the chairman of the Hawaiian Homes Commission from 1933 to 1935, Curtis P. Iaukea was against the HHCA at its inception. The rewriting of the Hawaiian national terrain and social fabric through American land legislation, Curtis P. Iaukea's engagement with and vocal opposition to the HHCA, and my own response to definitions of nativeness were all conditioned by the HHCA. The racialized and impoverished descriptions of land and people that it has perpetrated still fix Hawaiian identity in the eyes of the state. The debates almost a century ago signify native resistance to American classificatory systems of land and people. For

Curtis P. Iaukea, they also display the complexities of both participating in and speaking out against territorial landscaping agendas. Through his memory of international, national, and personal terrains, it is evident that the discursive movements from *'āina* to private property conditioned and still inform how we relate to space and one another.

The Republic of Hawaii firmly established and recognized by all of the Great Powers, with Sanford B. Dole as President, I was offered a position in the Public Lands Office as Sub-Agent under J.F. Brown. Whilst thus employed I accompanied Mr. Dole on a circuit of the Island of Hawaii, preparatory to the opening of Government lands for settlement under the Freehold and Right of Purchase Leases, a system recently adopted by the Legislature on the recommendations of Mr. Dole. Resulting in the taking up of many tracts of land on the Islands of Hawaii and Oahu. The Wahiawa lands on the latter island in particular with its flourishing town and community, and vast fields of pineapple as far as the eye can see.

I think this is an appropriate place to sit down my impressions from a long association with Sanford B. Dole, Hawaii's "grand old man," he was in later years.

It was my good fortune to know Sanford B. Dole and to be counted amongst the favored ones enjoying the intimacy of his home and friendship. A man of sterling qualities, cultured and refined, and at heart the friend of Hawaii and the Hawaiian.

I came to know him when he was serving his first term as a legislator and a Representative from the Island of Kauai at the session of 1884. He had introduced a Bill known as the "Homestead Law," under the provision of which the man of small means may acquire a tract of government land upon which to build himself a home and settle. A system of land tenure and occupation that up to that time was prohibitive, because of the existing statute requiring that all government lands of whatever nature, whether for sale or lease, be sold at public auction. Usually in such large tracts and at such an upset price or rental as only the wealthy and moneyed interests can acquire.

Suffice it to say, the Dole Homestead Bill was enacted into law and became operative on the 29ᵗʰ day of August 1884, when the King's sign manual "Kalakaua Rex" was affixed to the precious document. As a result some 3000 acres of land in the Hamakua District, Island of Hawaii were thrown open for settlement, the allotments averaging 20 to 25 acres. Then there was the Nuuanu Valley homesteads on the Island of Oahu, in easy access of Honolulu, comprising an area of a 100 acres, subdivided into 5 and 10 acres lots, now considered one of the choicest of the city's residential sites.

By this one stroke of diplomacy, Mr. Dole made for himself a name that won the love and affection of the Hawaiian people, for it was they that the law was intended to benefit and many availed themselves of the boon they had been waiting for these many years. A service, I have no hesitancy in saying that stood the author in good stead, when with the turn of the tide, Mr. Sanford B. Dole was called on to steer the Ship of States from the perilous rocks in which it had found itself after it had ceded the Monarchy.

So far so good. But now comes the rub where I was personally concerned. Balanced on the scale as it were, to test where my loyalty laid. With the old order or the new. A hard test it was. For all I owed and enjoyed, even from childhood, was due to royalty. To renounce which, spelt of ingratitude. Many an anxious hour, yea, many a sleepless night did I spend over my decision in the matter.

To explain. Mr. Dole on assuming the reins of Government, Queen Liliuokalani had surrendered under protest and had sent for me and made request of me to remain in office and continue in the administration of the Crown Lands, of which I was then and had been for many years past Commissioner and Land Agent. And saying that it was the magnanimous wish of the Executive Council; and as a personal request, added "I have need of your services."

Girding up my loins, I called on the Queen, informed her of what had taken place, stressing the point that my first duty was to royalty and not to those of her enemies. Much to my relief she responded by saying, "Stay where you are and keep an eye on the Crown Land revenues. They are mine, and I'm going to be restored to the Throne when the United States Government is fully informed of the wrongful manner the overthrow of the monarchy was accomplished by and with the connivance of the American Minister Stevens."

After expressing my deep sympathy with her at the turn of events had taken culminating in the overthrow and the surrender of her rights as sovereign, I bid her Aloha, and as I took her hand to kiss it with eyes filled with tears, I felt a slight tremor that for the moment inspired the feeling that the worst had come and all was at an end. This was the last time that I saw her to speak to until I called on her at Washington D.C. some four years later on my way home with Mr. S.M. Damon from London where we had been at the "Diamond" Jubilee of Queen Victoria's in 1892.

Needless to say, I notified Mr. Dole of my acceptance, took the oath of allegiance to the Provisional Government, and from that day to the formation of the Territory of Hawaii following the annexation of the Islands to the United States, I remained in the service of the Public Lands Department until I resigned to take office with the Oahu Railway and Land Company as Treasurer in succession to Mark P. Robinson [who] resigned in February of 1890.[1]

What surprised me most when I read this chapter was the apparently close personal relationship between Curtis P. Iaukea and Sanford B. Dole. Dole was a lawyer, formerly a legislator in the Hawaiian Kingdom, and then a leader in the illegal overthrow of Queen Lili'uokalani. He served as the president of the Republic of Hawai'i from 1894 to 1898. I didn't expect that Curtis P. Iaukea would like him so much on a personal level. The documents of this era point to interpersonal relationships between political actors that were complicated, and so easy definitions for "enemy" and "friend" are not available here. It will become even more apparent in later chapters that such a dichotomy simply did not exist. The political actors were operating in their own social context one hundred years ago. A reading of Curtis P. Iaukea's chapters suggests a blurring of interpersonal relationships with land legislation.

The collision between the personal, the political, and the geographic is probably most clearly reflected in the struggle over and vocal opposition to the HHCA in the public sphere. The HHCA was a culmination of various resolutions, acts, and debates in the territorial legislature and in the U.S. Congress. This act set aside "Public Lands" for "native Hawaiians" for "rehabilitation." In her book *Hawaiian Blood*, J. Kēhaulani Kauanui explains the genealogy of bills that created the HHCA. U.S. Senate Concurrent Resolution 2 (SCR 2), premised on native rehabilitation, and House Concurrent Resolution 28 (HCR 28), which sought to expand the leases for sugar planters on "Public Lands," were both introduced in February 1920. The two bills were then consolidated into U.S. House Resolution 12683, named the "Kūhiō Bill" because Prince Jonah Kūhiō Kalaniana'ole, Hawai'i's congressional representative to Washington, introduced it. This bill was recommitted as U.S. House Resolution 13500, and the issue was returned to the territorial legislature. Senate Concurrent Resolution 6 and SCR 8 were then created and linked planters' interests with blood quantum.

Under these resolutions, "available lands" were to go to the "native Hawaiian" or those with at least 50 percent Hawaiian blood quantum, as opposed to the "part Hawaiian" or those with less than 50 percent Hawaiian blood. The final resolution also revoked an Organic Act clause that had previously limited corporations from buying over 1,000 acres of land. Soon, sugar corporations were owning and operating on more than 1,000 acres of prime agricultural land, leaving the "worst" lands for native Hawaiian rehabilitation. Reintroduced then to Congress as HR 7257 and S 1881, the HHCA was signed into U.S. federal law on July 9, 1921.[2]

Public outcry against and support for the HHCA raged in the newspapers in 1922. One of the most prominent debates was between Curtis P. Iaukea and Lorrin Thurston, conducted in numerous letters to the editor. Lorrin Thurston was a lawyer for the plantation interests, the leader of the illegal overthrow of Queen Lili'uokalani, and the owner of Hawai'i's leading newspaper, the *Honolulu Advertiser*.[3] The tone of the debate mirrored a familiar type of political theater in the territorial government, as the faces of the political parties, Democrat and Republican, took shape.

Curtis P. Iaukea saved an entire three-ring binder of newspaper articles that presented this public debate with Lorrin Thurston. In 1922, Iaukea openly criticized the HHCA and the "doling" out of "Public Lands" to sugar interests, to the benefit of only a handful of native Hawaiians, and to the detriment of everyone else. He finally spoke out because, he said, "I owe a duty to the people." He explained further:

> All these twenty years and more, under our American Systems of government, I have enjoyed office paid by the people. My lips all that time have been sealed, so to speak. No man of any honor will openly criticize an administration of which he was part. The seal is broken now, and I mean to speak, which is the least I can do, in return for the honor and trust confided in me by the people.[4]

I interpret "the seal is broken" to be a reference to the passing of Prince Kūhiō, who died earlier that year.[5] "Trust confided in me by the people" is read as Curtis P. Iaukea's recognition of *kuleana* as an *ali'i* both to the people and to the *ali'i*.[6]

A triangular discourse concerning rehabilitation, yeoman capitalism, and nativeness emerged in Honolulu's newspapers in 1922. The focal point was the upcoming election of Hawai'i's congressional representative, and the presumed effect this decision would have on the HHCA. Prince Jonah Kūhiō Kalaniana'ole had died early in 1922 as the serving Republican member of Congress. He had also authored the HHCA, with the help of commission delegate and fellow Hawaiian John H. Wise.

After Prince Kūhiō's death, John Wise ran for Congress as a Republican against the Democrat William Jarrett. At the time, Curtis P. Iaukea had just served a term as the secretary of Hawai'i. Appointed by U.S. president

Woodrow Wilson, he was noted to be a faithful Democrat, and he came out in favor of William Jarrett in an article sent to the *Advertiser* entitled "FIGHT TO A FINISH; Wise or Jarrett for Delegate?" Lorrin Thurston then answered this article with seven consecutive articles entitled "FIGHT TO A FINISH; Iaukea vs. Thurston."

In the first article, Curtis P. Iaukea set forth the challenge: "I am with you in all things as far as John Wise's ability is concerned, but I can't help feeling that he is responsible for the Organic Act Amendments which I as a citizen highly disapprove, and regard as a battering away of the people's rights and safeguards."[7] In a subsequent article he spelled out his opposition to Wise in six parts, which culminated in Iaukea's disagreement with the repeal of the 1,000-acre law:

WISE HELPED REPEAL CORPORATION 1000-ACRE LAW

Lastly, but not the least: In doing away with the safeguard which the Organic Act provided in the interest of the people—I mean, the limitation placed on the acquiring by large corporations of land in fee simple, over and above the 1000 acres already possessed in fee simple.

Every acre of additional land acquired by a corporation renders it more and more difficult for the small man to acquire a holding.

REHABILITATION ACT DUE TO WISE

His was the head and brains that carried the Hawaiian Homes Act through Congress and with it the abortive measures and acts that I am more openly protesting in the name of the Democratic party in Hawaii.

The price paid for the rehabilitation of a few Hawaiian families was too dear and costly when the interests of the people are taken into consideration.[8]

Another article, entitled "Wise for Big Business," author unknown, continued to level accusations against Wise by pointing out his specific role in introducing and passing the amendment that altered the 1,000-acre law:

A few years ago when a large acreage of plantation leases was about to expire and, according to the mandate contained in the Organic Act, the land should be turned over to homesteading, the plantation lawyers realized that something had to be done and done quickly if those leases were to be retained.

Those clever plantation lawyers knew that it would never do to attempt to have the plantation leases renewed at the expense of homesteading. That would be altogether too raw, and the people that would protest loudest and longest would undoubtedly be the Hawaiian people above all others.

And so the very clever scheme was evolved by those plantation lawyers of creating a Hawaiian Homes Act, ostensibly for the purpose of "rehabilitating" the Hawaiians, but the real object of which was to enable the plantations to continue to control their valuable leaseholds on territorial sugar lands.

The homestead rights of the Hawaiian people were filched away from them by the efforts of those plantation lawyers aided and abetted by Wise. And in order to all the more cleverly deceive the people and make them believe they were scuring [sic] something tangible out of the new system of things, the Hawaiian people were fooled with the offer of some barren "homesteads" on the barren slopes of Molokai—lands so arid and unfruitful that a prairie chicken would starve to death if compelled to live on them—lands of such a character that even the lowest forms of insect life refuse to inhabit them—but lands good enough, so said Wise and the planters, for the Hawaiian people to live on.

And yet these lands, hitherto utterly useless and unproductive—lands good for neither beast, bird nor insect—were taken in hand by the plantation interests and offered as a means to rehabilitate the Hawaiians!

And it was John Wise who, knowingly and willingly, went to Washington to help put his Hawaiian people upon such and help the plantation interests to kill the provision in the Organic Act relating to homesteading, and to keep his own people from ever acquiring a single acre of land by the honest route.[9]

Many spoke out against the clause that allowed sugar corporations free rein with regard to land in Hawai'i, while some were clearly in favor of it. Thurston, a lawyer for the sugar interests at the signing of the Organic Act, not surprisingly favored the amendment. In 1922, responding to the opposition, he spoke freely of his initial dislike of the Organic Act, and the need to repeal the 1,000-acre law:

PIECE OF "BUNK"

In the first place, as a piece of effective legislation, it was the biggest piece of "bunk" ever enacted! It never did and never could have had any effect, except to hamper business. Second, that its only possible effect was to impose upon the sugar interests of Hawaii an unnecessary expense and burden, which reduced the available funds with which to make improvements and pay dividends. As the great majority of the people of Hawaii make their living, directly or indirectly, out of the sugar industry, it left that much less money to be divided among them. It was therefore a burden upon and an injury to the people of Hawaii.

INEFFECTIVE LEGISLATION

It was a rank discrimination against Hawaii, imposing restrictions upon us that are not imposed upon the people of any State.

It was ineffective legislation, because it was confined in its prohibition, to ownership in fee.

It imposed no restriction on leaseholds, for any number of years.

It did not prohibit the forming of a new corporation which purchased the land desired, its stock being in turn held by the real corporation in interest.

It did not prohibit such new corporation, or any number of new corporations, each owning just under 1000 acres, going into a partnership, the practical effect of which was to give title to one interest in as many thousand acres as there were corporations.[10]

Thurston argued simultaneously that the 1,000-acre provision in the Organic Act was not only bad for business, but that it also did not prohibit the monopolization of land and power in Hawai'i. His arguments that land should be used as the vehicle for rehabilitation of a race were therefore tied to a belief in the merits of fee-simple and unrestricted capitalism, and objection to any restriction of these resources as being bad for business. Native subjectivity therefore was placed for safety on the narrow precipice of unrestricted capital interests.

The Organic Act, which was the focus of the 1922 newspaper debates, took effect in Hawai'i on June 14, 1900. This act created the political entity known as the territorial government, which had jurisdiction over the eight substantial Hawaiian islands as well as thirteen lesser islands and atolls: "The Hawaiian group consists of the following islands: Hawaii, Maui, Oahu, Kauai, Molokai, Lanai, Niihau, Kahoolawe, Molokini, Lehua, Kaula, Nihoa, Necker, Laysan, Gardiner, Lisiansky, Ocean, French Frigates Shoal, Palmyra, Brooks Shoal, Pearl and Hermes Reef, Gambia Shoal and Dowsett and Maro Reef."[11] This act was designed to lay out every aspect of governance for the Territory of Hawai'i, and to define the procedural responsibilities of the legislative, executive, and judicial branches of government.

With regard to land management, the Organic Act imposed two restrictions on land:

1. The term of any agricultural lease was limited to no longer than five years; and
2. No corporation, including a sugar plantation, could acquire and hold more than 1,000 acres of land, subject to vested right.[12]

These restrictions made homesteading a priority of government, and although a 1908 provision to this act extended the allowable agricultural leases to fifteen years, a later provision established that agricultural leases would be subject to withdrawal if needed for homesteading or public purposes.[13] It was this clause that frightened many in the business sector.

The Organic Act also established the procedures for governance of "Public Lands." These were the Crown Lands and Government Lands of the Hawaiian Kingdom that were "ceded" to the United States in the 1898 Joint Resolution. It was the Land Act of 1895, passed by the Republic of Hawai'i, that treated Crown Lands as vested in the republic, and therefore renamed them "Public Lands." This made possible the sale of these lands, which had been restricted since 1865.[14] As Kamana Beamer explains, "The Law attempted to take two previously distinct land groups—those of the Government and those of the Crown—and reclassify them as one land base under the term 'Public Lands'" so that, as Donovan Preza notes, by "collectively calling them the 'Public Lands' the 'sale' of these lands was made possible."[15] Both writers also acknowledge that the opening up of the Crown Lands for public consumption in the 1895 Land Act was supposed to encourage outside American settlement of Hawai'i. The illegal overthrow of Queen Lili'uokalani created the biggest land displacement among Hawaiians; the Joint Resolution of 1898 continued this initiative by seizing approximately 1.75 million acres of Government and Crown Lands, now "Public Lands," for the United States.[16] I use the word "seize" deliberately. Since a joint resolution cannot legally annex another nation-state, the property of the Hawaiian Kingdom was not in fact ceded, but *seized*.

The genealogy of land use up to the Organic Act was discussed in the previous chapter. The Constitution of 1840 first declared that the "land of the Kingdom was not the private property of Kamehameha I" because the land "belonged to the chiefs and people in common, of whom Kamehameha I was the head, and had the management of the landed property."[17] The *Mō'ī* (king) governed according to *mana,* and since "[m]aka'āinana were never 'equal,' in terms of genealogy and social organizations to the *Ali'i,*"[18] an equal division of the land base was never anticipated. The *ali'i* were therefore in effect the landlords under the native tenant/land rights code, but native tenants maintained rights under the Kuleana Act—"a mechanism which allowed native tenants to divide out their previously undivided interest in land."[19]

The actual land division by Kamehameha III was known as the Māhele. As illustrated by the Office of the Regent in 1848, the land was sectioned off in the following ways: of the four million acres in the Hawaiian Islands, one-third to the Government class as "Freehold Estate of Inheritance," one-third to the Konohiki class as "Freehold Estate of the Konohiki," and one-third to the Native Tenant class as "Freehold Estate for the Life of the Konohiki."[20]

In 1850, foreigners were allowed to buy and sell land, thus opening it up to outsiders. But the land also remained deeply rooted in a native cosmology that recognized its importance for psychological survival. By insuring continuing land relationships for *maka'āinana* through the Kuleana Act and native tenant land rights, cultural connections to cosmology were preserved.

Under the constitutional law of the Hawaiian Kingdom, Government Lands were the property of the chiefs and people, while Crown Lands were the private property of the *ali'i*, and to be used to support the crown. Even after being renamed and redefined as "Public Lands," these approximately 1.75 million acres that were "ceded" to the U.S. government following the illegal overthrow of the Hawaiian Kingdom were still recognized as having been left in trust to the Hawaiian people.[21] Sixty years later, the 1959 Admission Act that made Hawai'i a state in the Union continued to recognize the trust nature of the Government and Crown Lands. But this trust relationship is different, because it relegates Hawaiians to a welfare status. The original trust relationship between *ali'i* and *maka'āinana*, one governed by *kuleana*, had been left behind.

Furthermore, the collapsing of Crown Lands into Government Lands, and the renaming of "Public Lands," effectively erased the private property rights of the *ali'i*. The Crown Lands were not public but belonged to the *ali'i* so that they could support themselves financially and maintain their trust relationships. These lands never were, and never became, legally or epistemologically public. Hegemonic writings after the illegal overthrow were used to reenvision these lands as "Public Lands." Calling these lands "public" supposedly made them so. But which public? Whose public? Public public? Meaning everyone?

The Queen made many trips to the United States to fight for the revenue of these lands. Working for the return of the Crown Lands revenues, so that she could support herself and her people, filled the remaining years of the Queen's life (see chapter 3). Thus, since Curtis P. Iaukea was appointed sub-agent of "Public Lands" on October 7, 1895, and later served as one of the first trustees of the Queen's estate, it was no wonder that by 1922 he had much to say about the use/misuse of these lands.

As the trust nature of land had been embedded in Hawaiian Kingdom laws since 1840, the concept of homestead was introduced in the Hawaiian Kingdom with the 1884 Homestead Law. This law granted 999-year homestead leases to those who met its restrictions, and 256 patents were issued.[22] Several years after the law's passage, Curtis P. Iaukea was involved as commissioner of Crown Lands in opening up these lands for rental by native tenants: "At the beginning of the year 1892, a new system of leasing was introduced, the main feature of which was to secure to small holders, more particularly native Hawaiians, the opportunity of acquiring under fair conditions suitable sections on the Crown Lands, for homestead and agricultural purposes."[23]

An example was the homesteading of Crown Lands at Puʻukapu, in Waimea, Hawaiʻi. In an 1894 report, Curtis P. Iaukea noted that the approximately 971,463 acres of Crown Lands held a value of about $2,314,250.00, and he described a new system of leasing to small landowners, mostly Hawaiians. Crown Lands at Puʻukapu in Waimea were specifically opened with "the intention being to afford them (native Hawaiians) every opportunity of acquiring suitable sections of land whereon they may build and establish permanent homes."[24]

Some years after Dole's Homestead Law for the Hawaiian Kingdom in 1884, a 1910 provision to the Organic Act stated that the territory should open land to homesteading when twenty-five or more qualified applicants applied for a particular parcel of land. But in 1921 the HHCA wiped out these amended homestead provisions and instead codified the status quo for Hawaiʻi's sugar industry, because "the managers of Hawaiʻi's large plantations feared that the net result of this homesteading experiment would be to destroy a thriving plantation enterprise."[25] The oligarchy that effectively ruled Hawaiʻi at the turn of the last century consisted of sugar corporations largely established by missionary families. Known as the Big 5—Castle & Cooke, C. Brewer & Co., Alexander & Baldwin, American Factors, and Theo H. Davies & Co.—these sugar planters leased large sections of "ceded" lands at very favorable rates. But after 1910, these corporations faced looming deadlines for these leases to expire.[26] Alan Murakami explains:

> Since the reign of King Kalākaua, large sugar interests in Hawaiʻi enjoyed the use of 26,000 acres of prime agricultural lands, largely Crown Lands, then under lease from the territory. These lands would become available for general homesteading once the leases expired. In all, government leases to some 200,000 acres of public land were due to expire between 1917 and 1921.[27]

The need to extend these sugar leases, and the possibility of gaining even more land in the process, therefore, fueled the 1921 HHCA legislation. But the issue of corporate acquisition of land had already been discussed on the floor of the U.S. Congress as early as 1900, when the 1,000-acre law had been a topic of debate. Some representatives wanted to limit the allowable acreage for corporations—among them, Senator Newlands:

> Mr. Chairman, the purpose of this amendment is to limit a tendency toward land monopoly in the islands of Hawaii. But this proposition reaches the vital question whether we shall allow in those islands a system which will gradually monopolize all the lands in large holdings either in the hands of individuals or of corporations, the mass of the population being attached to the soil in a semi-servile capacity without right to a foot of land upon which they stand. This amendment respects vested rights. It does not propose to interfere with any of the holdings of that island at the present time, though those old holdings are large. The general custom there is to organize a corporation for the purpose of running a sugar plantation. That corporation acquires a large tract of land, introduces extensive irrigation works, puts up a sugar factory, and commences business, and there is no doubt but that this kind of cooperation leads to the economical conduct of that business. This amendment does not interfere with that cooperation. It simply limits the holdings of any corporation to 1,000 acres. This amendment is not illiberal. It provides for holdings of a thousand acres, and it does not interfere with any existing holdings. I have already stated the tendency in all these possessions having tropical or semi-tropical climates to be toward land monopoly, and that tendency will increase as the value of these lands increases, by reason of the enlarged markets which annexation to our country will afford. It is the great evil now in Hawaii. It will be a greater evil in the future than it is now.[28]

The danger of monopolies was a major topic in these early congressional debates, but the strategies offered for combating them assumed that the beneficiaries of the trust did not have agency, and could not be self-governed. The only alternative to the rush toward corporate monopoly was apparently patriarchal mentoring by the governing entity.

Hawai'i's "Public Lands" were understood to be held in trust by the U.S. government and appeared explicitly this way in the Joint Resolution of 1898: "Congress would enact special laws for the management and disposition of Hawaii's public lands. And, that these laws were to be for the benefit of the inhabitants of the Hawaiian Islands for educational and other public purposes."[29] The Statehood Act of 1959 continued this genealogy of thought by also recognizing the trust nature of Government and Crown Lands.

The HHCA was fundamental in sustaining, promoting, and defining this trust as a land/race discourse. But at a great cost. The territorial legislature passed Senate Concurrent Resolution 8 in 1921. A compromise between ranching and sugar interests, this resolution repealed the 1,000-acre law of the Organic Act. By striking down this law, the HHCA changed the understanding of land

and citizen to accord with an American free-market enterprise and yeoman capitalist system, allowing the Big 5 to buy and sell as much land as they wanted without any restrictions. This was the trade-off for the establishment of the Hawaiian Homes Commission, and "Wise and Kalaniʻanaole participated in private negotiations in order to win the support of the Big Five."[30]

Initially the Hawaiian Homes Commission was to be a five-year experiment with 37,900 acres of land on the islands of Hawaiʻi and Molokaʻi.[31] Eventually, the act set aside between 188,000 and 203,000 acres for homesteading by native Hawaiians. But in return it also accepted the leases of sugar interests on "Public Lands," effectively exempting all sugar lands from homesteading.[32] "Through this resolution," Rona Halualani writes, "dominant sugar and rancher leases could continue, and Hawaiians could be reformed through land."[33]

By this time, then, both trust and homestead doctrines had been reinscribed with strictly American meanings, which continue to construct the Hawaiian citizenry today. In a 1922 newspaper article on Wise, Curtis P. Iaukea defended actual homesteading:

WISE OPPOSES HOMESTEADING

First: In betraying the people's trust by assisting the move to put an end to all homesteading in this territory for the next 15 years or perhaps for all time.

Homesteading is the mainstay of any American community in the building up of small homes and holdings, thereby establishing in the country what is termed "the bone and sinew" of the land.[34]

As Curtis P. Iaukea clearly knew, the "yeoman farmer" experience in the United States tied land and citizen together as one political unit. A Jeffersonian landscape divided land through the small farmer work ethic, as articulated in the Land Ordinance Act of 1785. Under this ordinance, the small yeoman landowner, by farming and tilling his acreage, gained the status of citizen: "In (this) new physical world a new human world might be created."[35] Within these new worlds of horizontal and vertical gridding, land further became viewed as landscape, and the small farmer's claim to citizenship was based on notions of equality.

As land becomes legible to and through the state, a national citizenry emerges that matches this national terrain. The Jeffersonian Land Ordinance of 1785 explicitly sought to produce a particular type of citizen who would produce and coproduce citizenship according to notions of democracy and equality based on an equal landowner citizenship and a yeoman capitalist farmer work ethic. Working together, the cartographer and the citizen/laborer informed and produced one another, and a national landscape was born that found its audience.

But it soon became clear that the production of a national citizenry is a highly complicated and densely bureaucratic endeavor, and cultural norms and identities become simplified in the process. Michel Foucault and Timothy Mitchell have suggested that subjects are created and institutionalized by the producers of the regimes of truth,[36] and modern governing entities therefore united to produce "the modern individual, constructed as an isolated, disciplined, receptive, and industrious political subject."[37] Such projects "all contribute to constructing a world that appears to consist not of a complex of social practices but of a binary order: on the one hand individuals and their activities, on the other an inert structure that somehow stands apart from individuals, preexists them, and contains and gives a framework of their lives."[38] Acting through legislation and bureaucratization, the inert structures neutralize and naturalize everything within the state system. Hence the irony that ultimately "It is not that the beautiful totality of the individual is amputated, repressed, altered by our social order, it is rather that the individual is carefully fabricated in it, according to a whole technique of forces and bodies."[39]

Hawaiians were definitely fabricated within a citizen/state homestead discourse in 1922. While Representative William Jarrett attacked the bill by claiming that it was really set in place to kill homesteading in Hawai'i for Hawaiians, in his rebuttal to Curtis P. Iaukea's attacks on the repeal of the 1,000-acre law, Lorrin Thurston explained that his own support for it was actually altruistic and moral, because he saw it as a force for the greater good for Hawaiians as subject/citizen homesteaders:

> Upon interviews with Kuhio after his return, and with other Hawaiians whom I considered the most sincere and responsible of the race, I found them so earnest and unanimous in their belief that the act would succeed in getting the Hawaiians "back to the land," and arrest the present appalling rate of decrease of the nation; so enthusiastic in their advocacy of the measure as the last hope of saving the full-blooded Hawaiian race from extinction, and so eager to make the attempt, that I did not have the heart to oppose them further; but agreed that, so far as I was concerned, I was willing that they should have the opportunity to try and see what could be done on the area and within the time proposed.
>
> That is the reason why I withdrew my opposition to the Rehabilitation Act.[40]

Thurston further criticized Curtis P. Iaukea for speaking out against the HHCA and charged him with betraying the memory of Prince Kūhiō by voicing his opinions. Hawaiians, under colonial and American national discourse, must always agree. Not to do so is dishonorable and might even threaten the image of friendly and nonconfrontational natives, essential for eventual full citizenship:

STRIKING AT KUHIO, TOO

Knowing all this, it comes with poor grace from Iaukea to lie back and acquiesce in the passage of legislation without a peep of protest, and now, after the leader, the creator, the soul of the measure, is dead and gone and his voice stilled forever, to malignantly attack the measure as "a betrayal of the people's trust."

The attack is on its face directed at Wise; but Wise was simply a man in the ranks, following and helping his leader-Kuhio!

If, in so doing, Wise was "betraying the people's trust," then by that same argument, Kuhio was doing likewise!

BITES THE HAND THAT FEEDS

I say that irrespective of the fact that Iaukea himself is a native Hawaiian, it comes with especial bad grace from him, for all his mature life he has been eating his poi out of the Kalakaua family poi bowl! He has been a "pet" of that family and even now is being given a living out of the Liliuokalani Estate.

I say that to now blacken the memory and motives of the last member of the family which during all his life has fed him pap from a silver spoon, is the act of an ingrate.

It makes no difference that Iaukea is making the attack in the name of John Wise. He is making it because Wise supported those who were principals in securing the passage of this law—that is, Kuhio and McCarthy.[41]

Thurston also responded by denying Iaukea the opportunity to speak. As the newspaper attacks continued, Curtis P. Iaukea found his responses either were not printed in the *Advertiser* in a timely manner or were altered in their form. The result was one-person editorializing by Lorrin Thurston on the subject of who Hawaiians should be and where they should be situated. Faced with this silencing, Iaukea then went to the other newspapers of the day, including the Japanese newspaper *Daily Nippu Jiji* and *New Freedom* to voice his grievances. But the *Advertiser* actually published one of his responses, which complained about Thurston's strategy:

In the conduct of a debate, it is not only unsportsmanlike for a contestant to interrupt his opponent while that opponent is endeavoring to make his points, but it

is unethical and reprehensible. When a host entertains a guest, it is unsportsmanlike and ungentlemanly for him to insult that guest in the course of an argument
which arises at the time.

This is precisely what you, or those in charge of your paper are doing. You accepted the challenge which I gave you, Wise vs. Jarrett. You stated in your paper
that I would be accorded the same consideration which you yourself would give
your answers to my charges. It is your newspaper, controlled by you. You are
therefore in the position of a host, or of a prize fighter possessed of an unusual
ability to use your feet.

Your printed edition of my letter is interlarded and adulterated with your own
comments, quotations, and criticisms. This I claim is not fair, sportsmanlike, or
in accord with the letter or spirit of the terms advanced by you in accepting my
challenge.

You have the advantage. The paper is yours. Come, be sportsmanlike.[42]

As this political bantering continued, who the native Hawaiian is was under
intense discussion, both in Hawai'i and in the U.S. Congress. Earlier definitions of native Hawaiian had fixed blood quantum at 1/32 Hawaiian blood, but
various forms of statistical analysis led to the raising of the blood quantum
requirement to 50 percent.[43] This sharply reduced the number of possible
participants in this process. Rona Halualani explains that informing the government's need to control was a "myth of extinction" that gripped policymak-
ers regarding Hawaiians: "It (was) estimated that by the year 1952, all pure
Hawaiians will vanish. An Extinction discourse therefore positioned Hawaiians as a dying population that only the (American) nation-state could save."[44]

In the HHCA itself there is only one statement of who the native Hawaiian is: "The term 'native Hawaiian' means any descendant of not less than
one-half part of the blood of the races inhabiting the Hawaiian Islands previous to 1778."[45] However fleeting this definition might be, the scope and terms
of 50 percent blood quantum had far-reaching socioeconomic aftereffects
thanks to the way that self and other were envisioned and executed.

Kauanui also notes that a "welfare discourse" accompanied the debate. In
the territorial debates, those with less than 50 percent Hawaiian blood were
seen as "almost white" anyway, and therefore not in as dire need of rehabilitation as those with more than 50 percent Hawaiian blood. Competence was
therefore tied to blood, and "the welfare discourse of protection and rehabilitation was the means by which a racialization of identity occurred."[46] In
this mind-set and through practice, Hawaiians were awarded a deficit citizenship, counted "only in relation to their welfare needs—as the logic of

'pitied, but not entitled' became ever more manifest. The result was to disqualify alternative discourses of native land entitlement."[47] Blood quantum discourse had previously helped to define American Indians, and it was used again to group and view Hawaiians through the same lens. The *native* is implicated here. Through blood quantum requirements, the state structure systematically detaches natives from the landscape and then reinscribes them in state-sanctioned ways within a capitalist system. This conscious separation of native people from land became a necessary state function: "The spatial energy of capitalism works to deterritorialize people (that is, to detach them from prior bonds between people and place) and to reterritorialize them in relation to the requirements of capital."[48] As a result, natives become placed and fixed in accordance with state agendas and priorities, as opposed to a sort of placeless reality formerly recognized in the eyes of the law. For example, hunting and fishing suggest a more nomadic and therefore unregulated existence in the imaginations of modernity than does a homesteading way of life. The process of fixing natives necessarily erases any type of cosmological, epistemic connection to ʻāina, and "epistemic erasures are not innocent; they justify political and territorial erasures."[49]

This habitual distinguishing of race, with class a supposedly insignificant by-product, is a necessary element in the racial imaginary of "Americanisation." As Antonio Gramsci recognized, the emphasis placed on gridding populations according to race/class categories in America determines citizenry, and this type of deficient citizenry granted individuals based on race has a lengthy genealogy and understanding.[50] Such designations, and especially the blood-based determinant, not only affected Hawaiians, forcing them into self-imposed measuring of degrees of Hawaiianness, but influenced all other citizens in Hawaiʻi as well. Under the Hawaiian Kingdom, "aboriginal Hawaiian" had signified a person having any amount of Hawaiian blood, while a "Hawaiian Kingdom subject" was a citizen of any ethnicity. The later determination of ethnicity, and the measuring of degrees of Hawaiianness, effectively Americanized the entire population by fixing racial categories, ignoring or rendering insignificant the influences of genealogy and the cultural experiences that constitute members of communities.

Designations of nativeness are inherently divisive. Who gets to be native? Which natives deserve to get back to the land? Furthermore, as part of the bureaucratic imagination, nativeness undergoes intense "performative procedures," because those designated as natives must prove and prove again their right to continue to exist as native in a contemporary context.[51] Nativeness, therefore, has been definitive as a social construction that renders "landscape a racial project."[52] The "who" allowed to be on the land, and in what capacities, becomes heavily guarded and inspected, and bureaucratic spaces are prescribed according to race/gender projects. In short, within this larger frame of matching deserving natives to rehabilitative lands, "nature's production is always entangled with much more than nature, including questions of class, race, gender, and sexuality."[53]

Nativeness and its designations have also allowed the surveillance capacities of both the territorial and U.S. federal governments in Hawai'i to intervene constantly into the emerging kaleidoscope of multiple cultural identities. However complicated setting blood quantum requirements or census taking might be, they are valued agents in sustaining the surveillance capacities of the state. Countable people and measurable portions of society have justified the exercise of bureaucratic power by the territorial and U.S. federal governments in Hawai'i in the emerging twentieth century.[54] The celebration of emergent institutional order over chaos, and the recoding of the landscape as a people-scape continued the process of establishing a national identity tied to a landed identity (possessing property), and eventually to notions of "equality." Western interpretations define both people and space, to establish close association between land and identity, so that through its owners, 'āina can be governed as land and natives can be governed as *native*. In this way, "social identity is inscribed, and thereby reproduced, in the physical landscape and in the way bodies move through space,"[55] and this movement of bodies through space is closely monitored.

As aboriginal Hawaiians, we now must see ourselves in this manner. And this is tiring—the constant proving of one's Hawaiianness. It is bureaucratically fatiguing—the continual requests for birth certificates to show lineage of Hawaiian blood—but emotionally taxing too. And in the process of fixing our Hawaiianess, American doctrine continues to distinguish and define us. Looking Hawaiian and being Hawaiian are already two different aspects of an impossibly complex social construction. As for Hawaiianness itself, it is not measurable, except in the bureaucratic imaginations of the status quo. In addition, one's state-made native identity is made and remade according to a whole host of shifting variables, such as the Census Bureau's changing definitions, the interpretations of the social whispers of otherness, and the particular political dictates of the power elite as it merges with economic output.

So, what does a native Hawaiian look like? My great-great-grandfather was fair-skinned, with hazel eyes and brown hair. Piehu—his middle name—was given to him by the reigning *Ali'i* because of his fair skin. Also, Piehu is "the spray that was sprinkled," to describe an incident at the ceremony performed by Kapihe when Kauikeaouli was born. My great-great-grandmother had a darker complexion and jet-black hair. As a Hawaiian today, I am fair-skinned, with blond/brown hair, and green eyes. Because of this, the questioning of my percentage of Hawaiian blood has been monotonous and continuous throughout my life. First comes the "You're Hawaiian?" Then comes the demand "How much Hawaiian are you?" On those days when I'm less than forthcoming, "Enough" is the answer. And don't let the blond hair fool you—there is enough. To provide the answer, and defend the exact percentage, only reinforces the divisive mind-set, one instilled by the American ideological and bureaucratic state system. Such obsessions with race seem mostly absent among our Polynesian cousins. As far as I'm aware, Tahitians aren't constantly asked "How much Tahitian do you have?" They simply are Tahitian: blood quantum is irrelevant. Ultimately, then, the posing and answering of questions about blood quantum reveal just how successful the American socialization process in Hawai'i has been.

My entrance as an on-campus seventh-grade boarding student at the Kamehameha Schools, which you have to have Hawaiian blood to attend, saved me not only from the constant questioning of my race, but also from assumption of the worst—that my heritage was the same one that for Hawaiians represents all that is wrong in Hawai'i. I happily avoided these charged interactions until I graduated from the Kamehameha Schools. And then it was back with everyone else, where race matters and is studied for clues as to how to proceed with personal interactions.

People still question my race and are surprised when they learn that I am Hawaiian and also the daughter of a very "Hawaiian-looking" father. But for my part, I have long stopped trying to qualify as a Hawaiian. I surf. I paddle canoe. I also completed service in the Peace Corps, I speak Spanish fluently, and I love to travel. I see myself in my great-great-grandfather sometimes. I also feel connected to place, and I know I am being watched and guided by forces greater than myself. Proving Hawaiianess does not play into this equation much.

Hawaiians in the early 1920s had much more to contend with immediately, as ʻāina continued to be retranslated by the various economic interests in Hawaiʻi. Because these actions bound native subjectivity tightly with a U.S. jurisprudence, the trust relationship that proceeded the hearings and that continues to inform the native citizenry today became confused, as the *kuleana* trust was silenced by a U.S. national paternalistic trust relationship. This later paradigm demands gratefulness from Hawaiians for a land base that should already be inhabited by Hawaiians, both native and part, as a by-product of the circular, all-encompassing trust of the *aliʻi*. Instead, this trust relationship today is configured to understand Hawaiians as recipients in a welfare state, as opposed to the stewards and beneficiaries of hereditary entitlements.

The documents surrounding the HHCA show that its agenda was complicated from its inception. Discussions were either vehemently opposed or passionately in favor of the passage of this act. But on both sides were, and continue to be, issues of being and proving oneself deserving enough to be counted not only as native, but also as able and willing to return to the land. Through this process, land as an ideological construct continues to reinterpret ʻāina—transforming it from a genealogical entity and mainstay to a product of racial discourse.

The HHCA required a whole host of performative and transactual maneuvers by part Hawaiians, native Hawaiians, and non-Hawaiians alike, with regard to land and livelihood. The bureaucratic procedures needed to continue this performative dance continue to unite and divide local communities, even as the homesteading agenda of getting Hawaiians back to the land continues its forward thrust. That many *kūpuna* (elders) wait and eventually die on the waiting list is part of this reality. When all is said and done, the "HHCA was used as a vehicle to continue the sugar and ranching leases."[56] Earlier versions stated that land could be leased to native Hawaiians, defined as those with 1/32 blood quantum, for 999 years at $1 a year. The final version both increased the blood quantum to 50 percent and shortened the lease time to ninety-nine years. Finally, the land set aside for rehabilitation was arguably in the least desirable spots. As Noel Kent notes, "The sugar planters managed to exclude any of the fertile sugar lands from the distribution process, and nearly all of the allotted acreage was rocky, arid, and sandy. Only two percent could be developed at a reasonable cost."[57]

My father's last family members now live and operate on Hawaiian homestead lands and are extremely knowledgeable about the process, and also very representative of the native. They manage to do so even while owning multiple other properties and running many businesses. It seems to me that they've been rehabilitated. They hold onto their homestead land and, I believe, would do anything to hold onto all the other lands in their possession as well—simultaneously exhibiting signs of being both good capitalists and good natives.

These public debates over American land discourse were embodied in and exhibited through the native population and served as the backdrop for more private struggles over land and inheritance. Queen Lili'uokalani's struggle to deed her private property as she saw fit, while also asserting her rights as *Mō'ī* to the Crown Lands revenue, further characterized the changing land discourse. Beyond the public realm, Curtis P. Iaukea recorded the intimate complications that affected the more personal land titling a century ago.

CHAPTER 3

A Story of Political and Emotional Maneuverings

Queen Liliʻuokalaniʻs Trust Deed and the Crown Lands

Land's value exists in its extension of the self from the past into the present and back. When capitalism enters into this relationship, contractual relations to property replace placial connections. Though contractual relations are not without emotional currency, Cole Harris notes: "The spatial energy of capitalism works to deterritoralize people (detach them from prior bonds between people and place) and to reterritorialize them in relation to the requirements of capital."[1] But even if capital and property attempt to take precedence over the connections of genealogy and *ʻohana*, one's lived experiences in a place and the lived experience of the self in the landscape are still present, because land is experienced as an extension of the self/body, thereby provoking emotional attachments to landscape.[2]

As capitalism's method for determining how life follows death, inheritance often further strains the triangular continuity of land, body, and memory. The questions and tensions surrounding inheritance—who will get what, when, and why—often deeply affect family relationships. The passing down of private property is often emotional, as complicated interpersonal relationships are played out over this extension of self—the land. Conflict over the passing down of land and resources to future generations can actually lead people to deny and ignore genealogical connections that are not breakable in and of themselves.

In 1909, the formation of Queen Liliʻuokalaniʻs trust deed was a highly emotional and bitterly contentious endeavor. For the Queen (fig. 7), the task of writing her trust deed coincided with her fight to regain revenues from the

FIGURE 7. Queen Liliʻuokalani, 1900. Hawaiʻi State Archives.

Crown Lands. Both the trust deed and the suit filed in U.S. Court of Claims entitled *Liliuokalani v. United States of America* seeking revenues from the Crown Lands were drawn up within days of one another in November and December of 1909. The Crown Lands revenue and the Queen's trust were also emotionally intense because Prince Kūhiō, Queen Liliʻuoklanai's nephew by marriage and second cousin, was Hawaiʻi's congressional representative in 1909. The Queen was always conscious of the danger of "antagonizing" the Prince when she embarked on her fight for the Crown Lands revenues, and their personal relationship was harshly tested by negotiations of land and inheritance rights.[3]

Even though the U.S. Court of Claims declared that Queen Liliʻuokalani did not have rights to the revenues of the Crown Lands, when the Queen died, both property issues were still unresolved. We are the inheritors of these troubled political, social, and geographic legacies—as contemporary Hawaiians, we learned how to negotiate private property, ʻāina, and ʻohana from these early court cases, and as such we have also frequently learned how to disconnect ourselves from our families and communities. However, our mastery of legalese and the related intellectual and political understandings, then and now, is a sophistication that the legal documents themselves often struggle to avoid.

Prince Kalanianaole and the Kealohilani Premises

Bordering the main driveway that fronts Washington Place on the makai side and within easy access from the south portico of the Mansion, stood a vine-covered Arbor where the Queen often sat of early mornings. And with an Autoharp or Zither, while away the time by singing softly to herself familiar Hawaiian songs and airs since the days of the Merry Monarch.

It was most fascinating to sit and listen to her, as she was still in good voice, the tone, expression and rhythm, perfect.

It reminded me of the days when, as a member of the Kawaihau Glee Club, sponsored by Prince Leleiohoku, the younger brother of King Kalakaua and Queen Liliuokalani, we used to go out of evenings with a new song the Prince had composed and make the rounds. First on King Kalakaua at Iolani Palace; then to Washington Place to serenade Princess Liliuokalani, and even as far as "Ainahau," the Waikiki residence of Princess Likelike. Reaching home again at "Kaakopua" on Emma Street, where the Prince made his residence with his Mother by adoption, Princess Ruth Keelikolani, half sister of the Fourth and Fifth Kamehamehas, in the "wee small hours of the morning." Happy days those were; the days when "Wine, Women and Song" were the rule of the day.

It was under such circumstances and happy auspices that I came to know Liliuokalani intimately. A relationship that endured through the years, and that enabled me to render her and mankind a service that will keep the memory of Queen Liliuokalani green for generations to come. By this I mean the execution of a Deed of Trust, known as the Liliuokalani Trust, under which she conveyed with certain reservations, all of her worldly possessions for the benefit of poor and destitute children, to take effect after her death.

I am not presumptuous enough to assume to myself the full credit for this gratuitous act on the Queen's part. There are others; but this I do say, that when the proposition was submitted, I was sitting behind the scene, as it were, to put in the final word at the opportune moment, without which the Deed of Trust would have had hard rowing.

As it was, it had to withstand the attack of those inimical to the trust, on the alleged ground of undue influence on the part of John Aimoku and myself. And for the one end and aim, to inherit the Queen's property and estate upon her demise.

To make a long story short, the issue was fought but in the Courts, the Trustees coming out of the smoke and fray with flying colors. Any one so inclined can find the full proceedings in the Circuit Court records.

In this connection it might be interesting to note that the "Bone of Contention" in so far as the contestants were concerned, centered in "Washington Place" and "Kealohilani," the beach residence at Waikiki, which the Queen under her deed of trust had bequeathed to John Aimoku and Joseph Kaipo Aea respectively, they having been brought up and reared by the Queen as members of the family and treated as such of the Queen's deed of trust of December 2, 1909. And Amendments made thereunder.

Some little time after Kaiponohea Aea had died, on July 28, 1915, the Queen addressed me a letter reading as follows:

Mr. Iaukea-Trustee.
I wish to bequeath to Prince Kalanianaole and his wife my residence known as Kealohilani, Waikiki, during their life, to take effect after my decease.
(Signed) Liliuokalani

July 28, 1915.

Washington Place.
In compliance with this request and with the consent and approval of the Trustees, a Deed to that effect was executed by the Queen on September 2, 1915, and a copy given to the Prince, the occasion being the Queen's birthday.

A few days later, September 7, the Trustees received a curt communication, couched in the following language:

Gentlemen:
I hereby refuse to accept the deed tendered by you dated Sept. 2, 1915, and herewith return the same.
Yours truly,
(signed) J. Kalanianaole.

The same day there was handed me a letter written in Hawaiian, signed by the Queen, and bearing the earmarks of having been drawn up by other hands than hers, to the effect that, Joseph Kaipo having died, it was her wish and desire that all of her lands makai of Kalakaua Avenue and Kuleanas embraced in what was known as Kealohilani, and the Fishery of Hamohamo, be conveyed to JK. Kalanianaole.

The exact language being (and I am quoting from the letter) "Under the power given me in said deed and because of my affection for my Alii (royal) relative, J. K. Kalanianaole, he being my nearest blood relative in this life now on this day of writing, I hereby direct you to forthwith convey by deed of conveyance, for the sum of one dollar ($1.00) the said lands and fishing rights to him forever, together with the houses and appurtenances and furnishings pertaining to said home; the deed possession to the lands and fishing rights to take effect upon my death," with the reservation to the Trust of a fifty foot front facing the sea and beach.

Surprised at receiving this letter, the Trustees called upon the Queen to confer with her about it. After reading over the type written letter the Trustees had received, the Queen stated that it was not her intention to convey the property to the Prince absolutely and forever, but only a life estate to him and his wife, (and survivor), upon the portion of the described in the amended deed of trust.

On October 14, 1915, J. Kalanianaole addressed a letter to the Trustees couched in the following language:

> A letter signed by Her Majesty Liliuokalani and dated September 7, 1915, was duly received by you through registered mail on the following day, directing you to make a conveyance of certain Lands named in said letter to me. It is now over a month ago and I request that you have the instrument prepared in accordance with the Queen's desire and deliver same to me at an early date as I expect to leave within a short time to attend to my duties in Washington.
>
> Yours truly
> (signed) Kalanianaole

To which the Trustees made reply:

> That, as Trustees, had separately called upon the Queen, and shown her his letter, and she again stated to each of them, that it was her wish and purpose to provide that he (the Prince) and his wife should have only a life estate in the residence portion of the premises. That as Trustees, they were willing to consent to the conveying of the life estate to him and his wife of the portion of the premises described in the deed, but were not willing that the beach portion on the Diamond Head side of the surveyed part should be included.

The amendment to the Trust deed, a copy of which was given to you, follows
precisely the wishes of the Queen as expressed to us on the several occasions above
named; this amendment has been recorded, and under all of the circumstances we
do not see how we can comply with your request of the 14ᵗʰ.
    (signed) W.O. Smith
    " " C.P. Iaukea

Speaking of Liluokalani and her Deed of Trust brings vividly to mind a similar
experience I had with Queen Kapiolani, consort and relict of the King Kalakaua.

The before [sic] I was leaving with the special Mission from the Republic of
Hawaii to the Diamond Jubilee of Queen Victoria in 1897, headed by the Hon.
S.M. Damon, as his Secretary and Military Aide, I called on Queen Kapiolani
to say Goodbye, and to ascertain if she had a Message to send to the British Queen.
Kapiolani having attended a similar celebration in 1887.

"Oh! Do!" she said. "Give Her Most Gracious Majesty my Aloha and warm
Greetings, and say that I will never forget the courtesies and attention I and Liliuokalani enjoyed at her hands and high officials of her Court and Government when
we were her honored guests in London in 1887.

Greetings over I stood up to take my leave. "Wait." She said, "There's something
on my mind that's troubling me, and I want your advice. "I'm Huhu (angered) at
the Boys." Meaning the young Princes, Kuhio Kalanianaole and David Kawananakoa. Her Nephews.

She went on to a great rate. Berating the Boys for not paying any attention to
her; associating with people she did not approve of; never home until late at night;
and so on. "I've made up my mind to cut them out entirely and leave everything to
the Maternity Home." [sic]

I then said to her, "Don't do that. There's enough to provide for the Home and
your Nephews too. They are your heirs and have position to maintain when they
grow up. They are young and sewing their wild oats. They'll get over that in time,
and realize that they have responsibilities they cannot avoid. The young Hawaiians,
growing up with them, will look to them as leaders. You can't deny them and cast
them off without a cent."

The Queen pondered for a while and said, "What would you advise me to do?"

Embracing the opportunity offered, I said "Relieve yourself of all responsibility.
You are not in the best of health. And place the management of your property and
estate in the hands of Trustees. They will see that your wishes are carried out. Make
provision for the Boys after your death, sufficient to keep them in comfort. The rest

of the income can go to the Maturnity Home. With proper handling and management, the property you now have will yield a large income and provide for you all and the Home too."

She seemed to think well of the suggestion and advice, and as I was leaving and kissed her hand as she took mine as an Aloha on parting, she leaned on my arms and whispered in my ear, "I'll do as you say."

On arriving at New York on our way home from the Jubilee, where I got the Honolulu papers, staring me in the face was the news that the Queen had deeded her property to her two Nephews, with some reservation for the payment of her outstanding liabilites.

Curious to know what led the Queen to dispense with her estate in the way she did, I learned from one of the parties concerned in the transaction, whom I knew well and intimately, that in her anxiety that the older of the two Boys, David Kawananakoa, should marry Princess Kaiulani, a union that she had set her heart on, she executed the deed as a means of overcoming the reflection and representations made to her, that unless she did so, Kaiulani would not entertain or consent to marry David as he had no visible means of supporting a wife.

That Princess Kaiulani ever entertained this proposition, I doubt. At all events, the union did not materialize, much to the Queen's disappointment. She then tried to recover the property, but proved unavailing. She died not long after.

I speak of this by way of comparison as between two Estates. Liliuokalani's and Kapiolani's. I know whereof I speak, being familiar with, and having had the handling of both Estates. The latter when Kalakaua was living, the source from which the bulk of what was later known as the Kapiolani Estates came; and of far greater value than Liliuokalani's.

Had Queen Kapiolani followed the advice I gave her to place the management of her Estate in the hands of Trustees, it would have been worth its millions today, with an income to maintain the Kapiolani Maturnity Home without its having to depend on the charity of its members and the public, to say nothing of the financial difficulties it is now facing.

On the other hand, the Liliuokalani Estate, heavily involved as it was when the Trustees took it over, is now paying a handsome dividend in the way of supporting and educating destitute children and orphans, to the number of sixty and more and in the course of the near future several hundred.

Well may one ask, What has become of the Kapiolani Estate? "Gone to where the Wood-bine twineth" might be the answer. A Pity—Tis true.[4]

When I found these chapters that my *kupuna* wrote about private property, inheritance, court cases, and ultimately, allegations of Queen Liliʻuokalaniʻs mental incompetence made by Prince Kūhiō, I soon developed a clearer perspective on my own experiences with interfamilial fights over the management of assets. Such squabbles are nothing new, and are instead historically inherited. As I know intimately and as the documents will further reveal, land and inheritance are contentious.

I worried at first about how to shed light on such volatile information after a century of silence, but I then realized that whatʻs surprising and even shocking is not that these legal and familial challenges occurred, but that we, both then and now, pretend they donʻt exist. After getting past my own discomfort, I came to understand that my great-great-grandfatherʻs account of these cases fought by our *aliʻi* against our *aliʻi* actually highlights their political and legal agency. They knew juridical discourse, and how to use the courts—by this point U.S. courts—for their personal agendas.

While these narratives illustrate sociopolitical agency, they also display competing land goals that were ultimately shaped by the U.S.-sponsored territorial government in Hawaiʻi. Instead of prior bonds based on genealogy and *kuleana*, holding and protecting land and inheritance rights now depended on appeals to and successes within these courts. Prince Kūhiōʻs goal was straightforward. He wanted to break Queen Liliʻuokalaniʻs trust deed so that he could gain control over the piece of land in Waikīkī known as Kealohilani, and he also wanted to inherit the Queenʻs residence named Washington Place in downtown Honolulu. The result of this desire was a dramatic tale of inheritance, land, and power in Hawaiʻi that played itself out in the juridical-political and emotional realms of the early 1900s. Much of the emotion was recorded in manuscripts and the letters between parties, which were often highly effective forms of political communication.

Since the formation and subsequent history of Queenʻs Liliʻuokalaniʻs trust deed comprises a densely bureaucratic narrative, the following time line of events, which highlights key dates, might be helpful:

December 2, 1909
    Queen Liliʻuokalani Trust formed. William O. Smith, Archibald S. Cleghorn, and Curtis P. Iaukea named as trustees.

January 21, 1910

While on a trip to San Francisco, Boston, Washington, and back to San Francisco, Queen Lili'uokalani revokes the trust deed.

February 19, 1910

Queen Lili'uokalani signs a bill of complaint in Honolulu to revoke the trust deed.

April 20, 1910

Queen Lili'uokalani sets aside revocation.

May 10, 1910

Power of attorney finally granted to Curtis P. Iaukea. This power had changed many times in 1909.

June 9, 1910

Reaffirmation and republication of the trust deed.

November 1, 1910

Archibald S. Cleghorn dies.

October 11, 1911

Samuel M. Damon named as trustee to replace Cleghorn. Amendments to the trust set boundaries on the land given away, and added "orphans" and "other destitute children" as beneficiaries.

November 30, 1915

Bill of complaint filed by "Next of Friend" Prince Jonah Kūhiō Kalaniana'ole (as next in succession to the Queen) against the trustees and others named in trust:

Acting as *best of friend* because of her assumed *mental incompetence*, Prince Kūhiō alleges that Queen Lili'uokalani did not know who was a friend or an enemy at the signing of her trust deed.

Prince Kūhiō asserts that the Queen's worry and anxiety over the illegal overthrow of the Hawaiian Kingdom, the charges of misprison of Treason, the six months imprisoned at 'Iolani Palace, and her prosecution and petitioning of the U.S. for the return of the Crown Lands revenues, had negatively affected the deeding of her property.

Prince Kūhiō makes personal attacks on Curtis P. Iaukea and others for "holding" the trust deed.[5]

Prince Kūhiō questions Queen Lili'uokalani's decision to sign a trust deed rather than a simple will, since this trust is irrevocable, and can only be changed by a vote of two-thirds of the trustees.

December 30, 1915

Queen Lili'uokalani speaks out in defense of herself and her trust deed.

January 10 and 25, 1916

Trustees answer the complaint formally, stating that her prior revocation of the deed occurred because she did not understand the terms of the trust completely. Her sanity is evident, because after she revoked her trust, she then amended the trust.

1915 and 1916

Constant attacks on her character and sanity ensue.

January 17, 1916

Next of Friend status of Prince Kūhiō is revoked by reason of interest.

August 29, 1917

Queen Liliʻuokalani signs a will, under the name Leiliuokalani, with James Kealoha and Samuel Kamakaia as witnesses, which seeks to formally revoke her trust deed of 1909. She gives Washington Place to Robert Keoua Wilcox, son of Robert W. Wilcox. She gives Kealohilani to Virginia Wilcox, daughter of Robert W. Wilcox. She gives Fred Iaukea, son of Curtis P. Iaukea, and also my great-grandfather, one lot at Ohua Lane in Waikīkī and various lots in Pearl City, island of Oʻahu. She also gives Prince Kūhiō five thousand dollars. One-half undivided interest to the Lele of Hamohamo is given to Fred Beckley. This will appoints John F. Colburn as executor, "in full charge of apportioning my estate." This version does not stand in court, and Virginia Wilcox is charged with forgery and imprisoned, even though the signature on this will looks to be Queen Liliʻuokalani's.

This will begins: "I Liliuokalani once, by the grace of God, queen of the Kingdom of Hawaii, now an American of times, residing in the City and County of Honolulu, Territory of Hawaii, being of sound mind and memory and aware of the _____ of this life, do make, publish and declare this to be my last will and testament, hereby revoking and canceling any and all former wills by me at any time made. First: I hereby declare that a certain trust deed signed by me on the 2nd day of December, 1909, in which Archibald S. Cleghorn, Curtis P. Iaukea, and William O. Smith were designated as trustees, and all papers signed by me ratifying the said trust deed, to be of no force and effect, the same having been obtained from me by misrepresentation and fraud."[6]

She asks that the trust deed be set aside, if not before her death, than after her death.

November 11, 1917

Queen Liliʻuokalani dies.

January 24, 1918

Myrah Heleluhe, a friend of Princess Kalanianaʻole, had a dream that a settlement should occur. The original trust deed of 1909 stands.

June 27, 1918

John F. Colburn, as attorney for the Kawananakoa minors, enters a plea in probate to contest the estate of Queen Liliʻuokalani.

The narrative began in 1909 when the Queen signed this nonrevocable trust deed, as distinguished from but in conjunction with an ordinary will, on November 1909, under Curtis P. Iaukea and W. O. Smith's counsel.[7] Queen Liliʻuokalani also gave personal power of attorney to Curtis P. Iaukea— revoked and reinstated several times.[8] She then revoked and subsequently reinstated the trust deed in 1910.

Here is what Curtis P. Iaukea wrote about the signing of the original trust deed:

Monday, November 29, 1909

Mr. Cleghorn called and had a talk with the Queen. I was not present at this interview. Mr. Cleghorn came to the office and informed me that Her Majesty had asked him to act as one of her Trustees with Aimoku and myself.

Whilst sitting with the Queen this morning under the Arbor in the front garden, where she often sat and mused by herself, no one else being around at the time and being desirous to know her real intentions as to the disposition of Washington Place which was to be left to Aimoku under the proposed Deed of Trust, I said to her, "You know, Your Majesty, that Prince Kalanianaole expects you to leave Washington Place to him, he being your nearest of kin. Have you given this matter any thought?" She cast her eyes to the ground without speaking for fully a minute and when she looked up said, "Yes, I know that the Prince would like me to give Washington Place to him. But the property came to me through the Dominis' and by right should go to the Governor's Keiki, Aimoku. Although an illegitimate child, he is of his own blood. This is why I am leaving this home to him to occupy as long as he is living and to his children, should he have lawful issue. Then, I want Washington Place to be kept up as it is for all time. I don't want to see it go as so many other residences of Hawaiian royalty have gone. I want it preserved and maintained as a monument to me and my beloved husband."

Wednesday, December 1, 1909

Gave the Queen a copy of the Deed of Trust which W.O. Smith gave me for Her Majesty to read over before signing. Read same to her in presence of Aimoku and left it with her. Before leaving the Queen this morning arranged the time when the Deed of Trust and will were to be executed. She named the next day at 2 p.m.

Thursday, December 2, 1909

The Queen executed a Deed of Trust of all her property to A.S. Cleghorn, C.P. Iaukea and W. O. Smith. She also signed her Will, witnessed by S.M. Damon and

Cecil Brown. They were also witnesses to the Deed of Trust. The Notary Public was Forbes.

Judge Humphreys, acting as the Queen's attorney, read the Deed of Trust to the Queen in the presence of Cleghorn, Damon, W.O. Smith, Cecil Brown and myself.

The following Saturday, December 4, Liliuokalani accompanied by J.D. Aimoku and her maid Rose Otis left for San Francisco on the Steamer Mongolia.[9]

In 1910, the Queen left for Washington, D.C. to engage the fight for the Crown Lands revenues. While away, she revoked her trust. In a number of letters to Aimoku, Governor Dominis's son and the Queen's stepson, Curtis P. Iaukea wrote about his shock and outrage at receiving word that the Queen had revoked her trust:

February 15th, 1910

My Dear Aimoku:

I have hardly gotten over my surprise of the past few days by having shoved under my very nose, without any previous warning or intimation from you or the Queen, the revocation of the Deed of Trust to Mr. Cleghorn, W.O. Smith and myself. It came like a thunderbolt out of a clear sky—it was so sudden. What possessed her Majesty to do this is beyond my comprehension.

I wonder if the Queen realizes what the consequences will be from this recent act of hers. It will mean an enormous expense to her in Attorneys fees and costs of Court, no less than fifteen or twenty thousand dollars when this matter is finally settled. The Trustees are not going to give up the Trust. They cannot do it even if they wanted to, because the Deed of Trust fixes responsibilities upon the Trustees which they cannot relieve themselves of. The mere fact of the Queen revoking her Deed of Trust doesn't relieve the Trustees of these responsibilities. There are vested rights under the deed of Trust which the Trustees are bound to protect, otherwise they might become personally responsible.

There is a way of changing or revoking any particular bequest that the Queen has made, but it must be with the consent of the Trustees or a majority thereof. If the Queen desires to revoke what she gave you or Kaipo or any other of the beneficiaries, paragraph 9 of the Deed of Trust, as our joint answer to the Queen points out, provides for it.

You will see from the copy of our letter to Her Majesty, which I enclose herewith, that the Trustees decline to reconvey the property as demanded of them by Thompson, _____ & Wilder, the Queen's attorneys, on the ground that they have not the authority to under the terms of the Deed of Trust, and furthermore that they do not recognize in the Grantor the right to revoke, the Deed expressly stating that it is irrevocable.

When Her Majesty, free from the influences of those who reduced her to take this ill-advised course, has had time to think and ponder over this matter, I have no hesitation in saying that she will see the folly of persisting in a course where no good can be accomplished and take early measures of rescinding the Deed of Revocation so as to put an end to any further expense which a contest of the case will involve.

Good bye, Aimoku. I have written you enough. I have no feeling in this matter except one of pity and sympathy for the Queen. When will she free herself of the influences that have caused her no end of trouble. Instead of true happiness and comfort in her old age, she must needs do something to destroy her own happiness.

My love to the Queen and your good self.

Your friend 'Iaukea[10]

Another letter followed:

Washington Place, February 27ᵗʰ, 1910

My Dear Aimoku,

Undeserved, and without any justifications for it whatsoever, the Queen, through her Attorneys, has brought accusations against me of the most serious nature, practically charging me with having abused her confidence, a fraudulent and designing person unworthy of the confidence of any one, in that I misled her and got the Queen to sign her Deed of Trust to Mr. Cleghorn, W.O. Smith, and myself, through a misconception on her part as to the provision of revocation.

Can anything be more absurd! If anyone knows and is more conversant with this matter of the Queen's Deed of Trust, it is you Aimoku; from its very first inception some three weeks before until its final execution on December 2ⁿᵈ last. Knowing every phrase of it as it proposes, can you or the Queen conscientiously say that she was misled in the matter. No, Aimoku, I did all I knew how to have her understand that a Deed of Trust as distinct from a Will, could not be revoked; but in order that she can change, alter, and cancel any part of it or revoke what she had bequeathed to this, that one or the other, a provision was inserted, as in C.R. Bishop's Trust Deed, enabling her to do this, with the consensus of the Trustees. Mr. W.O. Smith explained this feature of her Deed of Trust to her independent of me, and as did Mr. Humphreys the Attorney who drew up the Deed.

Then what is the sense of putting the Queen in this false position and who is forcing it upon her? Not the Trustees. Who then? You know who they are as well as I do. And the Queen also knows. Is she going to permit herself to be deluded into the influences of these people who have been trying to come into possession of the Queen's property, and particularly "Washington Place" whom the Queen until recently perhaps, has entertained fixed views what dispositions to make of it.

No! Aimoku. It cannot be. And if you have any influence left with the Queen, for God's sake, use it, and see if you cannot save her from the hands of these greedy and unprincipled men who will stop at nothing to gain their own ends, even to the risking of the Queen's health and very life perhaps. What a shame and a crying shame that Her Majesty whom we all love and respect so much, cannot be permitted to end the few remaining years left to her in this world, in peace and with ease and comfort.

My heartfelt sympathies go out to her when I think of the trying ordeal that she will have to go through as the result of her ill-advised action in signing the Deed of Revocation. And you, Aimoku, a party to the Deed too. What to think or say, I dare not. Your continued silence in the matter makes it all the more inexplicable and hard to explain.

Remember me kindly to Her Majesty. Very Sincerely Yours.

C.P. Iaukea[11]

The 1910 attempt at a revocation of the trust was a highly charged matter because it was irrevocable and could not be abandoned by the trustees. After Curtis P. Iaukea and the other trustees expressed their anguish and outrage, Queen Lili'uokalani reversed the revocation on April 20, 1910. Following these legal activities, including the revocation and reinstatement of the power of attorney, Curtis P. Iaukea, along with William O. Smith and A. S. Cleghorn, finally became confirmed as the first three trustees of the Queen Lili'uokalani trust and estate.[12]

The trust deed outlined the duties of the Queen's trustees, declared her intent toward two important pieces of property, Kealohilani and Washington Place, and listed other land awards and provisions for her close friends, granting property as life estates or fee simple.[13] Much thought went into these decisions, as evidenced by the papers I found placed between the more orderly documents, which contained names added, crossed out, and scratched over. As I move through the documents, and as I read the raw emotions from all parties, it seems the Queen was in emotional pain in deciding whom to trust. On October 11, 1911, the Queen made some amendments to the trust deed, naming Samuel M. Damon as trustee because Archibald S. Cleghorn had died. She also added the phrase "and other destitute children" to the word "Orphans" in paragraph "Fifth," article "I," with "the preference to be given to Hawaiian children of pure or part aboriginal blood."[14]

Aboriginal was a term used during the Hawaiian Kingdom era to connote *kanaka maoli* in full or part. *Kanaka maoli* was a term used to designate full-blooded Hawaiians in the nineteenth century. The later designation *native Hawaiian* refers to the race-based recipients of Hawaiian Homes in 1921, as already discussed, while *indigenous* is currently used by the United Nations to designate stateless peoples. These differing terminologies are important, because they contribute to an understanding of the mind-set of the various administrations as the naming and quantifying of Hawaiians across generations and multinational boundaries.

The property granted to Curtis P. Iaukea in the Queen's trust deed was later contested and condemned by the territorial government. This is the section of the trust deed that sent me on my own search through the documents, and ultimately to the halls of power, for answers to questions of my inheritance. I found none, but I did find answers about genealogy—and I learned a great deal. And I also learned that these halls of power are tainted by the actions of those who came before, and continue to be tainted by those there today. Power in Hawai'i is like a broken record stuck in the same groove, with no recognition that the groove itself was cut through habit and assumption. It is neither natural nor authentic, and therefore re-groovable for those up to the task. The information gathered here is the material presented in my copyrighted dissertation; it has forced me to meet with trustees, directors, judges, university officials, and an untold number of executive secretaries as part of my own quest simply to tell the story that I discovered and researched, as I push for an investigation of some in the upper echelons of power in Hawai'i who have wanted to appropriate and profit from the words of my ancestor. Intellectual property is at stake here—not real property in this instance, but property nonetheless, and subject to power plays similar to those of a century ago.[15]

In 1915, the trust underwent further revisions, including but not limited to the parcel of land known as Kealohilani:

WHEREAS it was provided in said original deed of trust that one Joseph Kaiponohea Aea was to have had and enjoyed the personal use and occupation of the premises at Waikiki known as "Kealohilani" with the appurtenances and the Fishery of Hamohamo during his lifetime and that on his death the same were to be enjoyed by the lawful heirs of his body for their lifetime (or so long after his death as the law would permit, with reversion then to the Trustees); and the said Joseph Kaiponohea Aea has since died and it is now the desire of said Grantor to further amend said deed of trust, and to withdraw the proposed disposition of the enjoyment of said premises by any heirs of said Joseph Kaiponohea Aea, and to also provide certain substitute beneficiaries of a portion of said premises after the death of the Grantor; all as hereinafter specified:

NOW THEREFORE, the said Liliuokalani, Grantor as aforesaid, by and with the approval and consent of her Trustees hereinbelow expressed, does hereby make the following further alterations and amendments of said deed of trust, namely:

(2) For Jonah Kuhio Kalanianaole and Elizabeth K. Kalanianaole his wife,

jointly during their lives, and the survivor of them for life, with reversion thereafter to the Trustees, the personal use and occupation of that certain portion of the
premises known as "Kealohilani," at Waikiki, in said Honolulu.[16]

This amendment to the Queen's trust, granting Kealohilani to Prince
Kūhiō and his wife Elizabeth as a life estate, as opposed to fee simple, set
the stage for the court challenges by Prince Kūhiō in 1915. Washington Place
was also at issue. Prince Kūhiō wanted control of this property, even though
it had already been granted to Queen Liliʻuokalani's stepson and Governor
Dominis's son, Aimoku. In his challenge to the Queen's trust deed, the
Prince sought revocation through the courts as her "next of friend." He
charged the Queen with mental incompetence.[17] In the ensuing battle, which
will be documented in chapter 4, Queen Liliʻuokalani's integrity, and that
of those closest to her, underwent extensive public scrutiny and constant
attack. A by-product of the insinuations that the sovereign was insane was
a questioning of the intelligibility of the Hawaiian nation, now being thrown
into a modernity that continued and deepened the desecration of the sacred.
"Enlightenment" attitudes about the rights of individual man and monetary
value became the judge and jury by which the Queen's mental state was
closely reviewed and analyzed, seeking to ensure that her personal estate
might be "better" divided.

Always in the background of these discussions about the Queen's trust
were her struggles in Washington, D.C., for the return of Crown Lands
revenues. Soon after August 12, 1898, when the joint resolution was passed
by Congress, she stopped receiving these revenues, when "the transfer of
sovereignty and the cession of all public lands including said Crown Lands
took place, and the legal title to said Crown Lands thereupon became and
is now vested in the United States."[18] The Queen repeatedly laid claim to
these revenues, ultimately leading to *Liliuokalani v. United States of America*,
which was filed in the U.S. Court of Claims on November 20, 1909.[19] Although seemingly separate from the trust deed, this unresolved land issue
was intimately connected with the trust and weighed heavily on the heart
of the Queen.

When Kamehameha III enacted the Māhele of 1848, the private property
of the King was separated from other lands. Known as the Crown Lands, they
were then inherited by Kamehameha IV and Kamehameha V as a life estate
and the private property of the *Aliʻi*. These lands were different from Govern-

ment Lands, which were specifically set aside for use by the government of the Hawaiian Kingdom. The Crown Lands were understood to be the private property of the reigning sovereign while alive, and the proceeds from these lands were used to support that sovereign.

As noted in chapter 2, after the illegal overthrow of the Hawaiian Kingdom in 1893, the Crown Lands were combined with Government Lands by the Republic of Hawai'i in 1894 and renamed "Public Lands."[20] After the joint resolution was signed on August 12, 1898, the now "Public Lands" were "ceded" to the United States. As the inheritor of the Crown Lands through the Republic of Hawai'i, the United States continued to use the misnomer "Public Lands" and to sustain the discursive practices that upheld this fictional entity. The apparent legal apparatus to cede these lands was contained in the Organic Act of 1900.[21]

The Queen's claim in Washington, D.C., in 1909 began with a statement about the Māhele division of Crown Lands in 1848:

> That heretofore, to wit, in the year 1848, Kamehameha III, King of the Kingdom of Hawaii, being owner and lord paramount of all the lands in said Kingdom of Hawaii, did surrender and forever make over unto the chiefs and people the greater part of his royal domain, reserving certain lands to himself as his own private property, which act was solemnized by an act duly passed by the House of Nobles and Representatives of the Hawaiian Islands in legislative council assembled entitled "An Act relating to the lands of his Majesty the King and of the government," copy of which act is hereto attached, marked "Exhibit A" and made a part hereof.[22]

She recalled that in 1865 an act was passed in the Hawaiian Kingdom entitled "An Act to Relieve the Royal Domain from Encumbrances and to Render the Same Inalienable." The 1865 act provided for a commissioner of Crown Lands and a board to manage the almost one million acres of Crown Lands. Under this act, lands were to be leased for not more than thirty years. This act also provided specifically for the revenue of such lands to be granted to the reigning sovereign:

> That under and by virtue of said last mentioned act said Crown Lands were rendered inalienable and all the rents, profits and emoluments derived from the said lands after deducting the necessary and proper expenses of managing the same, were declared to be for the use and benefit of the reigning sovereign.[23]

These lands were to be used "for the purpose of maintaining the royal state and dignity" of the reigning sovereign.[24] The Queen also stated that since the

United States was acting in a trust relationship at the time of its attainment of these lands, it should therefore turn over all revenues to the beneficiary of said trust, that being herself as the reigning sovereign:

> And, that the United States of America, having become so seized of the legal title to said Crown Lands, whereof, your petitioner has a vested equitable life interest, holds the same as Trustee for your petitioner to the extent of her interest therein, and ought in equity and good conscience to account to your petitioner for, and to pay to her, all the rents, profits and emoluments derived from said Crown Lands after deducting the necessary and proper expenses of managing the same, for and during the term of her natural life.[25]

A side note of this narrative, but highlighted in the decision of the U.S. Court of Claims, was the 1882 occurrence when Princess Ruth Keʻelikōlani, sister and personal heir to Kamehameha V, sold land rights from the Crown Lands to Claus Spreckels.[26] At that time, "the sovereign authorities hastened to dispute the transaction, and subsequent legislation by way of compromise restored the attempted conveyance to the general body of the crown lands" based on the 1865 act.[27] These lands were then returned to the office of the Crown Lands, and this specific law directed that all Crown Lands were to be used to support the office.

This instance was later used as the primary reasoning of the U.S. Court of Claims for rejecting the complaint from Queen Liliʻuokalani in May of 1910. The court maintained that the lands were not the sole personal property of the monarch, but rather connected to the *office* of the monarch, as the lands were used "for the purpose of maintaining the royal state and dignity."[28] By declaring that the lands belonged to the office and not to the individual, and with the supposed transfer of Hawaiian Kingdom sovereign power to the United States, the U.S. Court of Claims extinguished the rights of Queen Liliʻuokalani to the revenues from these lands.

The Queen's complaint in 1909 also explains why "public" is a misnomer for the Crown Lands:

> The crown land is described as a "portion of the public domain" whereas as we have already seen "it was clearly the intention of Kamehameha III to protect the lands from the danger of being treated as public domain" (Estate of Kamehameha IV, 2 Haw., 715), and in the entire history of Hawaii the word public had never been applied to the crown land, but on the contrary the word private had been repeatedly and emphatically applied. The crown land is then declared to have

been heretofore the property of the Hawaiian Government, a declaration absolutely opposed to every fact in the history of the crown land beginning with express separation of the reserved lands of Kamehameha III into government and crown land.[29]

Though she emphatically states that these lands were never part of the public domain, that these "Public Lands" were never to be used for the public became irrelevant, as multiple layers of meaning and use were placed upon them. What was therefore hidden in plain view was the original Hawaiian Kingdom use and function of these lands, as well as the stolen economic revenues from them, since they were being used largely for housing the U.S. military and for other purposes by the early 1900s.[30] Or, as the Queen put it in her complaint,

> That said portions of Crown Lands have been reserved by the United States of America for use as military and naval stations, that other portions have been proclaimed forest reserves, that other portions have been alienated and sold, and the remaining portions are in the possession, use and control of the government of the Territory of Hawai'i.[31]

Newly assigned hegemonic spaces were given the designation of national parks, forest reserves, and military bases by the United States. All of these spaces were on "Public Lands."[32] Today, the military continues to operate heavily on Crown Lands: "A large source of conflict stems from military control of former crown land and parcels seized during World War II; with their total Hawaii land use equaling 5%, while on Oahu a daunting 22%."[33] The borrowed ideology from the U.S. continent assigned a new use and function to Crown Lands, creating the entities "Public (Militarized) Lands" and "Public (Militarized) Body."

Silencing the voices of the *ali'i* and their claims to Crown Lands created a spatial silence that established and enforced new authoritative and geographic spheres. Access to such spaces relied, and continues to rely upon, realigned relationships within heavily guarded spheres of power. As Timothy Mitchell has observed, the creation of public/private spheres is a key strategy in appropriating the space of the other: "Rather than a fixed boundary dividing the city into two parts, public and private, outside and inside, there are degrees of accessibility and exclusion determined variously by the relations between the persons involved, and by the time and the circumstance."[34] On these newly

named lands, discursive practices associated with such a public are then prac-
ticed, and this innocence of the everyday creates a cultural amnesia and masks
the discursive practices of the power elite through a normalizing and mundane
relationality with space.[35]

For this ominous yet equalizing force known as the public, the homogeni-
zation of a citizenship and landscape is paramount to its continued existence.
A renationalizing of a people occurred in Hawai'i, and it happened to a large
extent through the renationalizing of the landscape away from Hawaiian
Kingdom epistemological definers and toward U.S. national allegiances.[36] In
Hawai'i, this nationalizing relied upon a well-defined and easily identifiable
U.S. public entity that could benefit from U.S. "Public Lands."

The Queen's claim in 1909 not only challenged the public-ness of the newly
emerging U.S. national terrain in Hawai'i, but also stated the obvious: that
the taking of private property is illegal under international law. Here the
Queen pointed to the actions of the United States with regard to Panama and
the North Pacific: "It did not take it from the existing Government. In both
cases there was a domestic revolution, and the revolutionary government
turned over to the United States the sovereignty desired."[37]

The Queen challenged the taking of private property in Hawai'i because
"private" is simply not public, and therefore cannot be transferred:

> When, however, the transaction involves the rights of private property not
> subject to confiscation under the rules of international law, we submit that a
> different question arises and one of which this court has jurisdiction. If this
> method of annexation can be used not only for the transfer of sovereignty, but
> also for the extinguishment while in the hands of the temporary revolutionary
> government of any inconvenient rights of private property, it may readily be
> imagined to what length the doctrine may be carried in the future. The United
> States takes the sovereignty and all public property appertaining thereto free
> from any obligation save that dictated by the conscience of the legislative and
> executive branches.[38]

The Queen's claim ended emphatically:

> That your petitioner is sole owner and the only person interested in this claim,
> that no assignment or transfer of said claim or of any part thereof or interest
> therein has been made; that said claim has not been presented to Congress or
> any Department, except that bills for the relief of your petitioner have been in-
> troduced in Congress from time to time and referred to committees, but no report
> of any committee either favorable or adverse has ever been made and no action

taken on such bills by either House of Congress, that claimant is justly entitled to the amount herein claimed from the United States, after allowing all just credits and set-offs; that the claimant has at all times since becoming a citizen of the United States borne true allegiance to the Government of the United States and has not in any way voluntarily aided, abetted or given encouragement to rebellion against the said government, and that she believes the facts as stated in this petition to be true.[39]

The claim focused on compensation, as opposed to the more obvious press-ing legal question—the return of the Crown Lands to Queen Liliʻuokalani's rightful legal control. The Queen's claim in 1909 declared that the United States owed "Four Hundred and Fifty Thousand Dollars ($450,000) for the net rents, profits and emoluments derived from said Crown Lands during the six years preceding the filing of this petition, after deducting the necessary and proper expenses of managing the same."[40] This amount represented the probable rents collected from the 911,888 acres of land in 1909 at approximately $22 an acre plus expenses.[41]

This 1909 claim was not the Queen's first legal attempt to make the United States return the rents of these lands. The following documents are just a small example of the hundreds of letters that circulated both prior to and after 1909 between Queen Liliʻuokalani and her allies as she repeatedly staked her claim to the Crown Lands revenues in U.S. courts and to U.S. delegations. Beginning in 1897, Queen Liliʻuokalani pleaded for the Crown Lands in an antiannexationist protest to U.S. president McKinley:

> BECAUSE it is proposed by said treaty to confiscate said property, technically called the crown lands, those legally entitled thereto, either now or in succession, receiving no consideration whatever for estates, their title to which has been always undisputed, and which is legitimately in my name at this date.[42]

In 1898, Queen Liliʻuokalani lodged a protest in Washington, D.C., for the return of the Crown Lands and the revenue:

> I, Liliuokalani of Hawaii, named heir apparent on the 10th day of April 1877, and proclaimed Queen of the Hawaiian Islands on the 29th day of January 1891, do hereby protest against the assertion of ownership by the United States of Amer-ica of the so-called Hawaiian Crown Lands amounting to about one million acres and which are my property, and I especially protest against such assertion of ownership as a taking of property without due process of law and without just or other compensation.
>
> Therefore, supplementing my protest of June 17, 1897, I called upon the Presi-

dent and the National Legislature and the People of the United States to do justice in this matter and to restore to me this property, the enjoyment of which is being withheld from me by your Government under what must be a misapprehension of my right and title.[43]

Letters shortly after this plea began to circulate to and from the Queen's attorney, J. O. Carter, as well as among her friends and allies of the Republic of Hawai'i. Here are a few of those letters:

10/27/1899

Hon. J. O. Carter

Dear Sir,

I wrote your opinion in regard to George Macfarlane's habit of procrastinating in his dealings. It is because partly from having so much on his hands at one time. He would want to undertake all the business that comes across his path and undertaking so many has little time for either. This procrastination of his allowing a whole year to go by on my part to wait for him is tedious to me. Not only that but allowing the best opportunity to slip by, and for the US Government to consider their claim to these Crown Lands as permanent and of course making any claim in future difficult since they have issued their protest against the sales of any more "Public Lands." Making known their actual possession. It has actually made my heart sick and tired. This long waiting & am discouraged. You hope he has either handed to me or sent me the desired document. He has done neither nor have I heard from him but I understand that he and Archie are in S. Francisco. He has not written me a line and I hope you will write and tell him to forward those papers to me as he told you he would.

Prince Kawananakoa is well and I fear already tired of Washington.

With kindest Aloha to Mary and all your family I remain

Yours Sincerely

Liliuokalani

April 24, 1908

My Dear Queen:

From time to time during this winter I have tried to get the committee on claims to give me another hearing so that I could present your claim for the Crown Lands.

As I have explained to you before, the leaders in Congress are opposed to allowing this claim, and the fact that it was defeated in the senate in February

1904 had made it impossible up to this time to get The House of Representatives to consider your claim and discuss your petitions.

Now at last I have a little encouragement from the Committee on Claims. The Chairman Hon. J. M. Miller has promised, as a personal favor to me, to try to get his committee to give me a hearing on your claim next week. Of course the committee may vote that they are not willing to consider the claim now, but I hope they will decide to hear me.

I wish my Dear Queen that you would realize that I have had more personal interest in your claim than in my measure I have had pending before the Congress. But it is unfortunately the fact that Congress year after year refuses to grant hundreds of claims whose merits are beyond question. It is also very hard to get Congress to consider your Claim favorably because of the rules of International law that apply.

You will remember that when your bill was discussed in the Senate in February 1904 both Senator Blackburn and Senator Mitchell who were fighting to pass your bill admitted that you had no claim that could possibly be established in this court of law or equity. They even went further and said that if an act were passed permitting you to sue the government in the Court of Claims, you could not possibly secure a favorable verdict there for any sum whatever. In short they admitted that any act of Congress to pay you any sum whatever would be merely an act of grace of a strong nation toward the former sovereign of a weaker nation. I am sure that your Majesty is keen enough to see that after such admissions were made by your own friends who were supporting your bill it is impossible to force any action in Congress; also that I have to depend on personally working among members to try to get them to act out of friendship for me and from a desire to show their good will toward the former monarch of what is now an American Territory.

The panic last year in the States makes Congress all the more strict in voting any money except what they have to. But I am going to press your Claim in spite of this and you may be sure that I shall never stop working on it until I persuade Congress to change its mind and vote you a generous sum of money to lighten your declining years.

I have now a great many friends in Congress, and you may rest assured that the Congress will reverse its former unfavorable action for me if they will do it for anyone.

We are both well and are now enjoying the summer weather. The foliage are all out and Washington, as you know in Spring is beautiful, it makes me feel at home to have sunshine again after going through such dismal weather as snow and sleet.

Both self and wife send best wishes for your Majesty health. I remain
Yours affectionately
J. Kalanianaole[44]

January 17, 1909.

Hon. Theodore Roosevelt,
President of the United States,
Washington, D.C.

Honored Sir:

I note in the telegraphic reports, that Ex-Queen Liliuokalani is now in Washington, pressing her claim for payment for the crown lands taken from her on account of the annexation of the Islands and the previous dethronement of the Queen.

It is without suggestion or solicitation on the part of the Ex-Queen, or any other person, that I take the liberty of addressing you in relation to her claim. I however feel that in the dethronement of the Queen and the incidents coincident therewith, a grave wrong has been done to the Hawaiians for which we have since repaid them only by additional wrongs; and that the payment of the Queen's claim is the very least our government can now do to, in a small measure rectify the outrage we have perpetuated upon the Hawaiians.

Suffice it to say, that as a former Vol. Army officer, and as a citizen, I consider that our people have perpetuated an unpardonable wrong upon the Hawaiians as a people, and an equally great wrong upon their queen. With six years residence on the Islands I have learned to admire much which I have observed in the Hawaiians, and also to regret to what low condition and depravity our modern civilization has reduced this noble people.

I cannot condemn too strongly the acts of the Americans in Hawaii, in dethroning this queen and destruction of this people. I have lived among them, and have many friends both among the Americans in Hawaii and the Hawaiians themselves. I feel that our Government has very sadly failed in its duty to the Hawaiians in permitting wealthy corporations to absorb the former happy homes of the Hawaiians, and to turn these homes into vast cane fields to be cultivated by foreign labor; driving the Hawaiians to the cities and to degredation, sin and death. It is a record upon which no American can look in any part with pride.

Feeling thus as I do, I write to ask, that you at least do all that you can to at last place one redeeming act toward these people to the credit of our Government, by paying to this former queen a small part of that to which she is justly entitled. I ask it as a citizen, and as one who in no possible way has the slightest opportunity to profit by your act, either directly or indirectly. We can at least repay to this Ex-Queen a small part of that which we have taken from her by force; and God knows the restitution is little enough.

Trusting that I have not encroached too much upon your valuable time, I am,
Yours very respectfully,
E. Tappan Tannatt, Professor
Department of Civil Engineering
Montana State College[45]

Besides these letters urging the return of some of the revenue from the Crown Lands, various bills were introduced in Congress as well. As early as April 23, 1901, House Bill 121 was introduced by Hawai'i delegate Nailima, entitled "Making an Appropriation to Satisfy the Claim and Demand of Her Majesty Liliuokalani against the Republic of Hawaii and the Territory of Hawaii." This bill sought to render $250,000 in full payment on all claims on the Crown Lands.[46] This failed, so again in 1904 Senate Bill 1553 was introduced "For Payment to Liliuokalani, formerly Queen of the Kingdom of Hawaii." This bill asked for $200,000 in compensation to the Queen "in full satisfaction and discharge of all claim, legal and equitable."[47]

This bill did not pass either, so in 1908 Queen Lili'uokalani petitioned President William H. Taft for the revenue of the Crown Lands: "That as such Sovereign I was the rightful owner of all the Crown Lands in the Hawaiian Islands, consisting about 911,888 acres, more or less, and therefore had the right to receive all incomes and proceeds, by lease or sale, derived from such lands."[48] Her petition to President Taft continued with an outline of the injustices done to her and to the Hawaiians with the illegal overthrow of the Hawaiian Kingdom, in response to her attempt to promulgate a new constitution. She stated that it was within her right, as reigning sovereign, to promulgate a new constitution in the first place, and therefore such action was not legally challengeable.

This petition also included sections of the confidential letter from Minister Stevens to Secretary Foster, dated Nov. 20, 1892, which marveled at the "nearly 900,000 acres of 'crown lands'" that could be co-opted and effectively rehandled by the American state.[49] The Queen ended her petition this way:

> In conclusion therefore, I must say that having given you the uncontroverted historical facts of how I was deprived of my throne and government, and stripped of all honors and dignities deriving therefrom; also my humiliation and shame which sorely affected my feelings and to the great injury to my character and health, I ask for relief in the lump sum of TEN MILLION ($10,000,000) DOLLARS in settlement of all my claims.
> And you petitioner will ever pray.
> Liliuokalani (signed)
> Honolulu, Nov. 1908[50]

The question of the Crown Lands was the backdrop for all of the Queen's legal and personal battles in her final years, and the labeling of Crown Lands as "Public Lands" made the epistemic and legal fight for these lands only that much harder to engage. That the Crown Lands are considered "ceded lands" to the United States is still a subject of contention for many Hawaiians. The missing revenue from, and the constant misuse of, these lands represent a continuing legacy of the political and emotional turmoil in Hawai'i at the end of the twentieth century, and a legacy that continues to inform Hawaiians' land displacement today. Ultimately, the Territory of Hawai'i did grant Queen Lili'uokalani a small annual pension of $1,250.00 each month for the remainder of her life—an amount obviously much less than what was legally due.[51] And the question itself boiled down to one of compensation alone; it did not broach the larger question of the illegal transfer of private property.

The wide array of documents and letters I have cited illustrates Hawaiian political agency in the early 1900s. Queen Lili'uokalani worked exceedingly hard to regain control of the revenues of the Crown Lands, and to question and challenge the designation of these lands as "public." In my research, I noticed the continuous and arduous labors of both Queen Lili'uokalani, who struggled to preserve her rights to these lands and to her personal private properties, and others who were trying to manipulate these lands and revenues further away from her control. It is heartbreaking to read some of these letters, even over a century later. The heartbreak does not escape notice, as these open wounds still await healing.

These letters and petitions are just a sampling of the enormous quantity of correspondence and manuscripts that passed between parties as the Queen formed her trust deed for the benefit of future generations of Hawaiians and continued her long fight for the return of the revenues of the Crown Lands. Even in Queen Lili'uokalani's later years, she never ceded her right to these lands, and the emotional costs of fighting for her right to the revenues influenced both her personal and her business decisions. This legal and emotional battle ensued with regard to her personal property. The emotional terrain was deepened and Queen Lili'uokalani's attachment to her land was further severed by Prince Kūhiō's allegations of her mental incompetence. I am resurrecting these words now because it is part of the story that Curtis P. Iaukea wanted to be told.

CHAPTER 4

"E paa oukou" (You hold it)

*Charging Queen Liliʻuokalani with Insanity
and "Holding" the Trust Intact*

In 1915, Prince Kūhiō put forth a bill of complaint that charged Queen Liliʻuo-kalani with mental incompetence, escalating the fight for the Queen's private property through what I call the "insanity trials."[1] This attack from within her own inner circle of family and friends was launched through western and American institutional forces that had been separating the Queen from her lands, and Hawaiians from place, resulting in a dismemberment of the parts from the whole. Questioning the Queen's mental capacity was part of the larger project of deligitimizing the entire social structure and multigenerational epistemology she embodied. If the sovereign is proven insane, the Papa/Wākea narrative, the Kumulipo, and other creation chants are rendered illegitimate, because the Queen is the embodiment of a genealogy that is all-inclusive and expansive. The insanity trials were an attempt to sever and make suspect this embodiment.

Like the references to her as ex-Queen Liliʻuokalani, the insanity trials leveled the Queen. But can genealogy and generations of knowing really be "ex-ed"? Through discursive practices, the insanity trials continued the project of keeping at bay the "restless ghosts of the national past,"[2] as the policing powers of the usurping state once again intervened in the Queen's private affairs. And nothing is more private than one's mental state.

Curtis P. Iaukea's handwritten chapters, which I found in the basement of the state archives some eighty years after their composition, confirmed that my ancestor wanted the story of the Queen's trust deed, and the defense of this trust in court to be told. The 1915 bill of complaint consists of well over one thousand pages of court documents and supporting testimonies. The magnitude of this case, and the multiplicity of voices and actors appearing in these papers, make it impossible to cover every aspect of the complaint here, so I will focus on key moments and details. My own voice punctuates this account of complicated legal texts, as I, and Hawaiians as a community, are fully implicated in these legal acts of *nā kūpuna* (our ancestors). And indeed one thing is certain—Queen Liliʻuokalani's personal life was implicated in the larger social narrative, and the intertwining forces of *ka ʻāina* and *mana* informed the legal and interpersonal proceedings.

I begin with a lengthy reflection on the case, by Curtis P. Iaukea. In this manuscript, he draws from Judge Humphreys.

The late Queen Liliuokalani's Deed of Trust with her last Will and Testament— And Revelations Behind the Scene.

Pending the preparation of the trust deed and will, and details incident thereto which took all of the ensuing six days to complete for submission to the Queen, let me digress a bit and give my readers an insight into the workings and manipulations that went on within the Queen's own family circle relative to the disposition of her property, with particular stress on "Washington Place."

Under the Queen's last will and testament, then under revision as afore mentioned, the historic home and mansion was given to John Dominis Aimoku, namesake of Governor John O. Dominis, the Queen's deceased husband, and from whom the property descended. As a matter of fact and within the knowledge of many then living and intimate with the family, John Aimoku was Governor Dominis' son, born through unlawful wedlock.

To this, and the mere thought of having the old and historic Home which had been officially known and recognized as "Washington Place," and named after the First President of the United States, turned into a private home, after the Queen's demise, for the use and occupation of one who was not legally entitled to it, the Prince and heir at law of the Queen, Jonah Kuhio Kalanianaole, made strenuous objection. Saying to the Queen, in my presence, that unless she left and devoted the Home in such a way as to keep up the memory and sanctity of the place and promises for some beneficent and public purpose, he, as next of kin, would move and take steps to set aside her last will and testament.

What the Prince threatened to do, only added fuel to the fire. For the Queen, from that time on, determined to adhere to what she had already decided on. To make a long story short, and notwithstanding all that was said and discussed about

Washington Place being devoted to the teaching and perpetuation of Hawaiian music and the Hawaiian language as has been already related by Judge Humphreys, was nothing more than a topic of conversation, and at a time when the Queen was displeased with Aimoku for something he had said or done. But at heart, the Queen's mind had been made up, and like the strong minded woman that she was there was nothing that could turn her from her purpose.

To resume the Judge's statement of the final act and scene when the deed of trust and will were signed, sealed and delivered on the afternoon of Thursday, December 2nd, 1909.[3]

> When I arrived on the front porch, the rest of the party, Mr. Smith, Governor Cleghorn, Mr. S.M. Damon, Colonel Iaukea and Mr. Cecil Brown, were sitting in a small room to the left, the library, and as soon as I arrived, Mr. Smith stated to the Queen that I would read over the trust deed which we had prepared at her request, and asked if that was agreeable to her. She said that it was, and I then drew a chair near her, handed Cecil Brown a carbon copy of the trust deed and asked him to check me as I read. I then read very slowly and as I thought in a clear tone of voice the trust deed, omitting not one word.
>
> During the course of the reading, the Queen interrupted me on two or three occasions and had me reread certain parts of the trust deed, she having been previously told by me that if there any objections at all to the instrument, that she should make it then, as it would be too late after it was executed to do so.
>
> The reading of the document over and concluded, the Queen subscribed, and asked Mr. Damon and Mr. Brown to subscribe as witnesses. Mr. A.S. Cleghorn, Curtis P. Iaukea and William O. Smith as trustees having also signed. Mr. Forbes, Notary who was present to take the acknowledgment, also subscribed his name.
>
> A will was drawn and executed contemporaneously with the trust deed immediately afterwards. After the trust deed was executed, I said to the Queen, we have prepared your last will and testament, in conformity with your instructions, and I will now read it over to you. Turning to Mr. Damon and Mr. Brown, she said, "I desire you gentlemen to witness my will." Mr. Damon spoke up and said, "It is unnecessary for us to remain present while the will is being read, as that is more or less confidential. We will retire and then can be called in."
>
> So Mr. Damon and Mr. Brown and the Notary retired to the veranda, and I read the will over. I think Mr. Smith and myself were the only ones in the room when the will was read. After I had read the will, the Queen said, "That is what I desire," and asked if I would call the witnesses to come in. I stepped to the door and asked Mr. Damon and Mr. Brown to return and witness the will. And when they came in, she said, "Will you gentlemen witness my will." And in the presence of her and each other signed the will as witnesses thereto.

Some six years later, after Prince Kalanianaole had brought suit to set aside the trust deed, it having been filed November 30, 1915, Judge Humphreys gave evidence as follows:

I called to see the Queen at Washington Place and was received by her alone. After making some respectful inquiries after her health, I then expressed regret that she should be annoyed by the suit. And she said, "Yes, Yes, it is too bad. I was at peace with all the world." I then asked her if she was satisfied with it. She said she was entirely satisfied with it; that it was just what she wanted; that all of the cares and burdens and worries of her business had been taken off her hands, and perfectly content with the situation.

She then pursuing the conversation, "The Bone of Contention", that was her precise language, "The bone of contention seems to be this place and the Waikiki place. These little boys, Aimoku and Joseph, I have reared and educated, and I have learned to love them as though they were my own. Is it to be wondered at, then, that I should wish to provide handsomely for them?"

And here she stated, I will observe parenthetically, "Now, do I talk like an insane person?" I replied, "You don't, Your Majesty." She then said, "My brother Kalakaua took all of the lands which belonged to our mother, and I made no fuss about it. When Kalakaua died those lands and all of his other property went to his widow Kapiolani. Kapiolani gave all of that property to Prince Cupid and his brother Prince David.[4] They are amply provided for." Again, "Now do I talk like a crazy person?"

I then asked her if Kuhio was related to her. She said, "He is my second cousin." She then asked me if I would act as her attorney in the litigation, and I told her that I had been offered a retainer by the Trustees, but had declined for the reason that I wished to say that my position was a neutral one; that I was not testifying with the bias of an attorney in the case, and for that reason I had declined the retainer which the Trustees had offered me, and for the same reason I felt I would rather not represent her.[5]

For the time being I will pass over the rest of the Judges' statement, and speak of an incident that occurred immediately after the deed of trust was signed, sealed and delivered.

As all had left "Washington Place" but the Queen, John D. Aimoku and myself, the Queen made the remark, "I hope they'll not put the deed of record until I'm gone. If Prince Kuhio knew that I have left this home to you," addressing Aimoku, "and all of my personal relics and family mementos to the Bishop Museum, he would be 'huhu' (angered) with me, and may not lift a hand to help me in my claim before Congress."

Fully sympathizing with her, I asked if I might run down to W.O. Smith's office and acquaint him of her wishes. "I wish you would," she replied, "it will relieve me of much anxiety." I then hurried to Mr. Smith's office only to find that the deed of trust was on its way to the Record Office, Mr. Smith feeling that the sooner that was done, the better.

On returning and informing the Queen that my errand was a fruitless one, she hung her head down and for a few moments said nothing. As I bowed myself out *of the room, she looked up and said, "I suppose I'll have to face the music when the Prince meets me in San Francisco." "Keep a stiff upper lip," I said jokingly, "It will all come out in the wash." She laughed, as I left her.*

The next morning the local papers came out with the announcement in glaring headlines; "Liliuokalani Disposes of Estate—Disposes her Property in Trust to Governor Cleghorn, W.O. Smith and C.P. Iaukea—Aimoku is to get Washington Place—Children's Orphanage to be Built."

That day, December 3ʳᵈ, and the following one when the Queen took her departure for the mainland on the S.S. Mongolia, were anxious ones. But the Queen kept her own counsel, busy as she was with preparations for the trip. Accompanying her to the steamer, I bid the Queen God-speed and a pleasant journey.

Two weeks later, on December 20, 1909, the Delegate and Princess Kalanianaole left for Washington D.C. on the Pacific Mail S.S. Korea. On the same boat was Colonel Samuel Parker, Foreign Minister under Queen Liliuokalani at the time of the Overthrow, 1893. Also Kaipo Aea, one of the Queen's charges and principal beneficiaries to whom she had devised the Waikiki residence of "Kealohilani." All on mischief bent to upset the deed of trust as later developments proved.

For no sooner had they joined the Queen in San Francisco when trouble began to brew. And on reaching Washington D.C. it took the form of a deed of revocation, which the Queen was induced to ascribe her name to, on the plea and pretext (as the Queen herself informed her trustees upon her return to Honolulu) that the deeding away of her property and estate would mitigate against her claim before the Congress.

At all events and in pursuance thereof, a suit was filed on February 19, 1910, in the Circuit Court of the First Judicial Circuit, Honolulu, alleging that the grantor, in executing the deed of trust, did so without a full and sufficient knowledge or understanding of the terms, provisions and effect thereof, and under a mistaken belief as to the character of the same, and praying that said deed be adjudged null and void, and that the Trustees be required to reconvey to the grantor, the legal title to all of the property described in the said trust deed.

To which claim, the Queen's Trustees, mindful of the trust and responsibilities reposed in them, naturally declined. As a result, the Queen on her return to Honolulu and after conferring with her Trustees, filed a discontinuance, on her own behalf, of the suit as of date April 20, 1910. Thus bringing to a close the first attempt on the part of the contestants to wrest control and management of the Queen's estate from the hands of her Trustees.

The second and final attempt came when, on November 20, 1915, a suit was

*instituted and filed in the Circuit Court, in the name of Liliuokalani by Jonah
Kuhio Kalanianaole as her alleged next friend, and also in the name of J.K. Kalanianaole individually, as petitioners therein, against Curtis P. Iaukea, William
O. Smith and Samuel M. Damon (Mr. Cleghorn having died in the meantime,
and Mr. Damon appointed in his place) and the Beneficiaries, as respondents. For
the purpose of obtaining a cancellation and annulment of the trust deed of December 2, 1909, upon the ground and claim that the said deed was executed by Liliuokalani as a result of a conspiracy on the part of Curtis P. Iaukea and John H.
Dominis, ("Aimoku" that was) and that the same was executed by her while she
was incompetent to do so, and as a result of undue influence exercized upon her to
that end.*

*On the 30th day of December following, the said Liliuokalani filed in the said
Equity suit the discontinuance of said suit and a further motion to dismiss the same
upon the ground that the suit had been filed without her authority, consent or
knowledge.*[6]

Here is the apex of interfamilial land fights, one making all others pale in
comparison. Here also is a narrative that has almost entirely escaped memory
and public review over the past one hundred years. Just as we are severed from
landscapes, we are severed from these memories, and from the sense of identity that they might sustain.

Let me take you back to the discovery of these papers. I am in the research
room at the Circuit Court (Oʻahu First Circuit). I had just made a triangular
journey—from the Bureau of Conveyances to the Hawaiʻi State Archives, and
now finally to the Circuit Court. This journey has been more than geographical; it has been emotional as well. I had learned much in the past few months—
more than I ever really wanted to know, really.

The material at the archives was both informative and explosive. By now I
am very familiar with the methods of discovery at the archives, and what at
first seemed like an impenetrable maze of information is now relatively easy
for me to navigate. How strange, though, that I would have to fill out request
slips, stand in line, and wait for files on my own *moʻo kūʻauhau*. I had only
recently discovered all the chapters that my great-great-grandfather had written for his own book on all that happened during the territorial era. I had
learned from him that a lot had happened, even though our history books on
this era are very few and strangely subdued or silent. A couple of the chapters
deal directly with some court case in which the Queen's sanity was questioned.

The Queen's sanity—what is he talking about? I asked the branch chief for historical records at the archives: "What's all this about the Queen's mental condition?" She and others suggested that I go to the Circuit Court, because all the territorial court cases from the early 1900s are held there. Well, it couldn't hurt to look, I thought.

So, where to start? Looking under my last name had been the ticket so far in this unbelievable journey; so I might as well continue there. In the files directory at the Circuit Court, "Iaukea" brings up what seems like an endless list of files and indexes. Of course, the first Curtis P. Iaukea, my great-great-grandfather, was at the center of some incredible historical moments. But he's not the only one listed here—each succeeding Curtis P. Iaukea is indexed at the Circuit Court (Oʻahu First Circuit). Besides his long career as a professional wrestler, my father had been a beach boy on Waikīkī Beach—he owned his own beach stand. My half brother owns and operates a catamaran off Waikīkī. My grandfather was a police captain and left his own trust deed when he died. My great-grandfather before him lived in Africa and worked on the rubber plantations. Go figure—I had no idea they were all so judicial. But I can always look into those other files at a later date, I thought.

And then I see it—*Bill of Complaint, 1915, Queen Liliuokalani with Prince Jonah Kuhio Kalanianaole as Next Friend v. Iaukea, et al.* I ask the clerk to find this case for me. It was filed before the cases were indexed and copied on microfilm, so the clerk has to pull up the actual files, and she comes back with a large binder of papers, with many more to follow. Oh no—here we go again! Didn't I just go through this at the archives? I had just spent the better part of a year reading through pages upon pages of material there, and the pages upon pages here at the court briefly give me pause, and for a second make me want to run out.

I open the binder and begin reading frantically. Where was Curtis P. Iaukea in all of this? Which side was he on? Was he for or against proving the Queen insane? Never really having read court cases before, I can't quite tell. Finally, after some tense moments flipping through the pages quickly, scanning and jumping ahead and back again, looking for clues in the language, I come to my *kupuna's* testimony in support of the Queen's mental state. "ʻE paa oukou" she told us. Hold the trust from attack." Oh, thank God. Relief.

On November 30, 1915, Prince Jonah Kūhiō Kalanianaʻole submitted a bill of complaint in the Circuit Court of the First Judicial Circuit, Territory of Hawaiʻi, as the Queen's "next friend." This case pitted Prince Kūhiō et al.

against the first three trustees of the estate of Queen Liliʻuokalani: W. O. Smith, who also served as her personal attorney in the complaint; Curtis P. Iaukea; and Samuel M. Damon. The bill of complaint charged the trustees with undue influence in preparing the trust deed, as well as manipulation of and conspiracy against Queen Liliʻuokalani with regard to the deeding of her private property. According to Prince Kūhiō, it was due to "impaired mental faculties and by reason of undue and improper influence" that Queen Liliʻuokalani signed her trust deed in 1909.[7] And, according to him, because of this influence, Queen Liliʻuokalani had not understood what she was doing in 1909 and thereafter with her land deeds.

The bill also pitted Prince Kūhiō against Queen Liliʻuokalani, because, as reported in court documents, she did not want to be a party to the bill. One month after receiving the bill of complaint, she and her trustees filed for a dismissal, and the Queen herself requested a preliminary hearing to prove her competence. When this motion was denied, Queen Liliʻuokalani appealed to the Hawaiʻi Supreme Court, and the Circuit Court's decision was reversed: "Upon the remand, W. O. Smith and his law partner, Louis Warren, successfully defended the Queen and the trustees of the Liliuo-kalani Trust. The Court's decision quotes W. O. Smith as trumpeting: 'The Queen is sane.'"[8]

In the battle that ensued in court and in the news media in 1915, the integrity of Queen Liliʻuokalani (fig. 8) and those closest to her underwent extensive legal scrutiny and public attack, thus separating the Queen further from the Hawaiian people, as the assumed Hobbesian contractual relationship between ruler and ruled created a distance that never existed. I was struck by the personal attacks and precise descriptions contained in the bill of complaint. It reads like a "he said/she said" account of the prior twenty years of the life of Queen Liliʻuokalani and the history of the Hawaiian Kingdom.

As I read the case, I knew I needed a copy of it. But it's hundreds of pages long! All of the testimony, by all of the parties, and all of the court documents—this case is a bear. And the copy machine charges $1 a page. At $1 a page, I will soon be out of money!

At the time I thought, Oh well, I might as well get started. I have $20 on me, and I'll just have to keep coming back. Maybe I can borrow some money from someone (the plight of the graduate student). I copied one page. Then another. Then another. Then I accidentally hit the Start button without putting in a dollar, and it made a copy. Wow—lucky me! Another page, no dollar,

FIGURE 8. Queen Lili'uokalani, 1915. Hawai'i State Archives.

and a copy. My only thought was, Ohmygosh! Get copying before one of the
clerks sees what's happening! The clerks glanced up, bored, and went back to
whatever they were doing. And luckily, the room is almost empty. No one is
waiting to use the copy machine. So, for over an hour, I sat at that copy machine
and methodically photocopied the pages of the court case—for free. Someone
really wants me to have this, I thought.

The bill of complaint meanders through descriptions of the Queen's mental state, the economic motives of the "conspirators," and an analysis of the
newly emerging territorial government. Above all, though, the bill seeks to
prove the mental deterioration of Queen Lili'uokalani as a way of opening the
door to breaking her trust.

"Do I speak like a crazy person?" was Queen Lili'uokalani's self-reflective
assertion of her own sanity. A ruling against her sanity would not stand precisely because of the Queen's assertion to the opposite. And the stakes were
very high. Had this case succeeded, the Queen Lili'uokalani trust deed would
have failed and the beneficiary of it, the Queen Lili'uokalani Children's Center, would not exist.[9] In addition to proving the Queen's sanity, the case was
important in safeguarding this economic lifeline for the Hawaiian people.

The bill of complaint begins by addressing the perceived physical and
mental (in)capacities of Queen Lili'uokalani:

That owing to bodily infirmities and troubles which the said Queen had suffered for and during the past ten years, her memory had become so impaired that it was difficult for her to recollect matters and things in connection with the details of her business occurring during recent years, unless such occurrences were impressed upon her memory by some particular reason or striking event.

That the Queen had been unaccustomed to attend to her own business, and that owing to her official position, her physical infirmities, the necessary result of age and illness, she had led a life of seclusion and retirement, seeing only from time to time her intimate friends and relatives, and taking no active part in the details of her own affairs, and that the said Queen had no recollection of the service upon her of said process, and that the Queen's mind was further affected and shaken, which allegations of said affidavits petitioners allege to have been and to be true; that she was greatly disturbed by the allegations set forth in said action, and that in the defense of the same and the protection of her interest she relied, as she declared in her affidavit filed in said suit, on her business adviser and relative, Prince J. Kuhio Kalanianaole aforesaid.[10]

The bill of complaint also identifies the agents poised for her undoing. Accusations of dominating the Queen are brought against the people who surround her on a daily basis:

Curtis P. Iaukea and John A. Dominis, because of their surveillance and her isolation, the said Queen is in fear and under the absolute domination of them, and cannot act freely and independently, nor at any of the times hereinbefore stated had been able so to act freely and independently, and that the said instruments of trust did not and do not express the wishes and desires of said Queen, and were not and are not her free and voluntary act and deed.[11]

The bill of complaint then focuses on Curtis P. Iaukea and his probable motives:

That said defendant Curtis P. Iaukea at all times herein mentioned was and now is a man of commanding presence, of suave manners, smooth ways, of wide and valuable experience in the affairs of State and otherwise of much culture, thorough education, had traveled in foreign countries, and generally was and is a man of the world; and that by said power of attorney to said defendant Curtis P. Iaukea, executed November 13, 1909, the said Queen had placed the entire care, management and control of all her property in the hands of said defendant, in the full belief that he would, in all respects, act for the benefit, advantage and protection of said Queen and her said property and interest, and from the date of said execution of said power of attorney the said Queen had been dependent upon the aid, advice and counsel of said defendant Curtis P. Iaukea, and he was her trusted agent, personal friend and adviser, in whom she placed and had the fullest trust and confidence, entirely forgetful of the fact that the said Curtis P. Iaukea had previously deserted her failing cause, to further his own interest.[12]

The modernity that Curtis P. Iaukea exhibited as "a man of the world" is portrayed negatively as being too knowing, too educated. The very qualities that he had been praised for were now his faults. His "desertion" of the Queen refers to his participation in the territorial government after the illegal overthrow. Modernity and the native supposedly lie at opposite ends of the spectrum. But historically it was not uncommon for the ali'i to embrace both for practical reasons. The fact that Curtis P. Iaukea worked for the territory at the same time that he was granted the Queen's power of attorney and named a trustee speaks to the emotional and political complications of the day, which muddied clear dichotomies between insiders and outsiders. In any case, the bill of complaint was filed by Prince Kūhiō and others who had also served as working members of the territorial government. Not surprisingly, then, the question "Who is the enemy?" was one posed many times by Queen Lili'uokalani herself.[13] To define "the enemy" simply as those who work for the occupier limits our own understandings and ignores intricate human and societal relationships.

In general, the overall tone of the bill of complaint intimated that Queen Lili'uokalani was helpless and easily malleable to the will of others:

> That the said Queen at all times during her life has been dependent on the aid, advice and counsel of some person other than herself for the proper management of her property, estate, business and affairs. That the said Queen, during a considerable portion of said time since her dethronement, suffered, as the petitioners are informed and believe, and for a long time was treated for a certain disorder, which has the effect of impairing her will; her mind and memory became so impaired that she readily came under the influence of any one near her and having her immediate confidence, and equally under the influence of another who might temporarily usurp that confidence. That the said instruments of trust did not and do not express the wishes and desires of said Queen, and were not and are not her free and voluntary act and deed.[14]

The bill spoke of a helpless and dependent *woman*. This move opened a "vacuum of knowing" on the Queen's part, to be filled by a "next friend" in the form of Prince Kūhiō, and after he was removed by the courts, by a guardian in the form of Lorrin Andrews. Infantilizing the feminine is common in western practice. In this system of knowing, any show of emotional weakness by a woman encourages/demands subordination to a masculine protectorate. The insanity trials denied Queen Lili'uokalani her voice and rendered her silent, further attempting to distance her from her *mana*.

In contrast, Hawaiian genealogy is one of female power. Strong women or *mana wāhine* abound in myths and legends of Hawai'i.[15] The Kumulipo, the Hawaiian creation chant, begins with the ancient Hawaiian world, when Pō, the female night, "gives birth by herself, and without any male impregnating element, to a son and daughter, Kumulipo and Pō'ele, who by their incestuous mating create the world."[16] The female deity is the darkness that is the beginning of creation. She is the primary source of consciousness and reality. Papa, the first female *akua* (god), is also the first ancestor of *ka po'e kahiko* (the people of old): "Papahānaumoku: Papa the woman who gives birth to islands, Papa the earth mother who mates with her brother Wākea, the sky father, and to whom are born the Hawaiian islands, the sacred *kalo* plant, and the Hawaiian people."[17]

Each of the four major *akua* in Hawaiian *mo'olelo* (narratives) is matched by an equally powerful female *akua*. "Kū, god of war; Lono, god of fertility and agriculture; Kāne, god of sunlight and male essence; and Kanaloa, god of the ocean—had a female counterpart. There was Kūho'one'enu'u, goddess of O'ahu island, Lonowahine, goddess of the Makahiki first fruit festival, Kāneikawaiola, goddess of fresh running water, and Nāmakaohaha'i, goddess of the ocean."[18] *Counterpart* connotes equal standing and equal responsibilities.

This system of knowing stands in clear opposition to western notions of the feminine. In 1915, the image and persona of a strong Hawaiian woman represented a *danger* to the social contract. Would her accusers have been so quick to argue for the emotional and physical dependence of a male monarch? This question remains unanswerable. What is known, in and of itself, is that the mental acuity Queen Lili'uokalani displayed earned her the reputation among her closest advisers of being a "strong-willed woman." Such a woman would be *too* strong for this social environment.

As I read through and started writing about this case years ago, I wondered, Won't I seem like a crazy female today for even talking about it? Talking about what one member of this family did to another member—who am I to think I can present this material? This goes beyond my role as an academic. This is about being a Hawaiian female, and not wanting to seem like a crazy Hawaiian female, which is how we are inevitably regarded if we draw too much attention to ourselves. It is also why I've felt I could never reveal my own family drama, which is enormous and beyond the scope of what is talked about here, to the legions of wrestling fans that my father still has. I suspected they wouldn't really want to know the truth and would think I was crazy for talking about it in the first place.

Questions such as these once made me doubt my own role as a Hawaiian researcher and writer. But I am now more comfortable in these roles. Even so, my experience is that we never want to point fingers within our own community—to do so is considered shameful. We also never really want to stand out from the crowd. It's especially shameful to speak out as a woman, even though we still have strong Hawaiian females at the forefront of our politics and social hierarchy.

In answer to the bill of complaint, Queen Liliʻuokalani exerted her legal independence whenever possible. Bless her for asserting it. What a strong woman!

One month after Prince Kūhiō filed the bill of complaint, Queen Liliʻuokalani answered with a motion to dismiss, and a discontinuance and motion to dismiss:

AFFIDAVIT IN SUPPORT OF MOTION TO DISMISS

Liliuokalani, being first duly sworn, on oath deposes and says: that she is the same Liliuokalani who was formerly Queen of Hawaii and who is named as a complainant in the Bill of Complaint in the above entitled suit by Jonah Kuhio Kalanianaole as her alleged next friend; that the said Bill of Complaint herein was filed and the above entitled suit was instituted without her authority, consent or knowledge; that she has not since its institution in any way ratified the bringing or the maintenance of this suit; that she disproves of its institution and its maintenance; and that she desires that the suit be terminated and dismissed.
(Signed) Liliuokalani[19]

DISCONTINUANCE AND MOTION TO DISMISS

Now comes Liliuokalani, who was formerly Queen of Hawaii and who is named as one of the complainants in the Bill of Complaint in the above entitled suit by Jonah Kuhio Kalanianaole as her alleged next friend, and says that the said Bill of Complaint herein was filed and this suit was instituted without her authority, consent or knowledge, that she has not since its institution in any way ratified the bringing or the maintenance of this suit and that she disapproves of its institution and does not desire its maintenance and that on the contrary she desires that the same be terminated and dismissed; and she, therefore, so far as it lies in her power to do so, hereby terminates, withdraws and discontinues the aforesaid and above entitled suit.

And she hereby moves that the said Bill of Complaint herein filed as aforesaid and the above entitled suit be terminated and dismissed on the ground that it was instituted without her authority, consent or knowledge and is being maintained without her authority or consent; that it has not at any time been ratified by this movant; and that she disapproves of its institution and does not desire its maintenance but on the contrary desires it to be terminated and dismissed.

An affidavit of the movant in support of this motion is hereto attached and is filed herewith.

(Signed) Liliuokalani[20]

She then followed these motions with an assertion of mental competency in 1916:

Pursuant to the decision of the Court filed herein on the 7th day of February, 1916, and the leave to amend therein granted, by way of supplement and amendment to her discontinuance and motion to dismiss heretofore filed herein, and not waiving her contention and claim that the said discontinuance and motion to dismiss are sufficient of themselves without this express denial of mental incompetency and assertion of mental competency, the above mentioned LILIUOKALANI, in whose name and behalf the above entitled suit purports to be brought by an alleged next friend, does hereby deny the truth of any and all charges, direct or indirect, that may be contained in the bill of complaint herein filed in the above entitled court and cause by Jonah Kuhio Kalanianaole in his own behalf and as her alleged next friend or that may be otherwise howsoever made herein, that she is or at the time of the institution of this suit was of unsound mind or mentally incompetent to protect her interests in this suit or in the property involved herein and does hereby claim and assert that at the time of the institution of the above entitled suit she was, ever since has been and now is of sound mind and mentally competent to terminate, withdraw and discontinue this suit and the bill of complaint herein, to move to dismiss this suit and the bill of complaint herein, to do all things incidental to the preparation and prosecution of the discontinuance and motion herein filed by her, to protect all of her interests in this suit and in the property involved herein, to transact all other matters of business and to take all other action whatsoever.

And all of this the said Liliuokalani is ready to prove and asks an opportunity to prove, without waiving her claim that the burden is, not on her to prove her sanity or mental competency, but on anyone, who alleges that she is insane or mentally incompetent, to prove the said alleged insanity or mental incompetency.

(Signed) Liliuokalani[21]

In addition, Queen Liliʻuokalani immediately rejected Prince Kūhiō's assumption of "next friend" status and asked for his removal on January 17, 1916, when she entered a motion in the First District Court entitled "Suggestion of

Disqualification of Jonah Kuhio Kalanianaole as Next Friend of Liliuokalani, and Motion for His Removal as Next Friend."[22] She and the trustees of her estate argued that Prince Kūhiō "is disqualified by reason of interest to act as such Next Friend of the said Liliuokalani," because, as her relative only and not as a recipient of said estate, he had no monetary and real interest in the Queen's estate.[23]

As the statements of W. O. Smith and C. P. Iaukea also make clear, Prince Kūhiō had no right to act as her "next friend," because the Queen had not wanted to file a bill of complaint in the first place, since she did not want to set aside her trust deed of 1909:

STATEMENT OF W. O. SMITH

At eleven a.m. this day I called upon Liliuokalani at Washington Place and talked with her about the above suit and asked her if she wished to have the Deed of Trust set aside. She answered very promptly that she did not.

I then asked her if she had given her consent to Kalanianaole to bring this suit, or had authorized it. She replied she did not, and did not know anything about it until it was brought.

We had further conversation upon the subject and she reiterated that she did not wish to have the deed set aside, and said in Hawaiian "E paa oukou," meaning "you hold it."

I then told her that we would prepare an answer to the complaint, stating the facts and I thought that it might be well to have a separate answer prepared for her to sign and file, and she replied that she would be guided by our judgment in the matter for she wished to have the trust continue; that she was well satisfied with the way her business affairs and property had been managed.

She went on to repeat what she had stated on a former occasion that her brother, Kalakaua, acquired a good deal of property and she got none of it, and those who had it were well provided for, and she wished to have her property go as provided in the Deed of Trust.[24]

DIARY NOTES BY CURTIS P. IAUKEA, SATURDAY, NOVEMBER 27, 1915

"Paa mai oukou" which interpreted means "you hold on." The Queen made this remark to me just as I was leaving the main house to return to my office. I immediately turned around and said "Yes, Your Majesty, your trustees will stand by you and your deed of trust."

We had been discussing for a half hour or more Kalanianaole's claim for a deed to the Queen's Waikiki residence and his proposed suit to set aside the Deed of Trust. Her majesty had repeatedly made the remark "What do they want to get my property for? Kalakaua and Kapiolani never left me any of their property. Why should they have mine?" This and the whole conversation that took place between the Queen and myself were made in the presence of Mrs. Heleluhe, who will testify to the fact if required. C.P.I.[25]

E pa'a 'oukou—hold the trust: do not set it aside. Maybe because these words are repeated so often or spoken with such emphasis by Queen Lili'uokalani, or because the undertones of strength and commitment are unmistakable, whatever the reason, these words echo through the generations and resonate with recognizable meaning. In stark contrast, the next friend speaks for another's voice that has been legally silenced for various reasons.[26] In this case, a next friend claims the legal right to speak for an individual who had apparently lost those rights due to perceived mental incompetence. But ultimately, the court recognized the problematic nature of letting Prince Kūhiō serve as Queen Lili'uokalani's next friend, and removed him.

Lorrin Andrews was then named as the Queen's guardian instead.[27] This was another combative relationship for the trustees, since Lorrin Andrews also charged that Queen Lili'uokalani was being manipulated and coerced by her trustees.[28] First posed by Prince Kūhiō, and then by Lorrin Andrews, at the root of the controversy lay the question as to whether or not Queen Lili'uokalani really knew what she was doing when she signed her trust deed in conjunction with her will in 1909:

> That as soon as said defendant Curtis P. Iaukea had been appointed the business agent and received said power of attorney and found that the said Queen relied on him for counsel and advice, the said defendant and the defendant John A. Dominis conspired together to obtain a testamentary disposition by plaintiff of her property in such form that they, the said defendants, might profit thereby, and, as the petitioners are informed and believe and therefore allege, within a few days after the said defendant Curtis P. Iaukea had received said appointment he procured the said Queen to consult Abram S. Humphreys, then and now a member of the bar of this Court, with reference to making a will, and the said Queen did consult the said Humphreys on the 26th day of November, 1909, and the said defendants also procured the said Humphreys to advise the Queen to execute an irrevocable deed of trust instead of a will, and to suggest to the Queen that the defendant W. O. Smith should be associated with him in the matter; that the said defendants Iaukea and Dominis procured the said Humphreys to make said latter suggestion and the said Humphreys made said suggestion for the reason that the said defendants and said Humphreys knew at the time the facts herein alleged, and being well aware of the condition of the mind of said Queen and the doubtful propriety of her executing either a will or trust deed under the circumstances, sought to strengthen the moral effect of such by the participation therein of the

said W. O. Smith, who was then and is now a man of high standing in the community and a member of the bar of this Court, that on the 27ᵗʰ day of November, 1909, the said Smith and Humphreys advised with the said Queen, and the said Smith suggested that if she wished to make a trust deed she might provide, instead of an irrevocable trust, a trust with the power of revocation with the consent of the majority of the trustees.[29]

The bill of complaint charges that she was confused,[30] but the archival records tell a different story. The letters between Queen Liliʻuokalani and her attorneys and trustees, as well as her statements taken in court and in chambers, reveal the Queen to be a feisty and independent woman. It is my conclusion that these documents show a purposeful endeavor by Queen Liliʻuokalani to safeguard her private property from attack, especially after her death. The establishment of the trust was done very conscientiously and was accompanied by great thought. According to the testimony of the trustees in response to the 1915 bill of complaint, the signing of a trust deed was explained clearly to the Queen at the initial signing. But only the participants in these unfolding events knew exactly how these juridical and emotional relations played out. I can offer only the following testimonies that speak to these issues. Here are portions of the complete testimonies taken in court in 1916, when the debate focused on the signing of a "will versus trust deed." They reveal why Queen Liliʻuokalani chose to pursue both.

W. O. Smith testifies:

I told the Queen that Mr. Humphreys had informed me that he had been sent for in the first instance to draft her Will, but that on conferring with her about her wishes he had suggested to her that a Deed of Trust might accomplish her desires better than a will. I then explained to her at some length the difference between a Trust Deed and a Will, telling her that a Will was an instrument which could be revoked at any time before the death of the testator, or could be amended by a codicil but that a Deed of Trust conveying the title of property to trustees was different, and unless it contained a provision that one could revoke the deed or reserving the power to alter or amend it, it would be binding.[31]

Question. Was she then in your opinion mentally capable to comprehend her own affairs?

Answer. Absolutely.

Question. Was she then in your opinion mentally able to understand the difference between the testamentary disposition of property, a will and unrevocable instrument in the nature of a trust deed?

Answer. Why she seemed to understand it.

Question. I am not asking you whether she did, I am asking you whether she
was mentally capable?

Answer. She was.[32]

Curtis P. Iaukea's statement to the court describes the day of the signing of
the trust deed:

> The next morning I asked the Queen if she would decide upon some attorney to
> draw up her will. And when she didn't respond, I mentioned Judge Humphreys.
> "Yes," she said, "I would like to have him." I telephoned Humphreys at Diamond
> Head, this being a holiday, and Thanksgiving Day, and made an appointment to
> meet him at his office for 10:30 a.m. that morning. Taking with me the draft of the
> will that I had prepared, and memorandum containing the changes that Her
> Majesty desired, I gave them to him and told him what the purpose of my visit
> was. Mr. Humphreys looked it over and said that there were a number of things
> not touched on and no mention made, such as the disposition of her personal
> property and so forth, and that he would not undertake to draw such an important
> paper as the Queen's Will without seeing her personally and ascertaining her
> wishes in this respect. Attorney Humphreys made out a statement of what infor-
> mation was further required and with it I returned to Washington Place, and
> reported the result of my interview with Mr. Humphreys. An appointment was
> then made for her attorney by the Queen, and set for the following morning
> (Friday) at 10 o'clock, November 26th.
>
> At this interview and consultation with attorney, the proposition of a Deed of
> Trust was first suggested to the Queen. After explaining fully the difference be-
> tween a Deed of Trust and a Will, the former irrevocable, whilst the latter could
> be changed at her will and pleasure, the Queen approved of the proposition, and
> turning to me asked what I thought of it. I told her that it was the best thing she
> could do.[33]

Testimony of Judge A. S. Humphreys to the Honorable William L. Whitney
at Chambers:

> I mentioned it previously in the conversation, that it would probably be better for
> her to provide for the charities which she had in mind by means of a trust deed,
> rather than by will, and I explained to her fully the difference between a trust deed
> and a will, not going into attenuated detail, but making such an explanation as
> would convey to the mind of an ordinarily intelligent lay person the distinction
> between the two. I said to her, for instance, that a will could be changed as often
> as she liked; that if it were attacked, if its contents became known and displeased
> any person, it could not be attacked until after her death, when she would not be
> here to defend it. I then told her that a trust deed, too, like a will, might be so
> drafted, that it could be so drafted that it could be revoked at the pleasure of the
> person making it, but, in the absence of some provision in the trust deed giving

her power to revoke it, it would be unalterable, and it would have this advantage over a will: namely, if any attack were made upon it, such attack would probably be made in her lifetime, and not, as in the case of a will, after her decease.

I said to her, "You know how many claimants there have been who have claimed to be heirs of Charles Kanaina, deceased, how many barefooted, taro patch Hawaiians there are who walk right up to the statue of Kamehameha and say, without batting an eye, 'He was my ancestor.' Now, when you die, there will be numerous people to find fault with the disposition which you make of your estate. You will be importuned, probably in life, as the years go by, by those about you to provide for them, they claiming that they have some call upon your bounty. If this trust deed is made, your answer to all these demands and all these importunities may well be, 'The book is sealed. I cannot change this trust deed without the consent of my trustees.'"[34]

W. O. Smith's memorandum regarding Lili'uokalani's trust deed:

I told the Queen that Mr. Humphreys had informed me that he had been sent for in the first instance to draft her will, but that on conferring with her about her wishes he had suggested to her that a Deed of Trust might accomplish her desires better than a will. I then explained to her at some length the difference between a Trust Deed and a Will, telling her that a Will was an instrument which could be revoked at any time before the death of the testator, or could be amended by a codicil but that a Deed of Trust conveying the title of property to trusts was different, and unless it contained a provision that one could revoke the deed or reserving the power to alter or amend it, it would be binding.

I told her about a provision which Mr. Charles R. Bishop had inserted in his Deed of Trust in which he could, with the consent of a majority of the Trustees, alter the Deed of Trust and make new provisions or substitute new beneficiaries, and suggested to her that if she decided to make a Deed of Trust instead of a Will that it might be well to have a somewhat similar provision in her Deed of Trust, as she might desire in the future to make some change.

Liliuokalani appeared very much interested in the matter and asked some questions and both Mr. Humphreys and I explained to her as clearly as we could the difference between a Trust Deed and a Will. We also talked with her further about the difference between the power to revoke a deed and the power to alter or amend it; also the qualifying provision requiring the consent of a majority of the Trustees. She stated that she would like to have a deed with the reservation suggested.

During the interview both Mr. Humphreys and I spoke to her about her claim against the U.S. government and about certain family mementoes, decorations, kahilis and other similar personal effects and suggested that it probably would be better not to convey to the Trustees her claim against the U.S. Government and that claim and the personal effects and any after acquired property could be provided for in a Will. That if she had definitely decided what she wished to have done with her lands and property other than the foregoing they could be conveyed by the deed to the Trustees and the other things could be conveyed by will, which devise could be changed at any time she chose.

The Queen talked about all these matters and called attention to the life estates she wished to give to Aimoku and J. K. Aea and provisions for their support.

She also talked quite at length about what should be done with the residue of the property and stated that she had had various projects in mind, one was to have her Washington Place used for library purposes. Another had been to use it for an institution for preserving a knowledge of the Hawaiian language and Hawaiian music, and said that she had also thought of other dispositions to make of the remainder of her property. She asked me what I would suggest and I told her that we desired to carry out her wishes, but she again stated that she would like to know what suggestion, if any, we would make. I said that there were many different ways in which the property could be used which would do good and be a public benefit; that for religious work, educational work and caring for the health of the people, quite liberal provisions have been made; and there was Lunalilo Home for indigent Hawaiians and the Children's Hospital which has just been established for children who are sick, but there was no adequate provision for orphan children. She showed much interest and said that she had thought of similar things before and that she would like, after providing for those whom she had specially named, to have the residue, or its income, used to help the orphans.

During this conference the list of the beneficiaries and provisions which she wished to make to each were referred to.

During the interview the matter of the difference between a Deed of Trust and a Will which might be revoked or changed was fully explained and with a great deal of care. And when the Queen had expressed her final wishes we suggested to Mr. Iaukea that schedules of property be completed as soon as possible. He stated that he would prepare them as soon as he could. This was all in the presence of the Queen.[35]

The testimonies continue, and continue to highlight the political and legal agency of Queen Liliʻuokalani and those connected to her in the drawing up of these documents, where Crown Lands are negotiated alongside her private property concerns. This barrage of questions regarding trust deed versus will fills many files at both the Circuit Court and the Hawaiʻi State Archives. When first reading them, I wondered how these documents had remained unknown, and literally hidden from view, for so long. They show that private property and juridical discourse had a sophisticated audience in the early 1900s in Hawaiʻi, and that the deeding of inheritance was not left to chance, but planned and executed knowingly by all parties.

The insanity trials prove a prime example of the use and leverage of law by knowing subjects on all sides. At the time of the trial, moʻo kūʻauhau and familial connections no longer guaranteed the passing down of resources, and the fight to gain property through inheritance instead took place in the courts. Today, juridical proceedings layered upon complicated personal relationships are still experienced to varying degrees in our families and communities.

There were moments when I thought, Why me? Why do I have to be the one who found this information, and what am I supposed to do with it all? There is too much heartache in this trial. There is too much heartache in all of Queen Liliʻuokalani's letters, and in everything that she had to go through in the last few years of her life, right up to her death. Why was she not allowed to die without this last attack on her property, her character, her sanity, and most of all, on her person?

Sometimes I am overcome with tears when I read all that she had to go through, crying openly in front of the clerks at the various repositories of our history. Other times I just feel sick to my stomach. Then I need to surf or walk or do yoga—anything to get the feelings out. My mother and my sister are the only other ones who have read some of this information. We have long discussions of what it all means.

I had pondered the "Why me?" question for so long because I didn't even talk to my father, or to that whole side of the family. And yet now I'm researching them. What started with simple questions concerning a simple map of the Lele of Hamohamo has turned into an entire endeavor to understand not only my own history, but Hawaiʻi's history as well. And following the name "Iaukea" through the files has unlocked so many narratives. It's like some perverse joke of my great-great-grandfather, as though he's saying: "You thought you were not connected to all of this, like you could ignore it, like you could ignore the family? Well, not so fast!"

Some people will not be happy with the discovery of this information. I'm guessing it will strike a nerve. Others will be shocked, and still others will wonder why we should even bother with it today.

And then one day, as I was asking the same question, "Why me?" a new thought came into my head—well, why not me? This is my reality, my experience. These were their experiences, their realities. Who else could do it? And then another thought. Wait, this isn't even really about me. This is about them. Our ancestors, whose stories were relegated to the basement of the archives. After everything they went through, their stories and their voices should be heard. They deserve that dignity.

At the heart of the debate was of course the Queen's sanity. Mental capacity qualifies recipients for private property. What follows are Judge Humphreys's answers to questions about the Queen's mental state:

> Q. Referring still to this interview in December, 1915, which you have just mentioned, I will ask if you noted any apparent change in the mental condition of the Queen, comparing that time with the time she had executed the trust deed?
>
> Mr. Cathcart: Objected to as incompetent, irrelevant and immaterial, and leading.
>
> A. I did.
>
> Q. Will you state what it was?
>
> A. I noticed that there were lapses in her memory, but such lapses were not specialized nor malignantly accelerated; they were not magnified abnormally, but were an essential phenomenon and a concomitant of her advanced years, and I attributed such—
>
> Mr. Cathcart: (Interrupting) I object to what witness attributed.
>
> A. I pause.
>
> Q. Have you now an opinion as to the mental condition of the Queen in this interview of December, 1915, when you had this last interview?
>
> A. I have an opinion.
>
> Q. Will you now state that opinion.
>
> Mr. Cathcart: Objected to as incompetent, irrelevant, and immaterial.
>
> A. My opinion is that she was then of sound mind, in spite of the lapses of memory to which I have referred. They no more, to me, indicated a weak mental condition than the loss of teeth or the diminution of eyesight or hearing would indicate a weakened mental condition in a man as he rises above fifty.
>
> Q. Referring yet again to that interview of December 8, 1915, I will ask you whether or not in your opinion the Queen was then mentally capable of transacting her own business?
>
> A. In my opinion she was.
>
> Q. In your opinion was she at that time of sufficient mental capacity to decide on any matter of disposition which she might wish to make of her property?
>
> A. My opinion is that she was. She was fully capable of discriminating between the natural objects of her bounty and third persons.[36]

This exchange was just one of many that sought to establish the Queen's mental capacity. That the Queen is seventy-seven years of age at this time is mentioned as a possible contributor to her perceived forgetfulness. But old age in itself is not spoken about at any length, except insofar as it may have contributed to the charge of mental incompetence. In juridical procedure, the mental competence of an individual is assumed, and a mental incompetence must therefore be proved. The Queen's attorneys point out: "All persons are presumed to be of sound mind and mentally competent to transact their business."[37] Otherwise, the question of sanity would always need to be proved prior to any action. In cases such as this, what results is a monotonous study of a person's everyday actions to ascertain any deviance from the norm. Although the bill of complaint of 1915 does not explicitly declare Queen Lili'uokalani insane, it does attempt to argue for mental incompetence and "mental weakness on the part of the Queen."[38] The case ended before outright insanity was raised or mental incompetency proven.

This sane/insane binary does not fit the mental variances of the human condition acknowledged in Hawaiian knowing. In a spirit-enhanced existence, the seeing of visions (akakū, hihi'o, and 'ūlāleo) and the physical possession of an individual (noho) by different akua are interwoven into every part of a person's life. Everything from eating to naming to dreaming is imbedded with spiritual qualities.[39] How then would one distinguish "sane" from "insane"?

In contrast, Michel Foucault has shown how the individual became an object of knowledge within western espistemology, and how this knowledge informed the ways that the biopolitics of a population became managed, surveyed, and criminalized under the jurisdiction of the state. In part, this process sought to bring a segment of the population within the circle of awareness of the state, and then to control this portion of society once invisible to the state's eye.

The criminal body and the "psychiatrization of criminal danger" were introduced into discourse as objects of knowledge in Europe in the nineteenth century.[40] The notion of a linkage between madness and crime, and the intervention of a public body presented as a source of social hygiene, were important to maintaining social unity, because "insanity is ultimately always dangerous."[41] Foucault traces this genealogy to the concept of the ship of fools that was widespread around Europe in the 1500s.[42] On this imagined ship, "deranged minds" were often lumped together with the "morally inept" (including drunks, adulterers, etc.) as they sailed from one continent to some unknown destination, as "highly symbolic cargoes of madmen in search of their reason."[43] Accordingly, the passenger on the ship of fools "has his truth and his homeland only in that fruitless expanse between two countries that cannot belong to him."[44] Theoretically, it was possible to set the insane out on the ocean in this way because "water as purification" and "wandering as redemption" acted as "formulas of exclusion" during the European Renaissance.[45]

These readings of ocean and water are very different from the understanding of *ke kai* (the ocean) in Hawaiian epistemology. *Kai* is an extension of *'āina* and informs *kānaka maoli* (people of old) of a space/place connected to cosmology and genealogy. The word *kai* also unites the dimensions and locations of self and environment. For example, *na kai 'ewalu* is the poetic expression for the channels that divide the eight inhabited islands, and *kai lalo* literally means the "lower sea" or "where the sun sets." To recognize water as a "formula of exclusion," as in western madness discourse, is to recognize the stark differences between such a theory and Hawaiian thought.[46]

In Europe, the seventeenth century saw the first "places of confinement," often in structures that had once been used to house lepers, but now assigned to housing the "criminal body." Confinement became a "police" matter.[47] These immense buildings housed extremely large populations of upward of six thousand people, where everyone was locked up together. Since the medical gaze had not been fully developed during this era, "poor and idle" populations were included in these ranks for confinement. With the rise of capitalism, these sites of confinement also served as work sites through forced inmate labor. It was during this era that confinement became a means for perpetuating and enabling a social happiness.[48]

As madness became the antithesis of reason, the state became both the definer and the confiner of madness. Its goal as a moral authority was to assure social happiness from the spectacle/threat of madness. Madness had progressed from the ship of fools, and shunning "animality" in the human experience, to being an integral instrument for defining the moral society. Through confinement and its display, madness helps determine the social fabric of a moral society.

Eventually, however, the "medical gaze" fully intervened, as the insane came to be seen as sick, and medicine was used to treat this population. The eighteenth century saw a separation of people considered mad from ordinary prisoners. As the literal chains of confinement were removed, the insane person gained the status of an object worthy of its own gaze of classification, observation, and surveillance. Foucault points to the patriarchal relationship between the caring patronage of the man of reason (sane) and the childlike deference of the insane during this era. This was to be expected, since the patriarchal family was privileged, and the moral uniformity of the state and the social morality of the family helped define the status quo.[49]

How would such structures respond to Prince Kūhiō's claims in 1915? The institutions governing populations of the insane in Hawaii were first established in 1862 under the Kingdom of Hawai'i, when the legislative session passed an act to establish an insane asylum in Honolulu.[50] This act determined that "the Judges of the Supreme, Circuit, Police and District Courts, shall have the power to commit any person to the said Hospital on a satisfactory complaint being made before them that such person is insane, and that the *public safety requires his restraint until he becomes of sane mind,* or is ordered to be discharged as hereinafter provided."[51] In the face of insanity, the policing power of the state was first called upon to insure "public safety" for the general population. Notions of confinement, reason versus unreason, and even "animality" were all enunciated in this initial act.

By 1864, sites were being scouted for an insane asylum in Hawai'i. An article in the *Pacific Commercial Advertiser* noted the need now more than ever for this type of facility. It is also significant that the article advocated placing such a hospital next to the police station, as opposed to next to Queen's Hospital:

> It does not appear exactly proper to place it near a sanitary institution, where its proximity may work injuriously to the patients of the hospital. Natives have a natural dread of crazy people, especially foreigners, and one result of such a location of it might be that it would prevent them from voluntarily going there to be cured of their diseases.[52]

The fear of somehow making the sane insane pervaded these early newspaper articles. Placing the asylum next to the police station would naturally assuage these fears, because of the safety and security that many, especially those with property, associate with the police. In any case, the first asylum was not built in downtown Honolulu, but at Pālama, Kalihi, for occupancy in 1866. Its incoming director, Mr. Davison, "already had considerable experience in like cases at the American Hospital."[53] But within two short years, the discourse on this subject shifted from a surveillance discussion to that of the "medical gaze," and in 1873 the minister of the interior appointed Dr. Georges Trousseau medical officer of the insane asylum.[54]

In 1875, King Kalākaua appointed the minister of the interior as the "Keeper of the Insane Asylum in Kalihi."[55] In 1889, the first inmates were discharged from the insane asylum with recommendations from the minister of the interior.[56] In 1883, a glowing report of the insane asylum was published in the *Pacific Commercial Advertiser*:

> The people of Hawaii are to be congratulated for their progressiveness in as much as many larger and wealthier commonwealths have almost neglected to provide suitable refuges for the unfortunate, while the most powerful civilized nations have not made, proportionately, a greater provision for those who demand public care and pity, than our insular but wise and beneficent Government.[57]

The Hawaiian Kingdom is congratulated for taking the plight of the insane seriously, and Hawai'i's mature state in the realm of western consciousness is thereby recognized.

Also noted in this article was the work ethic being instilled at the Kalihi asylum: "Those who are capable, physically, of light labor are kept busy among the taro patches, or about the garden grounds."[58] The proportionally larger population of native inmates to all others made work in the *lo'i* (taro) fields an obvious activity to "distract the inmates from their illusions by continual occupation."[59] Since this kind of laboring is culturally relevant in Hawai'i, it might prove particularly useful in the rehabilitation of the institution's largely native occupants. But this was only one universal method employed, while prior Hawaiian treatments were more varied and specific to particular illnesses. See *Nānā I Ke Kumu* for discussions of *ho'oponopono* (to correct), *hō'ailona* (signs), and *hō'ike* (revelations) that were used to treat specific illnesses.

A newspaper article of 1883 provides a contemporary analysis of Hawai'i's attitudes toward sanity, a moral society, and labor:

> The necessity for a well equipped Insane Asylum in this Kingdom is great. Isolated as we are from the rest of the world, with an ever increasing foreign population, the proper means for the care of this unfortunate class, which of late years has been rapidly increasing, is of paramount importance. In this age of strife and competition, when everyone has to work to his utmost to obtain and hold a position in the world, it takes only a trifling reverse of the wheel of fortune, acting upon an over-wrought nervous system, to unbalance the mind, that most wonderful of all wonderful creations, and the most delicately arranged, and cast it into a living tomb to await the day when nature would claim the rest of a being, which had perhaps years before gone out of existence. With proper care and attention at the critical moment the individual might, many times, be saved and placed back into the world to take his position in society, as before.[60]

In 1887, however, charges against the asylum were raised and examined by a Commission of Investigations.[61] Here, notions of rehabilitation and surveillance continued to inform one another. The government followed the direction of the Commission of Investigations and appointed Dr. S. G. Tucker to be the superintendent of the asylum.[62] In addition, S. B. Dole, J. O. Carter, and H. Waterhouse were appointed to a Committee of Inspection and Visitation in connection with the insane asylum.[63] Their task was to make quarterly reports on conditions and submit recommendations for maintenance and improvements.

In the next few years, the intersection of sanity, a moral society, and governance was fully achieved in both the Hawaiian Kingdom and the incoming territorial government, with the change to a political guard more clearly within the American scope. With the Constitution of 1894 and the Session Laws of 1893–1894, sanity as a qualification of citizenship was articulated in law. Article 44 of the Fundamental Laws of Hawaii, passed in the 1894 Constitution, highlighted a "Disqualification of Certain Classes."[64] Act 78 of the Session Laws of 1893–1894 was "An Act Giving to the Board of Health the Management and Control of the Insane Asylum."[65] Rehabilitation again fell slightly behind surveillance and the need to further control this population. What is clearly evident, then, is that Hawai'i entered into western madness discourse during the Hawaiian Kingdom, and that this discourse was streamlined by post-Kingdom governance that sought further control not only over this population, but over all populations in Hawai'i.

The tale of Queen Lili'uokalani's insanity trials closely parallels another historical narrative. Amitav Ghosh's novel *The Glass Palace* tells the story of King Thebaw, the last reigning king of Burma (Myanmar today), and his queen, Supayalat.[66] The royal couple was forced into exile after Mandalay, the capital of Burma, fell to the British in 1885.[67] King Thebaw and Queen Supayalat then lived in Ratnagiri, a town on the coast of India. The physical imprisonment of the sovereign and the questioning of his mental competency closely followed his violent expulsion from power.

What is telling in this particular tale is how the charge that King Thebaw is insane acts to justify the end of his reign both to the incoming occupiers and to his own people. In the novel, King Thebaw is imprisoned; he subsequently "sat in one of the armchairs [in his room] and watched the ghostly shadows of coconut palms swaying on the room's white plaster walls. In this room the hours would accumulate like grains of sand until they buried him."[68]

But the question this story raises is, What is insane—the person or the situation? The novel also records that the colonizers "declared that the King couldn't be trusted with money and enacted a law appropriating his family's most valuable properties."[69] As in the case of Queen Liliʻuokalani, the impairment of the king's mental state was read and represented as the king's inability to control his monetary state.

At this juncture, the monetary state of the country was not in question: only the monetary state of the sovereign. Where is his/her money going, and how can that flow be controlled? Like the Hawaiian aliʻi, King Thebaw, Burma's last reigning king, was a physical link between the cosmological realms of power and identity, and between the people and their physical environment and identity. Or as Ghosh puts it, "In certain places there exist invisible bonds linking people to one another through personifications of their commonality."[70]

In both instances, the attempt to render the sovereign insane was the final act of dispossession of people from place and of people from a prior, interwoven identity. Separated and disembodied from sacred connections during the insanity trials, the Queen's body itself became a sign for changing cultural identities and was reproduced in this discourse as criminal, incompetent, and weak.[71] This assault on Queen Liliʻuokalani contributes to our severed realities today—from ka ʻāina and ke kai, and from one another.

A tear still comes to my eye when I review all that transpired during the insanity trials. This last fight to preserve the Queen's property outlasted her own life, as the trustees did not settle the case until a year after she died. What must have it been like to die in this chaos and confusion? And what about the last will she signed, just three months before her death? What really were her final wishes? What would the Queen think of everything that transpired?

So many questions. So many more questions now than when I first started researching. And too many questions that only *they* knew the answers to. But the heartache. The heartache's still there. The heartache of the participants read through the generations. These charges were not instigated by faceless, all-powerful imperial entities. On the contrary, the case was fought over by close family and friends. This in itself is intriguing, because perusal of the case shows that the complications of wealth, private property, and inheritance acted to undermine cultural barriers, and institute fully capitalism's divisive agendas.

CHAPTER 5

The Final Insults

Kāhoaka, *Condemnation, the Lele of Hamohamo,* Projects of *"Reclamation," and Heartbreak*

The international travels of Curtis Piehu Iaukea, the Hawaiian Homes Commission Act of 1921, the fight for the Crown Lands revenues, the formation of the Queen Liliʻuokalani trust deed, and the 1915 bill of complaint—for me, the Lele of Hamohamo, and the connected properties Hooulu and Lei Hooulu, bring these significant events together and close this narrative. These concurrent historical, international, and personal events are obviously linked and related. But *Lele*, a "jump" that also refers to the linking of two discrete and even noncontiguous properties, is an especially fine metaphor for the ways that the bill of complaint, the Lele of Hamohamo's eventual condemnation, and my own family's history are tied together.

The bill of complaint came to an end in 1918 with a *kāhoaka*—a phenomenon defined as "a phantom, specter, spirit of a living person; sign in the heavens, kind of sorcery spoken in a moderate or natural voice."[1] Curtis P. Iaukea describes how such a vision ended the suit contesting the Queen's trust deed:

A FANTASY AND A DREAM

Look at it as one may, the strange spectacle remains of a "Dream" leading to the settlement of the long contested suit and litigation over the late Queen Liliuokalani's Trust Deed and Will. A "Kahoaka" as a Hawaiian would say. Meaning that the spirit of a living person had been seen, usually by a Priest or some intimate friend of the family.

The incident I am about to relate happened in this way.

One day early in April of 1918, I received a telephone message, saying that Kahanu, the wife of Prince Kalanianaole and Delegate to Congress, wished to see me on an important matter. Glad to see her, an appointment was made for the next morning, with my home near the Oahu Country Club Course as the place of rendezvous.

The Princess accompanied by an intimate friend of the family, and a life long retainer of royalty, Myrah Heleluhe, arrived in a closed car early, between six and seven a.m.

Comfortably seated on the front porch overlooking the Golf Course, the Princess opened the conversation by saying, "Myrah has had a dream. Let her tell it in her own way, and I will then tell you the object of my visit."

Myrah then told the story of her having seen the Prince standing by her bed and saying to her, "Tell Kahanu from me to take the initiative in compromising the suit, and when I return I will take it up with my Attorneys."

I looked at Kahanu and said, "Do you believe in dreams?" She replied, "Yes and No, but Myrah seemed so persistent that I made up my mind to come to you as Manager of the Trust Estate and find out whether or not the Trustees will entertain a proposition to settle the suit, as I feel that if some compromise is not made, it will cost no end of money. If you are in favor of it, I will write to the Prince and let you know what he has to say in the matter."

I said to her, "Do it by all means. If the Prince sanctions the idea, I will do all I can to further it." With this the interview ended.

Some three or four weeks later, the Princess called at my office at the Executive Building, where I was Secretary of the Territory of Hawaii, and showed me a letter from the Prince to the effect that he approved of the compromise.

To make a long story short, a compromise agreement was entered into and duly executed on the 21ˢᵗ day of June, 1918, under which the litigation between Jonah Kuhio Kalanianaole as sole heir at law of the late Queen Liliuokalani and the Trustees of the Liliuokalani Trust, was withdrawn and wholly terminated.

The Prince and his wife Kahanu getting the Waikiki beach premises known as "Kealohilani," in fee, with Hamohamo Fishery; the Trust Estate assuming all costs and Attorneys' fees in connection with the litigation on both sides, amounting to the round and tidy sum of a little less than twenty thousand dollars.

A happy ending as I thought. And all the result of a Dream or "Kahoaka" as a Hawaiian would say. Stranger things have happened. And I'm no dreamer.[2]

A *kāhoaka* like the one that guided Myra Heleluhe, could be a *'uhane* (spirit), a *hihi'o* (dream or vision), or a *hō'ailona* (sign or symbol). Whatever the case, it provided guidance for actions in the waking world. Understanding such visions helps Hawaiians direct immediate actions, solve existing problems, and forecast events and behavior. Freud famously evaluated dreams to throw light on past events and emotions. *Nānā I Ke Kumu* notes that Hawaiian dreams are different and display a much wider range of characteristics and applications:

> Hawaiians hear voices about as often as they see visual images. This is in complete contrast to most Western dreaming.
>
> Hawaiian dreams are usually about immediate concerns and about family or people and places close to home.
>
> Hawaiians feel responsible for their dreams about others. A dream that suggests coming harm to a relative is invariably followed by an immediate visit or phone call to warn the relative.
>
> Conflict and aggression are frequently present in Hawaiian dreams.[3]

Hawaiian dreaming was an active practice, useful for day-to-day living.[4] As John F. McDermott explains, "Hawaiians of the past had a system that was beautifully fitted to their culture. They were neither indifferent to their dreams nor terrified of them. They allowed their 'wondering spirit of sleep' to be a continuum of their daily lives. They made their dreams a creative and helpful force for the individual and for the group."[5]

A *kāhoaka* might have ended the bill of complaint, but its beginnings were very different. Prior to the filing of this bill, the correspondence between the trustees of the Queen Liliʻuokalani trust and the attorneys for Prince Kūhiō points to deception and fraud in Prince Kūhiō's attempts to gain control of Kealohilani. As noted already, a letter said to be signed by Queen Liliʻuokalani to her trustees on September 7, 1915, granted Prince Kūhiō the favored land in fee simple.[6] On October 14, 1915, Prince Kūhiō followed this letter up with a demand to know the status of the land conveyance.[7] The trustees replied at length, stating that the first letter was fraudulent because Queen Liliuʻokalani never recalled writing or signing it.

After reviewing this letter, Queen Liliʻuokalani reiterated that she wanted Prince Kūhiō to have Kealohilani as a life estate only, and not in fee simple. In fact, even when J. K. Aea was to inherit this property,[8] Kealohilani had always been deeded as a life estate. Furthermore, only the physical structure of Kealohilani was to be granted as a life estate to Prince Kūhiō, and not the beach fronting the area nor the fisheries of Hamohamo.[9] The trustees explained it this way:

Since the receipt of your letter of October 14th we have each separately called upon the Queen and shown her your letter and she again stated to each of us (the undersigned) that it was her wish and purpose to provide that you and your wife should have only a life estate in the residence portion of the premises. As Trustees we were willing to consent to the conveying of the life estate to yourself and wife of the portion of the premises described in the deed, but were not willing that the beach portion on the Diamond Head side of the surveyed part should be included.

The amendment to the trust deed, a copy of which was given to you, follows precisely the wishes of the Queen as expressed to us on the several occasions above named; this amendment has been recorded, and under all of the circumstances we do not see how we can comply with your request of the 14th.[10]

One month following this exchange, Prince Kūhiō entered his bill of complaint in the Circuit Court of the First Judicial Circuit seeking the dissolution of Queen Lili'uokalani's entire trust deed, and the insanity trials of 1915 soon followed. The chain of events that eventually put an end to the bill of complaint, and the personal and property effects of these cases, are the subject of this chapter.

After Queen Lili'uokalani's trust deed was upheld and enforced, Kealohilani and some surrounding property were given to Prince Kūhiō in fee simple. The Lele of Hamohamo, deeded to Curtis P. Iaukea by Queen Lili'uokalani, was condemned by the territorial government and became known as the Hamohamo Tract. The other adjoining properties of my *kupuna* were also simultaneously either condemned or feverishly sold off by my ancestors. Also condemned was Washington Place, the Queen's home and refuge. Converted into an "executive mansion" for the governors of the territory, and later the state, the property continues to serve this function today, although the governors no longer live in the Queen's house, but in an adjacent building.

A general mapping of Kealohilani and Washington Place will visually acquaint us with the properties being fought over. Kealohilani is easy to spot today, since the Marriott Waikīkī Hotel occupies the site. Prior to an update the Marriott's website noted that the hotel's two towers were named after Queen Lili'uokalani's summer homes, Paoakalani and Kealohilani.[11]

Here are Queen Lili'uokalani's own words about Hamohamo, her summer property:

Hamohamo is justly considered to be the most life-giving and healthy district in the whole extent of the island of Oahu; there is something unexplainable and peculiar in the atmosphere at that place, which seldom fails to bring back the glow of health to the patient, no matter from what disease suffering. In order to encourage the people who might be semi-invalids to resort there, I have always left open my estates on that shore, so that the air and the sea-bathing, the latter most essential in our climate, might be enjoyed without any charge by all who choose to avail themselves of the privilege. I have also caused trees to be set out, both those whose fruit might be of value and those of use for shade alone, so that the coast might become attractive to chance visitors. When it is the *malolo* season, the fishermen living in my neighborhood will go to my beach to launch their canoes, and push off two or three miles into the incoming surf to catch the flying-fish; it is a very exciting sport, and at the same time it is a means of livelihood to them. Nor are they the only people benefited by this free fishing-ground. Most of their catch is taken to the markets of the city. Some part is brought in, and landed on the beach at "The Queen's Retreat," where whole families of visitors are often to be found passing the day in rest or pleasure. These have brought with them an abundance of our national dish, the wholesome *poi,* and perhaps have added bread and butter and wine, and stores of other nice things; to these they may now, if they wish, join the sweet and toothsome flying-fish. Oftentimes they make a further purchase of the latter to carry home for the family supper. Political events have brought me leisure, and from the view through the porticos of my pretty seaside cottage, called Kealohilani, I have derived much amusement, as well as pleasure: for as the sun shines on the evil and the good, and the rain falls on the just and the unjust, I have not felt called upon to limit the enjoyment of my beach and shade-trees to any party in politics; and my observation convinces me that those who are most opposed to my system of government have not the least diffidence about passing happy hours on domains which are certainly my private property.[12]

This description displays the Queen's contentment, emotional connection, and appreciation for this place. For approximately four hundred years, the larger Waikīkī area was honored as a *wahi pana* (sacred site) because of its physical characteristics and long history of prominent *aliʻi* who resided here. Samuel Kamakau notes its significance in 1865 in a series of newspaper articles he wrote for *Ka Nupepa Kuokoa:*

WAIKĪKĪ

The Ahupuaʻa of Waikīkī is at the eastern side of Honolulu. On its southeastern side is a rounded hill with a kapu bathing place in it. Its "body" stands aloof, like a lion, and stretches into the sea. The east wind is warded off by its body, and it turns aside. Waikīkī sits proudly in the calm of the Kaʻao breeze.

Waikīkī was a land beloved of the chiefs and there many of them lived from remote times to the time of Kalaikūpule. Board surfing could be indulged in there, and for this reason the chiefs liked the place very much. At Waikīkī are the surfs of Ka-lehua-wehe, ʻAiwohi, Maihiwa, and Kapuni.

> Cultivating was a great occupation of the chiefs, and the land of Waikīkī was made productive through cultivation—from the inland side to the coconut grove beside the sea. The chiefs constructed many ponds and stocked them with fish, and they made irrigation ditches about the land that led into the fishponds and the taro pond fields. In ancient times no bulrushes were seen, but now—what has happened?[13]

What has happened? Geographically, the rain from Awawaloa flows into Pūkele (muddy water) Stream, and the rain from Puʻu Lahipo flows into Waiʻomaʻo (green water) Stream. These two streams flow into the Pālolo Stream, whose capacity is more than a million gallons of water a day on average.[14] Pālolo Stream flows toward St. Louis High School, through Kaimukī, and into Kapahulu, where it meets with Mānoa Stream in Waikīkī. Once in Waikīkī, the stream names change again, as Mānoa Stream becomes Kālia, and Pālolo Stream becomes Pāhoa. They meet near Kapahulu Library, then the stream divides again into three main streams: the Kuekaunahi, ʻĀpuakēhau, and Piʻinaio. Where these streams depart the land to blend with the ocean is called Waikolu, meaning "three waters."[15]

Along with the visible streams above ground, underground water spouts from fresh and ocean water gave Waikīkī its name, "spouting water." Before, Waikīkī was mostly the Kālia marshland, filled with different grasses (such as ʻakiaki), birds (ʻaukuʻu), plants (naupaka), and native trees (alaheʻe). All the waters of the streams and rivers are known as the Waters of Kāne. The Ala Wai Canal later trapped and directed these waters in order to develop and facilitate the massive visitor industry in Waikīkī.

Figures 9, 10, and 11, taken in the late 1800s and early 1900s, show Queen Liliʻuokalani's two summer homes, Kealohilani and Paoakalani at Hamohamo, and the pier fronting the property. Built in 1890, this pier was removed in 1934, "after being declared unsafe."[16] As will become more evident in this chapter, words like "unsanitary," "safety," and "unclean" dominated official discourse during this era.

The other highly contested property in the bill of complaint was Queen Liliʻuokalani's home Washington Place. Sitting across from the Hawaiʻi State Capitol, this property has served as the residence of all territorial and state governors since 1921. Kamehameha III originally named Washington Place after George Washington when U.S. commissioner to Hawaiʻi, Anthony Ten Eyck, who lived on these premises, asked permission from the King and

Mrs. Dominis, the owner, to name this home after the founder of the United States.[17] Building began in 1842 and was finished in 1846 by Captain John Dominis and his wife, the parents of John O. Dominis, who later married Queen Liliʻuokalani. Captain Dominis was said to be on a furniture-buying voyage to China for this house when his ship was lost at sea.[18]

The 5,000-square-foot home passed to John O. Dominis on the death of his mother, and then to Queen Liliʻuokalani after the death of her husband. She wanted Washington Place to pass as a life estate to John Aimoku Dominis, the son of her husband, John Dominis, upon her death. In her trust deed, she wrote:

> For John Dominis Aimoku, the premises known as "Washington Place," with the appurtenances, on Beretania Street, in Honolulu, for his lifetime, and on his death to the lawfully begotten heirs of his body during their lifetime (or so long after the death of said John Dominis Aimoku as the law will permit, with reversion then to the Trustees).[19]

It was also the Queen's constant wish to have Hawaiian music and language taught at her residence after her death.[20] Washington Place was special to Queen Liliʻuokalani; she spent most of her time there after the illegal overthrow of her kingdom and her subsequent arrest and imprisonment in ʻIolani Palace.

Many of the trees and flowers at Washington Place were planted by Mrs. Dominis. Following her death, Queen Liliʻuokalani continued to plant trees and flowers. A careful gardener, she spent many hours tending to the vast gardens that surrounded the house. A document at the Hawaiʻi State Archives begins: "Among the private letters and papers of the late Queen Liliuokalani, was the following compilation in the Queen's own handwriting of the varieties and names of trees and plants in the grounds of 'Washington Place,' her private home until her death in 1917."[21] This compilation lists sixty-four varieties of trees, forty-five varieties of flowers, and fifty-five varieties of Hawaiian plants and ferns on the premises.[22]

The images of Queen Liliʻuokalani's grand gardens at Washington Place in figures 12, 13, 14, and 15 could be compared to the "pruning back" and domestication of this property that began in the territorial era and continues today. Just as the Ala Wai Canal was imagined as a canal before its actual construction, Washington Place transitioned seamlessly from the Queen's

FIGURE 9. Hamohamo, home of Queen Liliʻuokalani at Waikīkī, Oʻahu, Hawaiʻi. Bishop Museum.

FIGURE 10. Paoakalani Hale, home of Queen Liliʻuokalani at Waikīkī, Oʻahu, Hawaiʻi, 1886. Photograph by Alfred Mitchell. Bishop Museum.

FIGURE 11. View of Kūhiō Beach, Waikīkī, Hawai'i, 1927. The pier was built as part of Queen Lili'uokalani's home Kealohilani. When the property passed to Prince Kūhiō, it was renamed Pualeilani. Bishop Museum.

residence to a home for the leaders of the territorial government. The time line of political and social events folded in easily with a territorial historiography and imaginary. Queen Lili'uokalani's house and home were appropriated by the territorial government not only through condemnation proceedings, but also through the transformation of the property into an organized landscaping project of the territorial government.

The ownership issues pertaining to both Kealohilani and Washington Place were decided with the settlement of the bill of complaint in 1918. The suit ended this way: Myra Heleluhe had a *kāhoaka* that emphasized a compromise; the trustees found a compromise with the attorneys of Prince Kūhiō; the compromise was to convey Washington Place to the territorial government for $20,000, but this legislation never passed, as the bills relating to it were tabled; finally, the territorial government condemned this property through eminent domain proceedings, and then used it as an "executive mansion" for the governors of the territory.

Curtis P. Iaukea's diary in 1918 notes the relief felt by both sides with the ending of this suit.[23] He also writes that Prince Kūhiō had been "averse to bringing the suit" in the first place but was convinced to do so by his attorneys and acquaintances to "establish his right as the heir and next of kin to the

FIGURE 12 (top left). "Washington Place," Honolulu, Hawai'i, 1899. Bishop Museum.
FIGURE 13 (bottom left). Exterior view of "Washington Place," Honolulu, Hawai'i, 1886.
Bishop Museum.
FIGURE 14 (top right). Reception at "Washington Place," Honolulu, Hawai'i, after
Queen Lili'uokalani's return from Washington D.C., August 2, 1898. Photograph
by Frank Davey. Bishop Museum.
FIGURE 15 (bottom right). John Owen Dominis and John Aimoku Dominis outside
"Washington Place," Honolulu, Hawai'i, 1913. Bishop Museum.

Queen." This one statement can be seen as representing the multiple pulls faced by Hawaiian Kingdom subjects as they entered into American jurisprudence.

In his diary, Curtis P. Iaukea wrote about the debates over the terms of settlement. The diary notes are similar to the section of his manuscript shared at the beginning of this chapter, and even though he makes no mention of Myra Heleluhe's dream, more is revealed here in the diary:

Saturday, March 2, 1918

Received telephone message from Princess Kalanianaole asking if she and Myrah might call at my home, Nuuanu, to see me on a matter pertaining to the Queen's Estate.

The appointment was made for the next day, Sunday, at 8:00 o'clock a.m. Sunday, March 3, 1918

About 8: o'clock this morning, Princess accompanied by Myrah Heleluhe, arrived in an auto, heavily curtained. It was raining at the time. After the morning greetings, we all sat down in the parlor, Mrs. Iaukea being present also. The Princess then stated that she had come to talk over with me the matter of compromising the Contest over the Queen's Estate, and see if some amicable settlement between Kuhio and the Trustees could not be reached. I asked her what Kuhio thought of it, and whether the proposition met with his approval. She said that she was proposing it on her own responsibility but felt Kuhio would approve of it if he thought that the Trustees would entertain a proposition of this nature. I told her that the proposition should emanate from Kuhio and not from the Trustees. The Princess then said that, she would write to him and urge him to adopt this course. The Princess and Myrah remarked that this suit may go on for years and we may all be dead before it was finally settled (referring to the beneficiaries). I then asked the Princess if Kuhio favored a compromise, whether Kuhio would like to have "Washington Place" in addition to the Waikiki residence "Kealohilani." She replied that Kuhio's idea was to have "Washington Place" kept up and maintained as a place of historical interest where all of the Queen's relics etc. might be preserved as is done with Mount Vernon the home of George Washington. Even suggesting that some of the King's relics and mementoes, her brother Kalakaua, now at their Waikiki home, be kept at Washington Place.

The conversation then drifted to the Queen's Waikiki residence which had been left by the Queen to Kuhio and herself as a life estate now left vacant and unoccupied by reason of the suit and Kuhio's declining to accept the deed. She remarked that she had her interest there and had no intention of giving it up.

After some further conversation as to how the compromise proposition was first suggested by Myrah when the Prince was leaving for Washington, and the remark that Kuhio made following it which was to the effect that, "Myrah said some sensible things at times," the interview came to an end with the best of feeling and expressions of confidence on the part of the Princess and Myrah that all will yet be settled amicably and to the satisfaction of all concerned.

The interview lasted about an hour and over.[24]

Subsequent letters between the law firm Castle and Withington, Attorneys and Counselors at Law for Prince Kūhiō, the trustees' attorneys (Smith, Warren, Whitney, and Perry), and C. P. Iaukea as executor of the trust deed hammer out a compromise:

April 26, 1918.

(From Attorneys for Prince Kūhiō to Attorneys for Queen's Estate)

Gentlemen:

1. Washington Place to be set aside in a form to be mutually determined as a perpetual memorial to Queen Liliuokalani and the Kalakaua dynasty, and the passage of any legislation necessary or advisable for this purpose to be requested of the legislature.[25]

April 29, 1918.

(From Attorneys for Prince Kūhiō to Attorneys for Queen's Estate)

Gentlemen:

As respects Washington Place, we do not understand how you propose to deal with the interest outstanding in the heirs of John Aimoku Dominis, nor in whom the fee is to be vested if not in the Trustees, nor whether it is contemplated that the Liliuokalani Trust would have any obligation for upkeep or maintenance in case the premises should be set apart and established as a memorial, nor what may be sought of the legislature in the matter, nor what is to be done in the event that the legislature shall fail to take action at the proposed special session, or if it acts and refuses to enter into the proposition.[26]

(From Attorneys for Prince Kūhiō to Attorneys for Queen's Estate)

Gentlemen:

Having conferred with Prince Kūhiō respecting your proposal of May 22, 1918 we are authorized to reply as follows:

1. The making of Washington Place a memorial to Queen Liliuokalani and the Kalakaua dynasty in some form seems to us an essential part of the compromise, and, as a tentative suggestion only, we propose that it be made an executive mansion for the Territory of Hawaii, which would dispose of the question of maintenance and might dispose of the question of acquiring the outstanding interest.[27]

In these early letters, Washington Place was to be conveyed tentatively as an "executive mansion." The attorneys on both side of this case agreed that

Washington Place would function primarily as a memorial to the Queen, with one option being that Washington Place would be known as the Queen Liliʻuokalani Memorial, owned and operated by a separate group specifically organized for this purpose, "With the proviso that in case Washington Place should cease to be occupied and used either for a public or charitable purpose, the same shall revert to those persons who would then be the heirs at law of Her Majesty."[28] Under these guidelines, an executive mansion would fulfill a "public" purpose.

The trustees responded as follows:

Gentlemen:

> With regard to Washington Place, the Trustees are favorably inclined to the idea of conveying their interest to the Territorial Government for a moderate consideration upon the understanding that the Government shall also acquire the interest of the Dominis minors and that the trust estate shall be relieved of all obligation of maintenance or otherwise with respect to the premises.[29]

An agreement was reached in 1918, and the trustees then attempted to convey Washington Place to the territorial government for a fee of $20,000:

> One of the most important provisions of the agreement is that within twenty-one months the Trustees shall dispose of the late Queen's residence at Washington Place to the Territory for a sum not to exceed $20,000. It is provided that if the Territory does not acquire the property in the time specified, then within three months of the term mentioned, a corporation shall be formed for the sole purpose of founding at Washington Place a Liliuokalani Memorial as a public and charitable institution. It is provided that this is made on the understanding that the Territory or the corporation if the Territory does not acquire Washington Place, will make provision for the rights of the Dominis minors, who have a life interest as tenants in the premises. If the Territory does not acquire the property and the purposes of the corporation referred to fail, then the property is to revert to the Trustees of the estate.[30]

The legislature of that year tabled the bill that would transfer the title,[31] but territorial leaders were already envisioning Washington Place as an executive mansion. The incoming territorial governor and his wife, Mrs. Charles McCarthy, leased Washington Place from the trustees and "enjoy(ed) the distinction among all governors of the states and territories of the United States of America of residing in a gubernatorial mansion in Honolulu that was once the royal abode of a sovereign of the Hawaiian monarchy."[32]

The bills that would transfer Washington Place never passed. Instead, the territorial government ended up condemning the home and the surrounding property. The *Honolulu Advertiser* reported that "condemnation proceedings under the law of eminent domain were instituted for the Territory by Lyman H. Bigelow, superintendent of public works,"[33] and $55,000 was paid to the trustees of the Queen Lili'uokalani estate for the property. The heirs of John Aimoku Dominis contested this in court,[34] but the case was withdrawn. The territory paid more than double the amount it would have if the property had been conveyed, which is perhaps why the exchange was said to have been completed "amiably" between the trustees of the Queen Lili'uokalani estate and the Territory of Hawai'i. It also secured legal title of "Washington Place" with the trustees, as opposed to setting title with the heirs of the son of John O. Dominus, John Aimoku Dominis.[35] But the taking of Washington Place by eminent domain, and use of these premises to house the leaders of the occupying state, were perhaps the final insult to both Queen Lili'uokalani and the heirs of John Aimoku Dominis. Because they lost all claims to the life estate, the trustees did not have to attend to the upkeep of the premises or pay interest to the Dominis minors, and the territory took ownership of this property in the name of the "public."

This confiscation incorporated the Queen's private residence into a historical time line that legitimized the territory. That few in our community today know that Washington Place was condemned shows the effectiveness of the legitimization process. The following excerpt from a 1918 news article shows that the narrative was already in place:

> Back in 1848 Washington Place, the home of royalty and the residence of the late Queen Liliuokalani, was nothing less than a curiosity to the people of Honolulu— a curiosity by reason of the fact that it was large and white and beautiful, without doubt the largest structure of its kind in the islands.
>
> Steps are being taken now to secure this historical old mansion as the territory's executive mansion and, if this is done, the structure will begin anew to serve Hawaii as it served the Alii of these islands for more than 70 years.[36]

This last sentence admits nothing—politically, economically, or socially. A tumultuous era in Hawai'i's very recent past disappears, smoothed over by the seamless continuation of a linear American narrative. In fact, the use of this house by leaders of the territorial government represents the territorial government's forceful invasion of the sovereign space of the Hawaiian Kingdom, through the symbolic taking of the Queen's private residence, and it occurred with the compliance of all.

The settlement between Prince Kūhiō and the trustees also dictated that Prince Kūhiō should have Kealohilani in fee simple. This property had a frontage of 213.1 feet and a side frontage of 302.9 feet and was located on Kalākaua Avenue. The settlement also granted to Prince Kūhiō the pier and beach fronting the area, as well as the fisheries of Hamohamo. The *Honolulu Advertiser* explains:

> According to the agreement reached and filed with the court the trustees are to give a deed to Prince and Princess Kalanianaole to Waikiki beach premises known as Kealohilani having a frontage of 213.1 feet on Kalakaua Avenue. They will also give deeds to a strip of land adjoining Kealohilani on the Diamond Head side having a frontage of 302.9 feet on Kalakaua Avenue and another piece of land beyond adjoining the premises of L. B. Kerr having a frontage on Kalakaua Avenue of about eighty feet.
>
> In addition to these grants the trustees agree also to give all rights and title in the sea fisheries of Hamohamo. It is agreed that in the property deeded a small piece of land, the location of which will have a width of fifty feet, is to be reserved to the trustees. This will give access to the beach to tenants on property owned by the estate across Kalakaua Avenue.[37]

The trust also agreed to pay all litigation expenses and attorneys fees on both sides. In return, Prince and Princess Kalanianaʻole waived all rights and title to any other property of the estate.[38]

Once this property passed to Prince Kūhiō, its name was changed from Kealohilani to Pualeilani,[39] and by 1938 the name of the pier as well as the beach area fronting it changed, becoming known as Kūhiō Beach.[40] After Prince Kūhiō's death in 1922, this area was donated to the Territory of Hawaiʻi. Today it is still known as Kūhiō Beach, and a statue of Prince Kūhiō was erected on the site in 2002.[41] The address of Kealohilani today is 2552 Kalākaua Avenue.[42] But ironically the surf break in front of it is still known as Queen's, because this was the Queen's home.

As documented in her letters to Curtis P. Iaukea, Queen Liliʻuokalani clearly did not want Prince Kūhiō to have fee-simple possession of Kealohilani. However, after almost three years of litigation and years of distress for Queen Liliʻuokalani, the bill of complaint ended amicably. Was the *kāhoaka* responsible, or would a neat ending hold off other suits? I'm afraid only the participants knew the answers to these questions.

Shortly after the resolution of the suit, however, the *Honolulu Advertiser* announced that "instead of ending litigation over the estate as has been planned, the announcement reached between Prince Kuhio and trustees of the Liliuokalani estate, it is known, opens the way for new lawsuits in connection with the Queen's property."[43] In fact, John F. Colburn, on behalf of the Kawananakoa minors, immediately contested the Queen's will, but this case was found to be "without merit."[44] Another more dramatic case involved the new will apparently written by Queen Liliʻuokalani that redivided all of her property just months before her death in 1917.[45] Signed "Leiliuokalani," this will never held up in court.[46]

Wills and estates are commonly a source of worry for those who would benefit. When you grow up with nothing, as my mother, my sister, and I did, and when not much is expected in your social environment—where drug dealers live, high school dropouts and pregnant teens are common, and the police patrol regularly—when you survive and then leave this environment of fear, isolation, and abandonment, there's remarkably little left to be afraid of, except perhaps these ghosts from the past. But these ghosts can instill a lifetime of fear and heartache without proper introspection. The challenge, therefore, lies in releasing and healing these past realities so that reconnections and new understandings are produced.

For survivors of these circumstances, inheritance is a whimsical idea, an unreal promise, and the business of other people. Struggle was the reality that taught us that we could endure—no matter what. My father once smugly predicted that my sister and I would end up "pregnant and tattooed" as teenagers. My whole life has been about proving him wrong, which inevitably led me to those papers of my *kupuna*—I would not have been so determined to track private property in my family, and in the process find his *moʻolelo*, if we had inherited or benefited from any of that property along the way.

But what would it be like to inherit based on lineage? I still can't fathom the promise, or even the possibility, and because of this, I'm not beholden to anyone's generosity or goodwill. Some of my family members feel they have to hide their money and real estate assets, and perhaps even live in fear of being identified as wealthy natives. When you have nothing, there's no need for pretending or hiding, even if the price results in a disconnect from genealogy. But what is contained in this genealogy today, when it has been reduced to monetary relationships? And how do we really recapture connections to *ka ʻāina* in this social reality? These questions are not easily understood or answered.

Which leads me finally back to the Lele of Hamohamo—that section of Hamohamo granted to my *kupuna*. This parcel of land, and the mystery surrounding it, are the final pieces in this particular puzzle. Upon discovering this land transfer in Queen Liliʻuokalani's trust deed, I not surprisingly wanted to know how much land my great-great-grandparents owned, where it was located, and what happened to all of it. Specifically, where is the Lele of Hamohamo, and why had I never heard of it, or of any of the other land, before? And finally, why all the secrecy surrounding land ownership? The search for the Lele of Hamohamo launched this entire project, and so I end this chapter and book with an account of this piece of property.

Though there might be other extenuating factors, I believe it is here that the territorial government finally recovered this piece of property, as some were against Curtis P. Iaukea obtaining this land in fee simple in the first place, and through this action they also got back at Curtis P. Iaukea for protecting the Queen's trust deed. Why else would they condemn this land? Perhaps it was also because he spoke out against the HHCA. Once condemned, most of the connecting properties known as the Iaukea Estate Land were rapidly sold off and developed. This complex narrative complicated native agency then and now, so much so that the actions of the contemporary actors who profited over the years bewilder me. I am still searching for answers but am now closer to understanding than I ever was, and the mystery-novel quality of my search has not escaped me. But now more than ever, I also sense that the land *itself* keeps track of our social interactions and ultimately reveals the truth of its secrets. We get away with nothing—*ka ʻāina* knows and holds the *moʻolelo* and narratives of generations past.

The Lele of Hamohamo was connected to my great-great-grandmother's properties called Hooulu and Lei Hooulu. Together, these properties of over twenty-three acres, consisting of duck ponds and rice fields, were partly passed down from my Chinese great-great-great-grandfather and my Hawaiian great-great-great-grandmother to Charlotte Iaukea, and partly deeded to Curtis P. Iaukea by Queen Liliʻuokalani. Today this area covers Date Street, running from Kapahulu Avenue to ʻIolani School, and Kaimukī High School.

In 1928, the Waikīkī Reclamation Project profoundly transformed this entire area. The project sought to contain the aquaculture of Waikīkī by controlling the waters from the three streams that enter into Māmala Bay (Waikīkī). It allowed for the dredging of the Ala Wai Canal, which dramatically affected the entire area by displacing the native population and altering the physical geography of Waikīkī. The project further affected my own family, as the once swampland sections of my great-great-grandparents' properties were partially condemned for the building of the Ala Wai Canal. Initiated and carried out by those who had never owned or lived in the particular areas, the reclamation project required the condemnation of acres and acres of prime agricultural land.

Royal Patent 5588/Land Commission Award 8452, Apana 3, Sections 2, 4, and 5, record the Lele of Hamohamo. Sitting alongside Kālia and Pāhoa streams, the property was finally turned over to Curtis P. Iaukea in accordance with the Queen's will in 1921. Less than one year after receiving title, he sold it to William Woon for $1 on May 11, 1922,[47] who then sold it to Charlotte Iaukea on the same day, for $1.[48] This was perhaps done to safeguard (hide) the property under my great-great-grandmother's name. In 1926, Charlotte K. Iaukea set up a trust deed for her heirs and named Albert Francis Judd and the Bishop Trust Company as the deed's executor.[49] Included in this trust deed were the fifteen acres of Hooulu, two acres of Lei Hooulu, and the eight acres of the Lele of Hamohamo:

Item 1: Land at Kaluaolohe, Waikiki, Oahu, City and County of Honolulu, Territory of Hawaii, containing an area of 15.94 acres being the same premises conveyed to the Settlor under the name of Kahaloipua by R.P. Grant no. 2615;

Item 2: Land at Hooulu, contiguous to the property described under Item No. 1, containing an area of two acres, originally granted to Akini, mother of the Settlor, by R.P. Grant no. 2016, and conveyed to the Settlor by deed of A. J. Cartwright, Trustee, dated December 6, 1878 recorded in the Hawaiian Registry of Conveyances in Liber 57, page 352;

Item 3: Land at Hamohamo adjoining the land described above under Item no. 1, being

a) portion of the Lele of Hamohamo described in LCA 8452, apana 3, section 2 to Keohokalole, RP No. 5588, and

b) portion of said Lele covered by LCA 8452, apana 3, section 4, area .34/100 acre, and apana 3, section 5 of LCA 8452, and

Item 4: All rights and property to which Curtis P. Iaukea, husband of the Settlor, became in any way entitled under that certain deed of trust made by the late Queen Liliuokalani as grantor to A.S. Cleghorn and others dated December 2nd, 1909, and recorded in said Registry in Liber 319, pages 447 et seq. and conveyed to the Settlor by said deed of William Woon dated May 11, 1922, recorded in said Registry in Liber 639, page 235.[50]

Trying to protect the property by transferring it to Charlotte Iaukea did not work. On July 12, 1929, a lien entitled "For Improving Insanitary Land in

Honolulu" was placed against the land of my *kūpuna*. This lien specifically targeted for eventual condemnation

> A portion of Grant 2615 to Kahaloipua; the whole of L.P. 8330, L.C.A. 8452, Apana 3, Section 4 to A. Keohokalole; the whole of R.P. 5588, L.C.A. 8452, Apana 3, Section 2 to A. Keohokalole; the whole of R.P. 8330, L.C.A. 8452, Apana 3, Section 5 to Keohokalole; and the whole of Grant 2016 to Akini.[51]

On February 27, 1936, the Territory of Hawai'i entered eminent domain proceedings in the Circuit Court of the First Judicial Circuit against Albert F. Judd, et al., as the trustee for Charlotte Iaukea.[52] This was one year after the death of my great-great-grandmother.

The final order of condemnation for the Lele of Hamohamo was passed on August 21, 1940,[53] just months after the death of Curtis P. Iaukea that year. The territorial government condemned the land that sits adjacent to Kaimukī High School and resold it in pieces, to be known as the Hamohamo Tract. On the record, this condemnation was recorded as property taken as part of the "Waikīkī Reclamation Project."[54] My speculation, however, is that the condemnation was personal.

After Charlotte Iaukea's death, some of the remaining fifteen acres was rapidly condemned or deeded in parts for the building of roads and other infrastructure for the "Ala Wai Canal, draining, wetland and reclamation and mosquito control projects," also known as the Waikīkī Reclamation Project. One example was a parcel of land deeded to the territorial government for $1,792.00 by the trustees of Charlotte K. Iaukea for the "extension of Date Street, from the Palolo-Manoa Drainage Canal to Kapahulu Road."[55]

Other properties of Charlotte's were also rapidly sold off in bits and pieces. Over twenty land deeds by Charlotte Iaukea, Trust et al. to other parties were dispensed in November 1929, August 1938, and in 1948 in Waikīkī. The deeding of property by her trustees and/or the condemnation of particular areas of her land in Waikīkī continued well into the 1940s. Before these dates, the deeding of land by Charlotte Iaukea and her trustees was very sparse and intermittent. And by the early 1950s, the names "Curtis and Charlotte Iaukea, by Trust," were no longer appearing in the land record books, even though this entire area was still known as the Iaukea Estate Land. After seeing their names so frequently displayed in the land grantor/grantee index books at the Bureau of Conveyances over a time span stretching for decades, I missed them when they were no longer present. No longer dominated by a number of familiar names of the territory, by the 1950s the grantor/grantee books included hundreds of names appearing for the first time. As a result of this process of change, an entire area dominated by the names of my *kūpuna* simply became known as "Date Street." And it was here that others in my family profited enormously by furiously selling off portions of the Iaukea Estate Land—an entire subdivision gone, and for what? Now we can never lay claim to this property, or to the meaning that this land provides, ever again. It would be a few decades before another Curtis P. Iaukea trust would be established, this one including some of the lands bought with the proceeds by my grandfather, Curtis P. Iaukea II. This is another trust that I know about only through my research.

The Waikīkī Reclamation Project was a dramatic event that changed the lifestyle and working environment of Waikīkī and the surrounding areas forever. My family was just one among many, many families affected by a desire to "reclaim" this area for a dream only just beginning to form in the minds and wallets of a few. Fueled by an innocence but really directed by a sense of self-righteous entitlement, the "reclamation" of a land base that had been neither owned nor operated by those doing the reclaiming proceeded.

As other examples throughout this book have shown, one effective method for the dispossession of people from place is the supposedly disinterested, unbiased, and therefore seemingly innocent apparatus of the law. And it was through juridical procedure that the marshlands and duck ponds of Waikīkī were transformed through the Ala Wai Canal into the massive tourist mecca known the world over.

Before the canal existed, there were imaginings of how nature, as well as how the native, should look and behave. A canal would fulfill longings for economic prosperity, for something "bigger and better" in Hawaiʻi. The canal was also a way to change the social landscape by altering the waterways of Waikīkī for "a new and better class of people."[56] "Nature cannot pre-exist its construction,"[57] Donna Haraway writes, and the rhetoric used to justify transforming the area in the late 1800s and early 1900s hinged on socially constructed images of nature—in this case as wild, ugly, and unsanitary.

This order of things was firmly established prior to the dredging of the canal.[58] George Chaney wrote of this area in 1880: "With such examples of the capacity of the land, what a pity it seems to find one's self soon surrounded by wretched marshes, disfigured—if their coarse face can be made uglier than the weeds and wild grasses make it—with muddy ponds of green and stagnant waters."[59] This attitude reflects the ideology associated with "seeing man," for whom nature is ugly if not controlled. What he does not see in Waikīkī at this time is the four hundred years of *aliʻi* rule, or the vast water and irrigation systems set up to feed the wetland taro started by Kalamakau, a much revered *Aliʻi Nui*, from the three upland streams that enter into Māmala Bay (Waikīkī), or the integration of the Chinese workforce and the proliferation of the duck ponds, or the native bodies that inhabited this environment and lived according to these various cultural codes.[60]

Once the otherness/ugliness of nature was established, and the native inhabitants removed from the equation, the supposed "sanitation" problems of the area were used as the primary justification for action. The marshlands and taro fields contained "restricted" water that resulted in Waikīkī being labeled "unsanitary." As a result, public health was the official reason given for the complete destruction of agriculture and aquaculture in Waikīkī in the early twentieth century.[61]

Sanford B. Dole, president of the Republic of Hawaiʻi, Lucius E. Pinkham, governor of Hawaiʻi and president of the Territorial Board of Health in the early 1900s, and Walter F. Dillingham, owner of the Hawaiian Dredging Company eagerly took on the task of "sanitizing" this area by controlling the flows of the rivers. Legislative action legitimized this transformation.[62] Act 61, passed in the 1896 legislature of the Republic of Hawaiʻi, was entitled "An Act to Provide for the Improvement of Land in the District of Honolulu Deleterious to Public Health, and for the Creation and Foreclosure of Liens to Secure the Payments of the Expense So Incurred."[63] It began the process of "reclaiming": "Act 61 (1896) soon became Chapter 83, sec. 1025 to 1034, of the 1905 Revised Laws of Hawaii. This law would be the justifying factor for the massive dredge and fill project in Waikiki in the 1920s, a project in which the main concern was real estate speculation and not sanitation."[64]

A "regime of truth" was being enunciated early, when Lucius E. Pinkham, as president of the Board of Health, submitted a 1906 report entitled "Reclamation of the Waikiki District: For the Making of Honolulu as Beautiful and Unique in Character, as Nature Has Endowed it in Scenery, Climate and Location."[65] Ironically, Curtis P. Iaukea was appointed as an agent to the 1907 Board of Health, where he helped to engineer this reclamation movement. Ultimately he was repaid for his efforts with the taking of the Lele of Hamohamo.

Other reports followed. In 1909, W. C. Hodby, chief quarantine officer for the U.S. Public Health and Marine-Hospital Service, submitted "The Outlook for Quarantinable Diseases in the Territory of Hawai'i."[66] Then "[a]fter a single case of yellow fever surfaced in Honolulu, a quarantine officer contracted the disease from a traveler from Mexico—Walter F. Dillingham and a group of other prominent businessmen issued a resolution against the offending insects."[67] Lucius Pinkham, who among other roles served as acting territorial governor when three reclamation laws were passed, also conducted the Pinkham Survey of 1917–1918 in Waikīkī.[68]

Within a span of slightly over twenty years, a canal was speculated about, studied, and mapped, and then quickly executed. Condemnation and eminent domain proceedings lodged against the private property of farmers in Waikīkī made the canal possible. Though the Hawaiian Kingdom had adopted laws regarding eminent domain as early as the 1840s, private property and "the common good" were and are two discursive entities that legitimize this process under U.S. jurisprudence, and in the name of that mythical creature "the public."[69]

In the massive land seizure required for the canal, if residents on the marshlands did not give up their land willingly, or if they filed court papers to stay on the land, further legal and financial maneuverings helped the state carry out its interests. Barry Nakamura notes:

> If the owners could not afford the costs of filling their lands or otherwise refused to do so, the Territorial government would pay to have the work done, from the money available in the Sanitation Fund. Then a lien would be placed on the filled land which, if not repaid by the land owner within a certain period of time, was foreclosed and the land auctioned to satisfy the lien.[70]

On the other hand, Walter F. Dillingham was in a perfect position to buy foreclosed land. He ended up owning some 145 acres in Waikīkī, land designated for "reclamation." Then he sold these acreages after his company dredged, filled, and "improved" this land—another example of conflict of interest as facilitated by legislative and economic actors in the territorial government.

As the land around the Ala Wai physically changed in appearance, the individuals who inhabited this land also changed, thanks to the disciplinary power of the state. A new era of relating to legislative power was established along the lines of subject/citizen.[71] This recoding of nature, along with the individual, is celebrated in the book *Building a Greater Waikiki*:

> Hundreds of acres of swamp lands reclaimed into what is now one of Waikiki's finest districts. Today there are beautiful homes, where once a swamp existed.

FIGURE 16. Waikīkī Duck Ponds and Diamond Head, Waikīkī, Hawaiʻi, 1904. Bishop Museum.

Hundreds of acres of land were filled in and a broad canal cut through from the sea to the Territorial Fair grounds. With the development of the boulevard which will run the full length of the canal, and the many fine homes and the palatial hotel, which are planned for this district, it will without doubt be one of the most attractive sections of the city.[72]

And accompanying these changes will be the "better class of people," as presumably these landscaping projects will directly contribute to a more "civilized" existence, both in land and in people. This myth is written into the text of "development" as celebration of an emergent order over chaos. This recoding of the landscape and the people-scape also emphasized a national identity tied to a landed identity (possessing property) and to notions of "equality." The images of Waikīkī and the Ala Wai Canal in figures 16 and 17 exhibit the imagined transformations from chaos to order, where "competing narratives are glimpsed in the photographs taken *before* and *after* the construction of the Ala Wai Canal. Both groups of photos were used to legitimize the incoming nation-state and modernizing agendas of the Territorial Government, as well as to disqualify existing epistemologies."[73]

Ultimately, the Ala Wai Canal killed the Waters of Kāne and produced

FIGURE 17. Diamond Head and the Ala Wai Boulevard with the Ala Wai Canal on the left, Waikīkī, Hawai'i, 1930. Bishop Museum.

the Waikīkī that we know today. Thanks to this process—and not only for my own family—epistemological understandings of *ka 'āina* and *'ohana* were strained and replaced with some of the more "practical" needs assumptive of contemporary capitalist epistemology that valorize the grabbing, the holding onto, and/or the selling off of as much land as possible.

In the 1920s in Hawai'i, those who were favorably positioned socioeconomically benefited from the concentration of land and power in the hands of very few. As for my own family, I believe they experienced both sides of this divide, as both property "losers" and financial "winners" simultaneously. This complicated their agency and produced an internal and profound confusion. In our current state of familial land affairs, land continues to be lost and won intermittently, always secretly, and usually with an eye for the "now," as opposed to safeguarding it for the future.

Left out of this narrative of the Waikīkī Reclamation Project, but included in others' readings (Nakamura, Ferguson, and Turnbull, among others), is the U.S. military's acquisition of significant amounts of reclamation lands at Waikīkī and Ala Moana. The military narrative presents Hawai'i as a welcoming, dependent feminized island entity that needs and beckons to the mighty male power of the hypermasculinized imperial state. The military, in short, will ensure native survival and existence in a violent world.[74] Each in their own ways, the U.S. military and the massive tourism industry have "reclaimed" and reinscribed Waikīkī according to desires and dreams based on their own consuming images, which are then reproduced by themselves for themselves. Waikīkī itself, a *wahi pana*, a sacred site, is now polluted by the massive tourism industry that has laid claim to her, the culture, and her people.

The Waikīkī Reclamation Project and the dredging of the Ala Wai Canal made all of these consuming imaginings possible. Gaye Chan and Andrea Feeser refer to the Ala Wai Canal as a "scar on the ʻāina."[75] Even as I celebrate the fact that canoe clubs and other local groups use this canal today for their practice and training, I could not agree with them more. The Ala Wai Canal displaced native and local livelihoods. And by literally stopping the waters, as others have noted, the canal has created the very health dangers and public health outcries that it was supposed to prevent. The Ala Wai is widely recognized as one of the most polluted bodies of water in Hawaiʻi today.

But this is only one example. Whether it is the physical reminder of unfairness showcased as the Ala Wai Canal, or the psychologically damaging remnants that still linger after the "killing of the waters" and the effects on work and livelihood, or the use of condemnation laws and eminent domain proceedings to secure properties like Washington Place and the acreages of my own family for some mythical "public good," or the changing of Kealohilani to Pualeilani and then to Kūhiō Beach, or all the land dealings and heartache that resulted from the insanity trials and the subsequent settlements, we still live with the effects of these land transfers and personal transactions. I have been affected by these proceedings, and our community has not escaped the "scar" of these occurrences.

As I finish this narrative with the lands of my *kūpuna* and so much more, I am no longer confused or even surprised by the ways that land is contested among families and in the larger society. This chapter is the culmination of a project devoted to learning and understanding what happened/happens to land/ʻāina under the societal pressures of occupation and capitalism in Hawaiʻi and using the complex and intertwining examples found in my own family as a guide to larger narratives and legal occurrences of a hundred years ago.

I am now completely convinced my *kūpuna* knew exactly what they were doing when they deeded land in the early 1900s. I'm also convinced that Queen Liliʻuokalani and Prince Kūhiō understood the land laws and used them to control their own property assets. Native agency, though extremely complicated and often subverted, was always present in all of these cases.

But as reassuring as this is to me, I must also reflect on the fact that the "ugliness" that these activities caused and still cause within our families and communities was also carried out knowingly, and with agency. Perhaps such contested relationships have always been present in Hawaiian historiography. Perhaps American jurisprudence only textured these transactions, as an occupying U.S. government facilitated the production of a territorial landscape alongside a territorial citizenry.

These historical relationships continue to influence our land-deeding decisions. A glimpse at the history of these eight acres affords us a window into the greater houses of deception, both within and outside my family unit. And some of these deceptions are truly heartbreaking.

As I've written this book, I've personally felt this heartbreak, from the past and the present that arises from the deception and fraud that accompany the institutionalization of land, private property, and inheritance. My emotional reactions have in turn guided "what I talk about" as much as "why I talk about it." To ignore this heartbreak, whether perpetrated by ourselves as Hawaiians upon ourselves, or by outsiders upon us, is to ignore a vital part of our collective narrative.

Through these narratives, the bureaucratic ledger in Hawai'i is opened wider and further explained. Knowledge of these past instances can only aid us in our future endeavors, since reorienting ourselves to our own histories further helps us explain and respond to our current realities. A healing also occurs, both in the individual and in the collective, from understanding entire narratives. The narratives presented here represent only a fraction of the mo'olelo from this era that are awaiting exploration. Much work therefore remains in our efforts to know who we are today based on who we were then.

Epilogue

"They know who you are, they see you coming," said Uncle Willy Iaukea as we visited places on Hawai'i Island that are not only special to our lineage—the 'Ī Clan of Hilo—but are fundamental to an epistemology that reaches back before time. Uncle Willy is happy we have arrived, and very open to sharing the *mo'olelo* from our 'ohana—stories that have come up orally through the generations. And it all feels so normal, so right, to be around this family at this time, and to be in these places that are familiar and welcoming, even though we've never visited them before. My mother, my sister, and I are meeting him and other members of the Iaukea 'ohana for the first time.

This is a very important reunion within the larger one. At this weekend-long family reunion in Hilo, the direct descendants of Kamehameha I have come together from everywhere, and we find ourselves happily meeting over sixty cousins, aunties, and uncles—again, all for the very first time. It's like watering a plant in the desert; there is so much to take in after so much drought. Over the course of a weekend, my perspective expands as I come closer to recognizing the magnitude of the greater *mo'olelo* from which we descend as Hawaiians. In this kind of knowing, there is no real distinction between land, body, and emotion. Any disruptions—what I've labeled *insanity*, for instance—arise from dismemberments of the parts from the whole. But trouble is simply a reaction to this felt displacement. The whole remains whole still, and in this continuum, "knowledge goes forward."[1]

This book recovers political memories, and for myself, resolves parts of my own identity lost because of such severing. Some of the inner workings of the territorial government are revealed here, providing more information about a difficult time in Hawai'i's history that has largely been presented as linear and progressive. In the unfolding stories of Curtis P. Iaukea, his Queen, and many others, the raw emotions and complex interactions that characterized territorial governance are revealed. I never knew how much happened during this period, because the history books tend to paint a brief and rather bland picture. Perhaps produced purposefully as part of American socialization, this narrative boredom might also have occurred because these personal stories, and others like them, are not accessible without dedicated and intensive research.

I've learned that early territorial history—chaotic, heartbreaking, but also intriguing and inspiring—covers a time and space when Hawaiians and citizens of the territory were trying to navigate multiple realities: American social and political influence, a strongly entrenched local ruling oligarchy, and the difficulty of retaining a Hawaiian identity in the face of dedicated landscaping and citizenry agendas designed to wipe out Hawaiian epistemology. Hawaiians actively struggled in each of these arenas as knowing agents, even when they were folded into these larger narratives. Native epistemology could not be eradicated, though it was sometimes appropriated by the outside to fit an unfolding development rhetoric.

Today Hawaiians are simultaneously marginalized from and incorporated within the larger occupying American narrative. We live in the shadows of the U.S. military and tourism industries, which do little to hide their contempt for the native population. Mass capitalism itself has also deconstructed our complex ties to ka 'āina, replacing them with one-dimensional transactions of private property that attempt to sever our connections to genealogy, often by provoking family dynamics into crisis.

But Hawaiians and our thought practices have survived, remaining unseverable at the source. As others have proclaimed, we are still here, and our genetic makeup still consists of interwoven understandings of land, body, and emotion. Assuming a separation between the three arises from a larger insanity that would see these entities and many others as separate and distinct. Ali'i, ka 'āina, and kānaka maoli, for example, are all links in a single genealogical chain. This is why what happened to Queen Lili'uokalani's personal and mental property is representative of all of our dealings with 'ohana and 'āina. This is why these events are important, and why we need to care— because as I've said throughout, the heart really does ache, and understanding how these events occurred and how we are still affected begins the process of putting the pieces back together. And the political, undeniable need to be on the land itself again must occur to actually heal the break.

Curtis Piehu Iaukea wanted us to know about some of these events and circumstances in detail; this book brings his memories and writings to the community. I've learned that my great-great-grandfather was a loyal and engaging man. He was well spoken, smart, and fiercely dedicated to serving government. I am proud to be his descendant. This alone is remarkable, because after many past experiences, I did not believe that I would ever be interested in writing about my own family. Nor did I believe that the yawning gaps could be closed, so that I would willingly recognize myself in my own *moʻo kūʻauhau*, let alone feel appreciation and wonder at it. I am now open to encountering and knowing more of my *ʻohana*, and more of the *moʻolelo* that make us whole. Curtis P. Iaukea's memories have helped me recover missing parts and stand in the light of my own agency, and for this I am grateful. Simple survival is no longer the end goal. Breaking the cycles of emotional and physical dispossession, healing, and doing the work to align brings some peace to an entire genealogy and must be constantly pursued.

Those with land and money in the family will continue to control and hide these things, but I care less about this now than I did before, because I've learned that things are far less personal than I had imagined. We are all operating within various power structures and institutional forces imposed a century ago. I've decided I want to believe that my family has been doing the best it can under the circumstances, at least within their own understandings of them, although I can't help but occasionally question some of their actions— marred as they have been by massive drug use and years of lying, stealing, cheating, running, and hiding. As for the taking and hiding of land and inheritance, I've learned that it is not entirely personal—we are all at the mercy of the social systems and the past individual experiences we find ourselves operating within. How events occurred has its own timing and sequence anyway. Dire circumstances motivated my own valuable search through the archives to arrive back at my own family. And in this process, I have finally made peace with my father and can recognize his pride in me as his daughter. There is much to be proud of in our genealogy—he began to realize this with my work, and he acknowledged my efforts to bring forth truth from a century ago.

The larger family has become important to me, and I bring my *kupuna's* words forward now because it is my *kuleana* to do so. Though others have wanted to tell my *kupuna's* story for monetary profit, and the University of Hawaiʻi has does nothing to protect me as a former doctoral student from my *moʻolelo's* co-optation, I am the one who possesses and has earned the ancestral and academic right to present my great-great-grandfather's papers in accordance with his own gentle and desired direction. This is my *kuleana*, put in my way long before I recognized the path as a path.

I have come to believe that the battle over property, private and intellectual, is the insanity itself. Power generally asserts itself predictably; our choice is usually to either engage or submit. The choice is never really an easy one. But the fact that many of those who have come before chose to engage speaks to their resilience and strength of character, even during confusing and unpredictable times and circumstances.

All summer long, I have seen the same turtle almost every morning when I go surfing. When I see my turtle, and it pops up to greet me, I know it's going to be a good day. Here is another sight. At the beginning of summer, I was swimming off a cliff near Diamond Head when I looked out and saw a whale. This is not unusual at this time of year, but the whale swam in relatively close to shore, stopped directly in front of my line of vision, and slapped its tail forty-four times. I counted.

At my family reunion, I learned much more about my genealogical connection to Kanaloa, a major god in Hawaiʻi and the god of the ocean. At one of the sites my uncle took us, I walked right up to a Hawaiian petroglyph, a *waʻa* or canoe, sitting humbly among the many rocks by the shoreline. Without anyone telling me it was there before I found it, I felt comforted by its presence. Maybe they—my uncle, my turtle, the whale, and the *waʻa*—really do know who I am, and see me coming.

List of Commissions and Appointments Received by Colonel Curtis P. Iaukea

As Compiled by Dr. Niklaus R. Schweizer

IN KING KALĀKAUA'S REIGN

1878, April 5
Royal Commission, CAPTAIN, Company A, Prince's Own Corps, Volunteer Military organized by King Kalakaua, November 3, 1875

1878, November 5
Royal Commission, COLONEL, King Kalakaua's Personal Staff

1880
CHIEF SECRETARY, Foreign Affairs

1883, April 9
Royal Commission, SPECIAL ENVOY to Court of St. Petersburg

1883, April 9
Royal Commission, SPECIAL ENVOY to Court of Servia (Serbia)

1883, April 9
Royal Commission, SPECIAL ENVOY to Court of Spain

1883, April 9
Royal Commission, COMMISSIONER for the Kingdom of Hawaii to the Great International Fisheries Exhibition, London

1883, April 10
Royal Commission, MEMBER, Our Privy Council of State

1883, July 28
Royal Commission, SPECIAL ENVOY to Court of Germany

1883, July 28
Royal Commission, SPECIAL ENVOY to the Republic of France

1883, August 27
Royal Commission, ENVOY EXTRAORDINARY & MINISTER PLENIPO-
TENTIARY for His Majesty the Emperor of Japan

1884, August 5
Royal Commission, MEMBER, Board of Health

1884, September 20
Royal Commission, COLLECTOR GENERAL of the Kingdom

1886, August 30
Royal Commission, DISBURSING AGENT for the Royal Guard

1886, August 30
Royal Commission, CHAMBERLAIN of Our Royal Household

1886, August 30
Royal Commission, COMMISSIONER of Crown Lands & Land Agent

1886, October 4
Royal Commission, GOVERNOR OF OAHU

1886, October 4
ADJUTANT GENERAL of the Forces of Our Kingdom

1886, October 4
Royal Appointment, PRIVATE SECRETARY to His Majesty the King

1887, April 12
Royal Commission, ENVOY EXTRAORDINARY & MINISTER PLENIPO-
TENTIARY to the Court of St. James at the 50th Anniversary of the Accession of
Queen Victoria

1887, August 7
Royal Commission, COMMISSIONER OF CROWN LANDS & LAND AGENT
of the Kingdom

IN QUEEN LILIʻUOKALANIʻS REIGN

1891, March 3
Royal Commission, COMMISSIONER OF CROWN LANDS & LAND AGENT
of the Kingdom

1891, March 7
Royal Commission, MEMBER, Our Privy Council of State

1891, March 12
Royal Commission, COLONEL on Our Personal Staff

IN THE PROVISIONAL GOVERNMENT
AND THE REPUBLIC OF HAWAII

1893, September 15
Appointment, MEMBER, Board of Prison Inspectors

1894, September 1
Appointment, SPECIAL CONSTABLE, District of Honolulu, Island of Oahu

1894, September 1
Appointment, MEMBER, Board of Prison Inspectors

1895, October 7
Appointment, SUB-AGENT of Public Lands

1895, November 27
Commission, MAJOR & QUARTERMASTER on General Staff of the Republic
of Hawaii. Sanford B. Dole, President

1897
SECRETARY & AIDE to Honorable Samuel M. Damon, Head of Mission of Republic of Hawaii to Queen Victoria's Diamond Jubilee

1898
Commission, SECRETARY & MILITARY ATTACHÉ to President Sanford B.
Dole & Mrs. Dole on their visit to President and Mrs. McKinley, Washington, D.C.

IN THE TERRITORIAL GOVERNMENT

1905, August 3
Appointment, MEMBER, Board of Trustees of Queen's Hospital. George R. Carter, Governor, Territory of Hawaii

1907, July 1
Appointment, AGENT, Board of Health

1917
SECRETARY OF HAWAII, appointed by President Woodrow Wilson

1933–1935
CHAIRMAN, Hawaiian Homes Commission

1937
MEMBER, Archives Commission

1937
CUSTODIAN—Throne Room, Iolani Palace

ELECTED OFFICES
1904
TAX ASSESSOR, County of Oahu on Democratic-Home Rule Ticket

1906
COUNTY SHERIFF (POLICE COMMISSIONER)

1912
SENATOR, 4th Senatorial District, Island of Oahu

TRUSTEESHIPS
1890
TRUSTEE, King Kalakaua Estate

1909
TRUSTEE, Queen Liliuokalani Estate

Queen Liliʻuokalani's Deed of Trust

This indenture, made this 2ⁿᵈ day of December, 1909, between Liliuokalani, widow of the late John O. Dominis, of Honolulu, Territory of Hawaii, party of the first part, hereinafter also called the "Grantor", and Archibald S. Cleghorn, Curtis P. Iaukea and William O. Smith, all of said Honolulu, parties of the second part, hereinafter also called the "Trustees",

Witnesseth: That whereas the said Grantor is desirous of placing all of her property in trust (save as below excepted) to be held and administered by the Trustees for the uses and purposes in this instrument set forth:

Now Therefore, the said Grantor, in consideration of the premises herein expressed and of the covenant hereinafter contained on the part of the Trustees to be kept and performed, and also of One Dollar to her paid by the said Trustees, the receipt whereof is hereby acknowledged, does hereby give, grant, convey, assign, transfer, set over and deliver unto the said Trustees all and singular her right, title, estate and interest what-soever in and to all her property, real, personal and mixed, of every nature and descrip-tion and wheresoever situate, in possession or in action, including all of the property described and referred to in the several schedules hereunder written, and also all other property whether included or described or referred to in said schedules or not; saving and excepting therefrom an estate for the life of said Grantor, hereby reserved, in and to her present residence premises known as "Washington Place" on Beretania Street in Honolulu, and also the premises at Waikiki known as "Kealohilani"; and reserving and excepting also all of the household furniture and furnishings and contents of each of said residence properties, and all personal effects of said Grantor, as now enjoyed by her, including all personal or family mementoes, heirlooms, pictures, bric-a-brac, crests, decorations, kahilis, and like property; and excepting further any claim said Grantor may have or claim to have against the United States:

To have and to hold the same, with all the rights, easements, privileges and appurtenances thereunto belonging or in anywise appertaining, and the reversion and reversions, remainder and remainders, rents, issues and profits thereof, unto the said Trustees hereinabove named and their successors in trust, heirs and assigns forever, subject only to existing incumbrances; but in trust nevertheless, to hold, use, manage, control and administer the same upon the following trusts, that is to say:

Except as this instrument may require the special holding, reservation or application of any particular parts or portions of the trust property to accord with the special use or disposition thereof, the Trustees shall administer the trust property according as to them shall seem most advantageous to all the beneficiaries hereunder and to most effectually accomplish the whole trusts thereof.

The Trustees shall at all times have the most ample power and authority, in their discretion from time to time to sell, lease, exchange, partition, mortgage, pledge and/or otherwise deal with and dispose of any of the lands and/or other property and interests of the trust estate, and to purchase any lands or other property and/or take leases thereof, for the benefit of the trust estate, as often and upon such terms and conditions or covenants and for such considerations as they may deem proper, and generally to make such investments as they may think best. They may exercise any and all of their powers by this instrument conferred or which may be necessary or convenient for the effectual administration of the trusts hereof according to the true intent and meaning of this instrument, without any order of any court first had or obtained, and without necessity of, any subsequent approval or confirmation by any court; and in every way invest and change the investments of the trust and administer under this instrument free from any restraint or limitation except as by this instrument prescribed. No purchaser of any trust property shall at any time be charged with any duty respecting the disposition of any sum or consideration moving from him to the Trustees on any sale or other disposition of property by the Trustees. The Trustees may also maintain an office or offices, and engage all necessary assistants and employees, and fix their compensation.

In all matters relating to the administration of the affairs of said trust, the vote of at least two of the Trustees shall be necessary to any action, and to execute any instrument required to be made. Provided, that the Trustees may appoint one of their number to act in the immediate management of the trust property and business, subject to their direction and control, whose duties shall be such as they may prescribe, and who for his special services as such managing trustee may receive additional compensation as determined by the Trustees.

The Trustees shall make annual report to the Grantor during her lifetime, and after her death to a court of competent jurisdiction, showing their administration of the affairs of the trust, the investments thereof, and the application of funds received, and a general statement of the condition of the trust.

The Trustees shall use and apply the income from the trust estate as follows:

First: For the payment of any and all taxes, assessments and charges lawfully imposed upon or with respect to the trust property or any part thereof or interest therein, by governmental authority, at any time during the continuance of this trust, including those against or with respect to the property wherein said life estate is reserved to said Grantor, and also all premiums for fire insurance, and all other necessary expenses for repair, maintenance and improvement of the trust property, and the expenses of administration of the trust hereof, including such compensation to the Trustees for their services as shall from time to time be fixed by the court having jurisdiction over this trust.

Second: To the discharge of the interest accrued and accruing from time to time upon the mortgage indebtedness of the Grantor, evidenced by her promissory note and mortgage for $70,000 to Claus Spreckels and Company, dated November 10th, 1908, said mortgage being recorded in the Registry Office in Honolulu in Liber 314, page 79.

Third: Annually or oftener, as desired by the Grantor, to pay to said Grantor the net income then remaining, or so much thereof as she may from time to time require for her maintenance and personal expenses, so long as she shall live.

Fourth: To the payment of the unsecured indebtedness of the Grantor existing at the date of the execution of this instrumental, in full or in part to any creditor or creditors from time to time as the Trustees may deem necessary, and also to the reduction and final payment of the principal of said mortgage indebtedness.

Fifth: For the cause of Orphans, as hereinafter provided.

II.

Upon the death of the Grantor, the Trustees shall make, execute and deliver to Curtis P. Iaukea, of Honolulu, a deed conveying to him, absolutely and forever, (subject only to said mortgage if the same be not then discharged with respect thereto) all of the land and improvements thereon known as the Lele of Hamohamo, at Waikiki, adjoining his wife's land at Kaluaolohe, containing eight acres a little more or less.

III.

The Trustees shall also, upon the death of the Grantor, set apart certain portions of said trust property, as below specified, for the personal use and occupation of the following named persons, during their lives only, respectively, namely:

1. For John Dominis Aimoku, the premises known as "Washington Place", with the appurtenances, on Beretania Street, in Honolulu, for his lifetime, and on his death to the lawfully begotten heirs of his body during their lifetime (or so long after the death of said John Dominis Aimoku as the law will permit, with reversion then to the Trustees).

2. For Joseph Kaiponohea Aea, the premises at Waikiki known as "Kealohilani", with the appurtenances and the Fishery of Hamohamo, for his lifetime, and on his death for the lawful heirs of his body for their lifetime (or so long after the death of said Joseph Kaiponohea Aea as the law will permit, with reversion then to the Trustees).

3. For Nakanealoha, and J. Mana her husband, of Pauoa, Honolulu, and the survivor of them, all those premises on Ohua Land, Waikiki, designated on the Map of Hamohamo as Lot No. Two (2); reversion to the Trustees.

4. For Anaole, and her daughter Keliiakahai, of Honolulu, and the survivor of them, Lot No. Five (5) on said Ohua Lane, Hamohamo, Waikiki; reversion to the Trustees.

5. For John Kiaaina, and Keoki his wife, of Kamoiili, Oahu, and the survivor of them, Lot No. Four (4) on said Ohua Lane; reversion to the Trustees.

6. For Robert von Oelhoffen, and his wife, of Lahaina, Maui, and the survivor of them, Lot No. Four (4) on said Ohua Lane; reversion to the Trustees.

7. For Naheana Paia, of Honolulu, Lot No. Seven (7) on said Ohua Lane; reversion to the Trustees.

8. For Mainalulu, and Nauhane his wife, of Honolulu, and the survivor of them, Lot No. Eight (8) on said Ohua Lane; reversion to the Trustees.

9. For Loe (w), of Honolulu, the house and premises now occupied by her at Muolaulani, Kapalama, Honolulu; reversion to the Trustees.

10. For Hakaui, and Kainalu his wife, of Honolulu, and the survivor of them, the lot of land now enclosed and occupied by them at Muolaulani, Kapalama; reversion to the Trustees.

11. For Mary K. Kahalepuna, of Waikiki, Lot No. Three (3) on said Ohua Lane; reversion to the Trustees.

12. For S.K. Mahoe, and Emalia his wife, of Waialua, Oahu, the premises known as "Punamoenui" and "Punamoeike", at said Waialua; reversion to the Trustees.

Such of the foregoing parcels of land as are affected by said mortgage shall remain subject thereto pending payment thereof unless previously released therefrom.

The taxes and expenses of maintenance of said several properties described in the foregoing paragraphs numbered from "(1)" to "(12)" inclusive, shall be borne by the Trustees as part of the general expenses of the trust administration; and the Trustees shall use their discretion regarding the necessity of the same.

It is hereby expressly provided, that if for any cause, legal or otherwise, anyone or more of said specific portions of property hereinabove numbered as paragraphs (1) to

(12) inclusive, shall fail to be available for the use of said several persons as above intended, the Trustees may in their discretion make some substitute provision therefor; and their power and discretion in making such other provision shall not be reviewable by any person.

IV.

The Trustees shall also, upon the death of the Grantor, make absolute payments of One Hundred Dollars ($100) to each of the persons next hereinafter named, to-wit: (a) Mahiai Robinson, (b) Aki, the sister of said Mahiai Robinson, (c) Mrs. Mary Auld, the widow of Wm. Auld, (d) Mary Pahau, and (e) Mrs. Kahae Kalehua; for the sole and separate use of each of them, respectively.

V.

The Trustees shall also, after the death of the Grantor, and after the payment of the taxes, charges, insurances, and all other administrative expenses, as hereinbefore provided, pay the following annuities, in equal monthly instalments, to the several persons next hereinafter named, respectively, during their lives, to-wit:

(a) To said John Dominis Aimoku, Six Thousand Dollars ($6,000) per annum.

(b) To said Joseph Kaiponohea Aea, the sum of Eighteen Hundred Dollars ($1800) per annum.

(c) To said Nakanealoha and J. Mana her husband, jointly, and the survivor of them; the sum of One Hundred Eighty Dollars ($180) per annum.

(d) To said Anaole and her daughter Keliiakehai, jointly, and the survivor of them, the sum of One Hundred Eighty Dollars ($180) per annum.

(e) To said John Keaaina and Keoki his wife, jointly, and the survivor of them, the sum of One Hundred Eighty Dollars ($180) per annum.

(f) To said Robert von Oelhoffen and his wife, jointly, and the survivor of them, the sum of One Hundred Eighty Dollars ($180) per annum.

(g) To said Naheana Paia the sum of One Hundred Eighty Dollars ($180) per annum.

(h) To said Mainalulu and Nauhane his wife, jointly, and the survivor of them, the sum of One Hundred Eighty Dollars ($180) per annum.

(i) To said Loe, the sum of One Hundred Eighty Dollars ($180) per annum.

(j) To said Hakaui and Kainalu his wife, jointly, and the survivor of them, the sum of One Hundred Eighty Dollars ($180) per annum.

(k) To said Mary K. Kahalepuna, the sum of One Hundred Eighty Dollars ($180) per annum.

VI.

The Trustees shall have full power and authority, anything in this instrument contained to the contrary or inconsistent therewith notwithstanding, if in their judgment they shall deem it necessary or expedient for the best interests of the trust estate as a whole and of all the objects thereof, to sell any part or parts of the trust property, howsoever by this instrument otherwise intended to be disposed of or used, for the purpose of payment of the said mortgage indebtedness of the estate; or they may renew, or extend, or add additional property to, said mortgage, or any mortgage given in lieu thereof.

VII.

From and after the death of the Grantor, all the property of the trust estate, both principal and income, which shall not be required for any of the special provisions or payments in this instrument before mentioned, shall be used by the Trustees for the benefit of orphan children in the Hawaiian Islands, the preference to be given to Hawaiian children of pure or part aboriginal blood.

The manner and extent of such provision and the number and selection of such children shall be determined by the Trustees from time to time in their full discretion.

As soon as practicable and due regard, always, to the retention and investment of sufficient of the corpus or principal of the estate in income-producing property or securities to provide for the continued maintenance thereof, the Trustees shall extend such work by the establishment and maintenance of an institution or institutions for such orphans, and provide for the government thereof. It is the desire of said Grantor that any building or buildings used for such purpose shall be constructed of fire-proof materials, as nearly as may be.

Every such institution so established shall bear the name of "Liliuokalani."

In such work, whether before or after the establishment of any such institution, the Trustees may exercise their entire discretion how far to care for or assist in caring for or educating or otherwise providing for any child or children, according to the circumstances of such cases, whether such child or children shall reside within or without any such institution.

VIII.

As often during the continuance of the trust hereof as anyone or more of the Trustees shall die, or go abroad to reside or shall desire to retire from, or refuse, or become incapable to act, or any vacancy shall otherwise occur, a new trustee or trustees shall be appointed by the judge of a court of competent jurisdiction, but only upon the written nomination of the remaining trustee or trustees, if any. Upon any failure so to nominate the appointment shall be made by the court, notwithstanding, upon the application of any trustee or beneficiary hereunder.

Upon every appointment of a new trustee or trustees the trust property and all title therein and thereto shall immediately vest in such new trustee or trustees, and he or they shall thereupon have all the powers and authority, and perform all the trusts of these presents, in like manner as the trustee or trustees in whose place he or they shall have been appointed, as fully as though originally named as a trustee herein, and without necessity in any case of any written conveyance or transfer of such title.

No trustee shall be answerable or liable for any loss occasioned to the trust estate except as may arise from his own willful misconduct or gross negligence; neither shall any trustee be personally liable for any obligation contracted or incurred in his capacity as a trustee.

IX.

It is hereby expressly conditioned, that at any time during the lifetime of the Grantor, the said Grantor may, with the consent of a majority of the Trustees, such consent to be expressed by their joining in writing with her to effect the same, make and/or change any of the provisions of this instrument; to alter the same, and new provisions make; or add, withdraw or substitute beneficiaries hereunder.

That said Archibald S. Cleghorn, Curtis P. Iaukea, and William O. Smith, parties of the second part, in this instrument named as the Trustees hereunder, do hereby join with said Grantor in the execution hereof, in token of their acceptance of the trusts hereof; and they hereby jointly and severally covenant and agree with the said Grantor that they will faithfully discharge the duties of said trust to the best of their ability.

The Schedules hereinbefore referred to, of property included in this trust conveyance (but not to be taken as exclusive of any property not mentioned or referred to) are the following:

Schedule "A"

All of the right, title and interest of said Grantor in and to the lands described in and conveyed to her by the following deeds; recorded in the Registry office in said Honolulu, to-wit:

(1) Deed of A. Keohokalohe, et al., dated May 13, 1859, Liber 12, page 26; Hamohamo, Waikiki, Oahu.

(2) Deed of Hiikua, dated May 7, 1864, Liber 18, page 145; Ahupuaa of Puelelu, Kona, Molokai.

(3) Deed of Umalele, June 17, 1864, Liber 18, page 218; Apanas 1, 2 and 3 of R.P. 2284, Waialae-iki, Oahu.

(4) Deed of Administrator Est. of C. Kapaakea, August 3, 1867, Liber 24, page 198; Apana 2 of R.P. 4449, Kamookahi, Waikiki, Oahu.

(5) Deed of Richard H. Stanley, April 21, 1870, Liber 31, page 27; Ahupuaa of Honohina, Hilo, Hawaii.

(6) Deed of Makanahelehele, et al., April 17, 1873, Liber 36, page 489; L.C.A. 2085, R.P. 2828, at Kaneloa, Waikiki, Oahu.

(7) Deed of Kailikole, December 27, 1873, Liber 38, page 406; L.C.A. 2492, R.P. 2795, Hamohamo, Waikiki, Oahu.

(8) Deed of Hokii, September 2, 1876, Liber 46, page 348; L.C.A. 1446, R.P. 6239, Waikiki, Oahu.

(9) Deed of Kalela, et al., November 1, 1880, Liber 66/476; houselot at Hamohamo, Waikiki, L.C.A. 1433, R.P. 1272.

(10) Deed of S. W. Mahelona, March 12, 1881, Liber 159/402; land at Kamookahi, Waikiki, Oahu.

(11) Deed of D. Malo, March 26, 1881, Liber 68/118; Apanas 1 and 2 of L.C.A. 1926, R.P. 2590, Kolowalu Manoa Waikiki, Oahu.

(12) Deed of Haumea, June 7, 1861, Liber 67/454; L.C.A. 11047, R.P. 6391; L.C.A. 7397, R.P. 7045; L.C.A. 6176, R.P. 5698; Keauhou, Kona, Hawaii, and Waikiki, Kona, Oahu.

(13) Deed of Mary Ann Conradt, October 1, 1881, Liber 75/83; L.C.A. 1437, R.P. 3920, Kalia; L.C.A. 1437 at Pahupahupuaa; Waikiki, Oahu.

(14) Deed of M. Kuaea, May 2, 1862, Liber 74/136; L.C.A. 8183, R.P. 1321, at Hauula, Koolauloa, and land described in Liber 66/605 at Haleaha, Koolauloa, Oahu.

(15) Deed of D. K. Fyfe, Com'r of Estate of W. L. Moehonua, dec'd, November 29, 1882, Liber 82/248; Apanas 1, 2, 3 and 4 of L.C.A. 5230, Lahaina, Maui.

(16) Deed of Sarah Kahookaamoku, March 5, 1883, Liber 78/418; L.C.A. 2557 at Kamookahi, Oahu.

(17) Deed of Herman Kockemann, March 26, 1883, Liber 77/404; land at Hamohamo, Waikiki, Oahu.

(18) Deed of Kalanialii, June 23, 1883, Liber 81/149; R.P. 2557, Kamookahi, Oahu.

(19) Deed of Kuhinia, September 1, 1883, Liber 82/406; in the Kuleana of Ohuohu, L.C.A. 1451, R.P. 6123, and L.C.A. 1450, R.P. 6805; Hamohamo, Waikiki, Oahu.

(20) Deed of D. W. Pauahi et al., January 26, 1884, Liber 84/437; Apana 2 of L.C.A. 1468, R.P. 2508, Waikiki, Oahu.

(21) Deed of Tamar Kuaea, Admx. Estate of M. Kuaea, August 15, 1887, Liber 89/264; land at Waikahalulu, Honolulu, Oahu.

(22) Deed of Albert G. Bliss, December 3, 1884, Liber 90/342-3; land at Kapalama, Honolulu.

(23) Deed of Kapunani et al., April 9, 1885, Liber 109/82; Apana 2 of L.C.A. 2027, R.P. 2575, Hamohamo, Waikiki, Oahu.

(24) Deed of Chas. B. Wilson, Feb. 11, 1886, Liber 96/482; and also by deed of Cecil Brown, June 17, 1896, Liber 159/431; lots Nos: 9 and 11 of Macfarlane lots on Young Street, Honolulu.

(25) Deed of J. Aea, July 17, 1886, Liber 108/23; land on upper side of public road at Waikahalulu, Honolulu, (See Liber 72/377).

(26) Deed of Deborah Mahoe, December 20, 1886, Liber 98/467; Apanas 1 and 2 in the Ili of Kapahaha and Keoneula, on King Street, Honolulu.

(27) Deed of Ioela Kane et al., March 18, 1887, Liber 107/11; land near Kapiolani Park, Kapahulu.

(28) Deed of Kalawaia, April 14, 1887, Liber 104/157; land at Kauluwela, Honolulu, portion of Apana 49 of L.C.A. 7713; land at Nahiku, Maui R.P. 1818; land at Kapalama, Honolulu L.C.A. 1081. R.P. 2491.

(29) Deed of Emma Buchanan, Guardian, July 25, 1887, Liber 108/189; L.C.A. 1452, R.P. 5060, Hamohamo, Waikiki, Oahu.

(30) Deed of Puu, et al., May 28, 1886, Liber 110/334; Apana 1 of L.C.A. 1475, R.P. 1275, at Hamohamo, Waikiki, Oahu.

(31) Deed of Keamalu, et al., October 1, 1888, Liber 112/213; L.C.A. 2030, R.P. 5585, at Kauluwela, Honolulu.

(32) Deed of John Kaelele, October 12, 1888, Liber 113/306; L.C.A. 2030, R.P. 5585, at Kauluwela, Honolulu.

(33) Deed of Wm. R. Castle, August 31, 1889, Liber 118/314; Palolo, Oahu; Kuleanas of: Mahoe, R.P. 2545; Kalakuaole, R.P. 3480; Kilohana, R.P. 2413.

(34) Deed of A. S. Cleghorn, January 31, 1890, Liber 122/193; L.C.A. 1450, R.P. 2839, Hamohamo, Waikiki, Oahu.

(35) Deed of Kahae Aea (releasing dower), April 29, 1890, Liber 108/23; land described in and conveyed by deed of J. Aea, dated July 17, 1886, L. 108/23.

(36) Deed of Trustees of Estate of R. W. Holt, June 16, 1890, Liber 125/215; R.P. 136, Manoa, Oahu.

(37) Deed of Kalela, et al., August 8, 1891, Liber 133/164; L.C.A. 1433, R.P. 1272, Hamohamo, Waikiki, Oahu.

(38) Deed of Oahu Railway & Land Co., October 21, 1891, Liber 154/262; Lots 1, 2 and 3 in Block 25, Pearl City Lots, Ewa, Oahu.

(39) Deed of W. R. Castle, December 3, 1891, Liber 133/445; L.C.A. 1923, R.P. 6867, Manoa, Oahu.

(40) Deed of Estate of Kalakaua, February 18, 1892, Liber 136/29; R.P. 3424, Kamanaiki, Kalihi, Oahu.

(41) Deed of Kealoalii, October 8, 1894, Liber 148/384; 1 share in Hui Land of Holualoa 1 and 2, North Kona, Hawaii.

(42) Deed of Lau Chong, April 16, 1894, Liber 167/121; L.C.A. 10295, R.P. 6637, Hookena, South Kona, Hawaii.

(43) Deed of Kaoaopa, June 28, 1895, Liber 155/151; L.C.A. 735, R.P. 5722, Honolulu.

(44) Deed of Helen Boyd, Trustee, January 7, 1896, Liber 159/33; Apana 1 of L.C.A. 1454, R.P. 2558, Waikiki, Oahu.

(45) Deed of Kahakuakoi, et al., September 3, 1898, Liber 178/267; Interest in Estates of Charles Kanaina, W. C. Lunalilo, Bernice P. Bishop, and Queen Hokaleleponi.

(46) Deed of Kaehuahanui Kuihelani, October 8, 1898, Liber 186/259; Lots 190 and 203, Kulaokahua Plains.

(47) Deed of Kapiolani Estate, Ltd., January 31, 1901, Liber 219/163; part of Waikiki residence.

(48) The Ahupuaa of Keohuole, at Kailua, Hawaii, L.C.A. 8452, R.P. 6851.

(49) Leasehold interest, under lease from Keelikolani, July 1, 1882, Liber 74/383; 40 years from July 1, 1882, R.P. 2057, Pawaa, Honolulu.

Schedule "B"

The following lands by Royal Patents to said Grantor:

(1) R.P. 3550, June 29, 1891, Book 18 of Grants. Lot 11 at Honuakaha, Honolulu, 5000 square feet.

(2) R.P. 3575, December 22, 1891, Book 18 of Grants. Lots B and C at Kaauwailoa, Palolo, Oahu.

Schedule "C"

The following lands by descent or devise:

All of the lands and interests in lands devised to the Grantor by the Will of her deceased husband, John O. Dominis, Probate No. 2749, May 27, 1867 (probated September 30, 1891), including hereunder the following: the same being theretofore conveyed to said John O. Dominis by the following deeds, to-wit:

(a) Deed of Wahinelii, May 18, 1864, Liber 18/434; 1/2 of R.P. 2822.

(b) Deed of Kanui, December 2, 1864, Liber 18/435; 1/2 of R.P. 2822.

(c) Deed of Estate of L. Haalelea, May 6, 1865, Liber 19/319; Ahupuaa of Naiwa, Molokai.

(d) Deed of Makini, June 6, 1865, Liber 19/366; land of "Lanilua", Hilo, Hawaii.

(e) Deed of J. W. Keawehunahala, June 11, 1867, Liber 23/378; Apana 4 of L.C.A. 2699, R.P. 876, at Lokoea, Waialua, Oahu.

(f) Deed of Ki and James Robinson, October 7, 1868, Liber 26/293; Apana 3 of L.C.A. 3373, R.P. 2895, at Lokoea, Kawailoa, Waialua, Oahu.

(g) Deed of Charles Pouzat, February 17, 1874, Liber 39/127; Interest in land at Waiakea, Hilo, Hawaii, conveyed to him by deed of Kamakina, May 12, 1866.

(h) Deed of Naunauna, Liber 39/499; Apana 2 of R.P. 909 at Alapii, Waialua, Oahu.

(i) Deed of R. Keelikolani, August 26, 1874, Liber 40/207; Lot No. 1 on Diagram of Ahupuaa of Kawailoa, Waialua, Oahu.

(j) Deed of Herman Kockemann, March 26, 1883, Liber 77/404; land at Hamohamo, Waikiki, Oahu.

(k) Deed of Trustees of Estate of Bernice P. Bishop, September 4, 1889, Liber 116/386; land at Paalaa, Waialua, Oahu.

(l) Royal Patent No. 3462 to John O. Dominis, January 22, 1890, Book 17 of Grants; "Washington Place", on Beretania Street, Honolulu. (See also devise of interest in same to him by Will of Mary Dominis, Probate #2619).

(2) All of the lands and interests in lands devised to said Grantor by the Will of Bernice Pauahi Bishop, deceased, dated October 31, 1883, probated December 2, 1884, probate #2425.

(3) All of the lands and interests in lands devised to said Grantor by the Will of H.R.H. Likelike, deceased, dated April 15, 1884, probated April 25, 1887, probate #2512.

IN WITNESS WHEREOF the said parties hereto have hereunto and to another instrument of like tenor and even date set their respective hands and seals the day and year first above written.

Executed in the presence of
S.M. Damon (sgd)
Cecil Brown (sgd)
(sgd) Liliuokalani (Seal)
(sgd) A.S. Cleghorn (Seal)
(sgd) Curtis P. Iaukea (Seal)
(sgd) William O. Smith (Seal)
Territory of Hawaii
City & County of Honolulu ss.

On this 2nd day of December 1909, before me personally appeared Liliuokalani (widow), A.S. Cleghorn, Curtis P. Iaukea and William O. Smith, to me known to be the persons described in and who executed the foregoing instrument, and severally acknowledged that they executed the same as their free act and deed.

(sgd) WM.J. Forbes
Notary Public, First Judicial Circuit.
(NOTARIAL SEAL)
Recorded
2nd December 1909 at 3:40 P.M.
Liber 319 on pages 447–459

Queen Liliʻuokalani's Petition
to U.S. President William H. Taft

His Excellency William H. Taft,
President-elect of the United States:

Esteemed Friend:

I have the honor to address you this petition in my own behalf, to wit as follows:

-FIRST-

That on the 29ᵗʰ day of January, Anno Domini 1891, I, LILIUOKALANI, petitioner herein, was proclaimed Queen of the Hawaiian Kingdom.

-SECOND-

That as such Sovereign I was the rightful owner of all the Crown Lands in the Hawaiian Islands, consisting about 911,888 acres, more or less, and therefore had the right to receive all incomes and proceeds, by lease or sale, derived from such lands. See Exhibit A, annexed herewith and made part of this petition. That since my ascension to the throne of Hawaii to January of the year 1893, when I yielded my authority as Sovereign of the Hawaiian Kingdom to the superior armed forces of the Government of the United States, which had been landed at Honolulu at the request of the minister plenipotentiary of your Government here at that time to support the establishment by some of my subjects a Provisional Government in direct conflict with the Constitution of the Kingdom of Hawaii, I have always received and earned my due proportion of the proceeds and income from said Crown Lands.

-THIRD-

It is a painful tale for me to rehearse here how I was deprived of my Government by some of my subjects aided by the armed forces of the United States, acting under the authority of His Excellency John L. Stevens, minister plenipotentiary of the United States; but suffice for me to call your attention to my protest.

On the 17th day of January, A.D. 1893, at 6 p.m. of that day I signed the following protest:

"I, LILIUOKALANI, by the grace of God and under the constitution of the Hawaiian Kingdom, Queen, do hereby solemnly protest against any and all acts done against myself and the constitutional government of the Hawaiian Kingdom by certain persons claiming to have established a Provisional Government of and for this Kingdom.

"That I yield to the superior force of the United States of America, whose minister plenipotentiary, His Excellency John L. Stevens, had caused United States troops to be landed at Honolulu and declared that he would support the said Provisional Government.

"Now, to avoid any collision of armed forces, and perhaps the loss of life, I do under this protest and impelled by said forces yield my authority until such time as the Government of the United States shall, upon the facts being presented to it undo the acts of its representative and reinstate me in the authority which I claim as the constitutional sovereign of the Hawaiian Islands."

This protest was countersigned by my Cabinet Ministers, and addressed to the President and other gentlemen composing the said Provisional Government of the Hawaiian Islands.

-FOURTH-

That on the 19th of January, I wrote a letter to President Harrison, making an appeal that justice should be done; a copy of which is herewith annexed, marked Exhibit B, and made part of this petition. It appears that President Harrison could not have taken notice of your petitioner's appeal, or perhaps he was as anxious as the Provisional Government to annex these Islands, for on the 16th, of February your petitioner finds that he sent a message to the Senate transmitting the treaty, with a view to its ratification, without having first investigated or inquired into all the conditions or points of our situation, or that of the United States itself.

-FIFTH-

That on the 31st of January (1893), I also wrote a letter to Mr. Grover Cleveland, President-elect of the United States, as follows:

"His Excellency Grover Cleveland,
"President-elect of the United States:

"My Great and Good Friend: In the vicissitudes which happened in the Hawaiian Islands, and which affect my people, myself, and my house so seriously, I feel comforted the more that, besides the friendly relations of the United States, I have the honor of your personal friendship and good will.

"The changes which occurred here need not be stated in this letter; you will have at the time at which it reaches you the official information, but I have instructed the Hon. Paul Neumann, whom I have appointed my representative at Washington to submit to you a precise of the facts and circumstances relating the revolution in Honolulu, and to supplement it by such statements which you may please to elicit. I beg that you will consider this matter, in which there is so much involved for my people and that you give us your friendly assistance in granting a redress for a wrong which we claim has been done to us, under color of the assistance of the naval forces of the United States in a friendly port. Believe me that I do not veil under this request to you the fulfilment [*sic*] of which could in the slightest degree be contrary to your position, and I leave our grievance in your hands, confident that in so far as you deem it proper we shall have your sympathy and your aid.

"I am, your good friend,

(Sig.) "Liliuokalani R."

-SIXTH-

That on the 31st day of January the Hon. Paul Neumann received his appointment as envoy extraordinary and minister plenipotentiary to the United States of America. On the 1st of February he departed for Washington, with the late Prince David Kawananakoa, brother of Prince C. K. Kalanianaole, Delegate to Congress, to negotiate for a withdrawal of the annexation treaty which was then pending in Congress and to restore to me and my people what had been taken away by the actions of some of my subjects assisted by the United States armed forces. At my request Mr. E. C. Macfarlane kindly consented to accompany the Hawaiian Royal Commission. The commission arrived at Washington to stay the progress of the annexation treaty. The members of the Senate became doubtful as to the correctness of the actions of the commissioners of the Provisional Government.

-SEVENTH-

President Harrison's term expired, and President Cleveland's inauguration took place, and his first official act has been to withdraw that annexation treaty; and the second, to send a commissioner to investigate the then situation in Hawaii nei.

-EIGHTH-

That the people who were against me and my government accused me of attempting to promulgate a new constitution; although that such attempt was in answer to the prayers and petitions of my people the native Hawaiians. These native people had sent petitions for a new constitution to King Kalakaua and to the Legislature ever since 1887, the year when those same people who were against me had forced on King Kalakaua the Constitution of 1887, known as the bayonet constitution. I believe that under that constitution there is no clause or provision stating "that there should be no other constitution but this," Article 78 of that Constitution reads that

"Whenever by this constitution any act is to be done or performed by the King or Sovereign, it shall, unless otherwise expressed, mean that such act shall be done and performed by the Sovereign by and with the advice and consent of the cabinet."

It is also given in that Constitution, Article 41, last clause, that—

"No acts of the King shall have any effect unless it be counter-signed by a member of the cabinet, who by that signature makes himself responsible."

I would state here that it was within my prerogatives to answer the prayers and petitions of the majority of my subjects requesting me to grant them a new constitution and do away with the obnoxious constitution of 1887. My ministers encouraged me to listen the urging petition of my people, then afterwards advised me to the contrary. Let me say here, that in yielding to the protest of my ministers I claim I have not committed any unconstitutional or revolutionary act, and having with-drawn, why should those that were against me and my government have gone on making preparations for war as they did, and actively aided and supported by the armed forces of the United States? And in support of the statement here—inbefore mentioned in this paragraph relating to the wish of my people for a new constitution, I call your attention to a statement of facts made by the Hui Kalaiana (Hawaiian Political Association) in behalf of the people to J. H. Blount, the United States Commissioner, showing why the people urged me to promulgate a new constitution for the Hawaiian People, a copy of which is herewith annexed, marked Exhibit C, and made part of this petition.

-NINTH-

That when the representative of your government recognized the provisional govern-ment, that such recognition was sufficient to impress upon the mind of any *persona compos mentis* that the aid of the United States Government was really at the back of it; although it was neither a government *de facto* nor *de jure*. And yet this wrongful recognition of the said provisional government by a Minister of the United States placed my government in a position of most perilous perplexity.

-TENTH-

What then the real and true cause of my overthrow; my being deprived of all I had as Sovereign of the Hawaiian Kingdom? In answer, permit me to call your attention to the following extracts from Minister Stevens' letter to Secretary Foster, dated Nov. 20, 1892. Don't forget to notice that it was marked "Confidential."

"An intelligent and impartial examination of the facts can hardly fail to lead to the conclusion that the relations and policy of the United States toward Hawaii will soon demand some change, if not the adoption of decisive measures, with the aim to secure the American interests and future supremacy by encouraging Hawaiian development and aiding to promote responsible government in these islands.

"There are nearly 900,000 acres of 'crown lands,' and these in the main, are among the most valuable of the islands. The rent paid for them goes to the Sovereign, and the amount of the income received is no doubt much less than it would be if these lands were owned and managed by private individuals.

"Well handled and sold at fitting opportunities, the proceeds of the crown lands would pay the national debt, provide adequate pensions for the two or three royalties, in case monarchy should be abolished, etc, etc.

"Directly and indirectly, the palace probably costs the little Kingdom $150,000 per year. A governor, at $5,000 a year, acting in harmony with the responsible men of the legislature, would be far better for the islands than the present monarchical Government. In truth, the monarchy here is an absurd anachronism.

"Americanize the islands, assume control of the 'crown lands,' dispose of them in small lots for actual settlers and freeholders for the raising of coffee, oranges, lemons, bananas, pineapples, and grapes, and the result soon will be to give permanent preponderance to a population and a civilization which will make the islands Southern California, and at no distant period convert them into gardens and sanitariums, as well as supply stations for American commerce, thus bringing everything here into harmony with American life and prosperity. To postpone American action many years is only to add to present unfavorable tendencies and to make future possession more difficult.

"The present Sovereign is not expected to live many years.

"What should be done? One of two courses seem to me absolutely necessary to be followed either a bold and vigorous measures for annexation, or a 'custom union,' an ocean cable from Californian coast to Honolulu, Pearl Harbor perpetually ceded to the United States, with an implied but not necessarily stipulated American protectorate over the islands. I believe the former to be the better that which will prove much the more advantageous to the islands, and the cheapest and least embarrassing in the end for the United States.

"I cannot refrain from expressing the opinion with emphasis that the golden hour is near at hand.

"Which of the two lines of policy and action shall be adopted our statesmen and our Government must decide. Certain it is that the interests of the United States and the welfare of these islands will not permit the continuance of the existing state and tendency of things. Having for so many years extending a helping hand to the islands and encouraging the American residents and their friends at home to the extent we have, we can not refrain now from aiding them with vigorous measures, without injury to ourselves and those of our 'kith and kin' and without neglecting American opportunities that never seemed so obvious and pressing as they do now."

-ELEVENTH-

And that same representative of your government avowedly declared in his letter to Mr. Foster, dated February 1ˢᵗ 1893, the following words:

"The Hawaiian pear is now fully ripe and this is the golden hour for the United States to pluck it. If annexation does not take place promptly, or is held in doubt and suspense for six or ten months there certainly will be here a revulsion to despair."

#Note-See Mr. Stevens' letter to Mr. Foster, dated Nov. 20ᵗʰ, 1892.

-TWELFTH-

I am not asking you for the restoration of my Kingdom. I am satisfied and pleased with the present conditions. And I will, in all most the same words uttered by that great American statesman, Daniel Webster, say: "I was forced to be an American, and I shall live an American, and I shall die an American." But I must crave of you and the American people the recognition of my claim and to grant me a substantial pecuniary sum in settlement of all my claims.

Permit me to call your attention to the declarations announced in the platforms of the three great Political Parties in this Territory, as follow, to wit:

"We endorse the measure introduced by our Delegate in Congress asking the appropriation of the sum $250,000 for former Queen Liliuokalani"—Territorial Republican Party, adopted at Honolulu, September 4ᵗʰ, 1908.

"We pledge our candidates to the Legislature to a renewal of the appropriations for former Queen Liliuokalani, and our Delegate to Congress to introduce and support a measure looking to a Federal appropriation for the payment to her of a lump sum in settlement of all existing claims on her part.—Adopted in Territorial Convention (Democratic) September 10, 1908.

"We pledge our Delegate to actively press the justice of special recognition by (the) Congress of the United States on the ground both of moral principle and human law, of the entire equity and magnanimous courtesy of granting to our beloved ex-Queen Liliuokalani, a substantial pecuniary sum commensurate with her former position and dignity." Adopted in Territorial Convention of the Independent Party for Home Rule, August 31ˢᵗ, 1908.

-PRAYER FOR RELIEF-

I believe that the value of the Crown Lands, the total area of which is 911,888 acres as already mentioned in Paragraph Second of this petition, rating on an average price of about $22.00 per acre, would foot up to the amount of $20,000,000.

In conclusion therefore, I must say that having given you the uncontroverted historical facts of how I was deprived of my throne and government, and stripped of all honors and dignities deriving therefrom; also my humiliation and shame which sorely affected my feelings and to the great injury to my character and health, I ask for relief in the lump sum of Ten Million ($10,000,000) Dollars in settlement of all my claims.

And your petitioner will ever pray.

Honolulu, T.H.   (sig) *Liliuokalani*

Nov. 1908.

EXHIBIT A

Summary for the Crown Lands for 1893

ISLANDS	DISTRICTS	AREAS
HAWAII	Hilo	256,939
	Hamakua	18,864
	Kohala	57,680
	Kona	2,000
	Puna	66,000
	Kau	187,990
Total for Hawaii	589,473	Acres
MAUI	Lahaina	2,984
	Olowalu	17,040
	Kula	16,283
	Hana	610
	Koolau	17,408
	Kahakuloa	10,523
Total for Maui		64,848
MOLOKAI		21,383
LANAI		17,370
OAHU	Kona	5,581
	Koolaupoko	9,958
	Koolauloa	6,672
	Waianae and Ewa	41,367
Total for Oahu		64,178
KAUAI		154,636
Total Area of Crown Lands	911,888	

NOTES

INTRODUCTION

1. A list of Curtis P. Iaukea's commissions and appointments is found in appendix A. Curtis Piehu Iaukea and Lorna Kahilipuaokalani Iaukea Watson, *By Royal Command: Biographical Notes on Curtis Piehu Iaukea*, ed. Niklaus Schweizer (Honolulu: Hui Hanai, 1988), 230–32.

Curtis P. Iaukea notes his especially high regard for U.S. president Woodrow Wilson in papers found at the archives, and wanted this to be noted in "any book" that would include portions of his manuscript.

2. Iaukea Collection, U-33, Hawai'i State Archives, Honolulu, Hawai'i.

3. This dream was recorded by Lorna Kahilipuaokalani Iaukea Watson. Iaukea Collection, U-33, Hawai'i State Archives, Honolulu, Hawai'i.

4. Iaukea Watson. Niklaus Schweizer, editor of *By Royal Command*, explains the "History of the Manuscript" (i) and his role in editing that portion of the manuscript. Schweizer's university course is also where I first began to learn about my *kupuna*.

CHAPTER I. FAMILY SECRETS AND CARTOGRAPHIC SILENCES

1. "The 'Lele of Hamohamo' and the Attempt to Deprive of It," Iaukea Collection, U-33, Hawai'i State Archives, Honolulu, Hawai'i.

2. W. D. Alexander, *A Brief History of Land Titles in the Hawaiian Kingdom*. Interior Department, Appendix 1, Surveyor General's Report (Honolulu: P.C. Advertiser Co. Steam Print, 1882), 6.

3. Bureau of Conveyances, Honolulu, Hawai'i, *Queen Liliuokalani Deed of Trust, December 2, 1909*, Book 319, pp. 447–59, section II, 4–5; see appendix B in this book.

4. Bureau of Conveyances, Honolulu, Hawai'i, Helu 2615, Palapala Sila Nui, Kuleana Helu 128, Land Grant 2615, April 1856.

5. George Huʻeu Sanford Kanahele, *Kū Kanaka Stand Tall: A Search for Hawaiian Values* (Honolulu: University of Hawaiʻi Press, [1986] 1986), 190.

6. Place and space discourse stems from a cultural geography perspective that acknowledges both the physical parameters and the emotional ties to land. Place represents the lived experiences of people in these spaces, while space signifies the measurable geographic entity. See Denis Cosgrove, *Social Formation and Symbolic Landscape* (Madison: University of Wisconsin Press, 1984); David Carmichael, *Sacred Sites, Sacred Places* (New York: Routledge, 1994); Paul Carter, *The Road to Botany Bay: An Exploration of Landscape and History* (London: Faber and Faber, 1987); Timothy Mitchell, *Colonising Egypt* (Berkeley: University of California Press, 1988); David Turnbull, *Masons, Tricksters, and Cartographers* (New York: Routledge, 2000); Yi-Fu Tuan, *Space and Place: The Perspective of Experience* (Minneapolis: University of Minnesota Press, 1977).

7. Mary Kawena Pukui, Samuel H. Elbert, and Ester Mookini, *Place Names of Hawaiʻi* (Honolulu: University of Hawaiʻi Press, 1974), x.

8. Kamana Maikaloni Beamer and T. Kaeo Duarte, "I palapala no ia aina—Documenting the Hawaiian Kingdom: A Colonial Venture?" *Journal of Historical Geography* 35 (2009): 73.

9. Alexander, 4.

10. Cosgrove, 14–15.

11. Turnbull, 92.

12. Joseph Singer, *Property and Values: Alternatives to Public and Private Ownership* (Washington: Island Press, 2000), 4.

13. Keanu Sai, "The American Occupation of the Hawaiian Kingdom: Beginning the Transition from Occupied to Restored State" (Ph.D. diss., University of Hawaiʻi, Mānoa, 2008). Keanu Sai's dissertation is a complete analysis of early land laws in Hawaiʻi and the subsequent illegal occupation of the United States of Hawaiian Kingdom sovereign territory.

14. Alexander, 7.

15. Alexander, 6.

16. Beamer and Duarte, 68.

17. Beamer and Duarte, 74.

18. Michel Foucault, "Truth and Method," in *The Foucault Reader*, ed. Paul Rabinow (New York: Pantheon Books, 1984), 31–120.

19. Clifford Geertz, "Deep Play: Notes on the Balinese Cockfight," in *Interpretive Social Science: A Second Look*, ed. Paul Rabinow and William M. Sullivan (Berkeley: University of California Press, 1979), 196.

20. Jamaica Kincaid, *The Autobiography of My Mother* (New York: Farrar, Straus, Giroux, 1996), 181.

21. Kincaid, 181.

22. *Hawaii Hochi*, "A Great Man Passes," March 7, 1940.

23. Iaukea Collection, U-33, Hawaiʻi State Archives, Honolulu, Hawaiʻi, "Iaukea to Speak at Visitors' Club: To Give Reminiscences of Monarchy Days," *Honolulu Advertiser*, March 23, 1937.

24. Iaukea and Watson, viii.

25. Iaukea Collection, U-33, Hawaiʻi State Archives, Honolulu, Hawaiʻi, "Believe It or Not by Ripley (Reg. U.S. Pat. Off.)," *Honolulu Star-Bulletin*.

26. Benedict Anderson, *Imagined Communities* (New York: Verso 1991), 183.

27. Iaukea Collection, U-33, Hawaiʻi State Archives, Honolulu, Hawaiʻi, "Comments from E. W. Miller to John Balch, President of the Mutual Telephone Company in Hawaii."

28. Iaukea Collection, U-33, Hawaiʻi State Archives, Honolulu, Hawaiʻi.

29. Milan Kundera, *Ignorance: A Novel* (New York: Harper Collins, 2000), 10.

30. Pierre Nora, "Between Memory and History: Les Lieux de Memoire." *Representations* 26 (Spring 1989): 9.

31. Nora, 9.

32. See also chapter 8 in Iaukea and Watson, *By Royal Command*.

33. This diary was addressed to Mrs. Edward B. Watson (Lorna Kahilipuaokalani Iaukea Watson), Iaukea Collection, U-33, Hawaiʻi State Archives, Honolulu, Hawaiʻi.

34. Iaukea Collection, M-70, Hawaiʻi State Archives, Honolulu, Hawaiʻi, Box 2–7, Historical Notes on Hawaiʻi.

35. Susan Scheckel, *The Insistence of the Indian: Race and Nationalism in Nineteenth-Century American Culture* (Princeton, NJ: Princeton University Press, 1998), 15.

36. Edith McKinzie, "The Kumulipo" in Kumulipo: Hawaiian Hymn of Creation, Visual Perspectives by Joseph Feher, Honolulu, Hawaii, 1988, 1.

37. Kumulipo, Hawaiian Hymn of Creation, 1.

38. Kumulipo, Hawaiian Hymn of Creation, 1.

39. Kumulipo, Hawaiian Hymn of Creation, 5.

40. Martha Warren Beckwith, *The Kumulipo: A Hawaiian Creation Chant* (Honolulu: The University of Hawaiʻi Press, 1984), 179.

41. Liliuokalani, *Hawaii's Story by Hawaii's Queen* 1898 (Honolulu: Mutual Publishing, 1990), 196.

42. *Nā Kūʻauhau ʻO Kahiwakāneikopōlei*, Newsletter for the Grand Convention, Hilo, Hawaiʻi, 2010.

43. Iaukea and Watson, 1.

44. Michel Foucault addresses the production of discourse and the historical aspects that contribute to knowledge in *Power/Knowledge*. He notes that historical moments influence discourse, and that the body is the receptor and transmitter of discourse. Michel Foucault, *Power/Knowledge: Selected Interviews and Other Writings, 1972–1977*, ed. Colin Gordon (New York: Pantheon Books, 1981).

CHAPTER 2. LAND AS THE VEHICLE

1. Opening paragraphs of Curtis P. Iaukea's chapter 6, Iaukea Collection, M-70, Hawaiʻi State Archives, Honolulu, Hawaiʻi, Box 2–7, Historical Notes on Hawaiʻi, n.d.

2. J. Kēhaulani Kauanui, *Hawaiian Blood: Colonialism and the Politics of Sovereignty and Indigeneity* (Durham, NC: Duke University Press, 2008).

3. In 1921, Lorrin Thurston renamed the *Pacific Commercial Advertiser* the *Honolulu Advertiser*. His son, Lorrin P. Thurston, took over control of the *Advertiser* in 1931 when he became president and editor (*Honolulu Advertiser* archives online). The *Honolulu Advertiser* officially closed on June 6, 2010, after its longtime rival, the *Star-Bulletin*, bought the newspaper.

4. Iaukea Collection, M-70, Hawaiʻi State Archives, Honolulu, Hawaiʻi, "The Colonel on Party Harmony," *Pacific Commercial Advertiser*, June 1922, Box 1–9, Scrapbook, Campaign Folder.

5. Prince Kūhiō passed away on January 7, 1922, at the age of fifty from chronic nephritis.

6. The definitions for the concept of *kuleana* are wide and varied, including "right, privilege, concern, responsibility, title, business, property, estate, portion, jurisdiction, authority, liability, interest, claim, ownership, tenure, affair, province; reason, cause, function, justification," etc. As these definitions suggest, responsibility and property are interchangeable. *Kuleana* can refer to one's rights and privileges as easily as it might refer to one's estate or land tenure. Mary Kawena Pukui and Samuel H. Elbert, *Hawaiian Dictionary* (Honolulu: University of Hawaiʻi Press, [1957] 1986), s.v. "kuleana."

7. Iaukea Collection, M-70, Hawaiʻi State Archives, Honolulu, Hawaiʻi, "Curtis P. Iaukea 'Runs Amuck' on Lorrin A. Thurston, Challenges Him to a 'Fight to a Finish!'" *Commercial Pacific Advertiser*, Box 1–9, Scrapbook, Campaign Folder.

8. Iaukea Collection, M-70, Hawaiʻi State Archives, Honolulu, Hawaiʻi, C. P. Iaukea, "Wise or Jarrett for Delegate? Which? A Reply to Lorrin A. Thurston's Analysis," *Commercial Pacific Advertiser*, June 1922, Box 1–9, Scrapbook, Campaign Folder.

9. Iaukea Collection, M-70, Hawaiʻi State Archives, Honolulu, Hawaiʻi, "Wise for Big Business," Box 1–9.

10. Iaukea Collection, M-70, Hawaiʻi State Archives, Honolulu, Hawaiʻi, Lorrin A. Thurston, "Fight to a Finish: A Reply to C. P. Iaukea's Charges against Wise," *Honolulu Advertiser*, June 1922, Box 1–9 (g).

11. Territory of Hawaii, *The Organic Act: Legal Periodicals, Historical Note*, April 30, 1900, C 339, 31 Stat 141.

12. Alan Murakami, "The Hawaiian Homes Commission Act," in *Native Hawaiian Rights Handbook*, ed. Melody Kapilialoha MacKenzie (Honolulu: Native Hawaiian Legal Corporation, 1991), 45, as found in *An Act to Provide for a Government for the Territory of Hawaii*, ch. 339, 31 Stat. 141 (1900) (amended in 1908, 1910, and 1921).

13. Murakami, 45.

14. Murakami, 1.

15. Kamana Beamer, "Na wai ka mana? ʻŌiwi Agency and European Imperialism in the Hawaiian Kingdom" (Ph.D. diss., University of Hawaiʻi, Mānoa, 2008), 277; and Donovan Preza, "The Empirical Writes Back: Re-examining Hawaiian Dispossession Resulting from the Māhele of 1848" (master's thesis, University of Hawaiʻi, Mānoa, 2010), 163.

16. Murakami, 26.

17. Hawaiian Kingdom, Office of the Regent, *An Historical Overview of the Events Surrounding the Great Māhele*, vol. 2. Honolulu, Hawai'i, Dec. 1998.

18. Preza, 148.

19. Alexander, 27; and Preza, 117 and 148.

20. Jon Chinen, *The Great Mahele: Hawaii's Land Division of 1848* (Honolulu: University of Hawai'i Press, 1958).

21. "Hawaii Organic Act: Congressional Debates on Hawaii Organic Act," http://libweb.hawaii.edu/digicoll/annexation/organic.html, p. 1054.

22. "Hawaii Organic Act," Special Collections Libraries, page 1054.

23. Curtis P. Iaukea, *Commissioners of Crown Lands, Biennial Report, 1894* (Honolulu: Hawaiian Gazette Company, 1894), 4.

24. Iaukea, *Commissioners of Crown Lands*, 40.

25. Melody Kapilialoha MacKenzie, "Historical Background," in *Native Hawaiian Rights Handbook*, 17.

26. Rona Tamiko Halualani, *In The Name of Hawaiians: Native Identities and Cultural Politics* (Minneapolis: University of Minnesota Press, 2002), 62.

27. Murakami, 45.

28. "Hawaii Organic Act," Special Collections Library, p. 1067.

29. U.S. Congress, Joint Resolution of Annexation, July 7, 1898, 30 Stat. 750.

30. Kauanui, 156.

31. Murakami, 47.

32. Murakami, 43.

33. Halualani, 62.

34. Iaukea Collection, M-70, Hawai'i State Archives, Honolulu, Hawai'i. Iaukea, "Wise or Jarrett for Delegate?," Box 1–9 (g).

35. Cosgrove, 161.

36. Foucault, "Truth and Method."

37. Mitchell, xi.

38. Mitchell, xii.

39. Michel Foucault, *Discipline and Punish: The Birth of the Prison* (New York: Pantheon Books, 1977), 217.

40. Iaukea Collection, M-70, Hawai'i State Archives, Honolulu, Hawai'i, Lorrin Thurston, "Wise or Jarrett for Delegate? Seventh and Final Installment of Reply to Charges by Iaukea against John Wise," *Honolulu Advertiser*, 1922, Box 1–9 (k).

41. Iaukea Collection, M-70, Hawai'i State Archives, Honolulu, Hawai'i, Lorrin A. Thurston, "Wise or Jarrett for Delegate? Which? Sixth Installment of Reply to Charges by Iaukea against John Wise," *Honolulu Advertiser*, June 1922, Box 1–9 (k).

42. Iaukea Collection, M-70, Hawai'i State Archives, Honolulu, Hawai'i, C. P. Iaukea, "Col. Iaukea's Letter to the *Advertiser*," *Honolulu Advertiser*, June 1922, Box 1-9 (l).

43. Murakami, 47.

44. Halualani, 65. The idea of Hawaiians as a dying race is noted in numerous texts, including MacKenzie, *Native Hawaiian Rights Handbook*, 17, which quotes from *The Hawaiian Homes Program, 1920–1963*, Legislative Reference Bureau Report,

No. 1, 1969: "Available social statistics indicate that as of 1920 the position of the Hawaiian community had deteriorated seriously. The general crime rate for people of Hawaiian ancestry was significantly higher than that of other groups. The rate of juvenile delinquency was also higher, an ominous omen for the future. Economically depressed, internally disorganized and politically threatened, it was evident that the remnant of Hawaiians required assistance to stem their precipitous decline" (6).

45. Territory of Hawaii, "Hawaiian Homes Commission Act, 1920," Title 2, Hawaiian Homes Commission, Sec. 201 (7).

46. Kauanui, 168.

47. Kauanui, 168.

48. Cole Harris, "How Did Colonialism Dispossess? Comments from an Edge of Empire," *Annals of the Association of American Geographers* 94 (1) (2004): 172; see also Richard H. Schein, "Teaching 'Race' and the Cultural Landscape," *Journal of Geography* 98 (4) (1998).

49. Derek Gregory, *Geographical Imaginations* (Oxford: Blackwell Publishers, 1994), quoted in Bruce Braun, *The Intemperate Rainforest* (Minneapolis: University of Minnesota Press, 2002), 8.

50. Antonio Gramsci uses the term "Americanisation" to distinguish the "particular environment," "particular social structure," and the "certain type of State" needed to produce the entity America. The particularities include a well-defined and controlled labor force, one that is both productive and regimented while socially structured and adjusted for "the negro question." Antonio Gramsci, *Selections from the Prison Notebooks* (India: Orient Longman, 2004), 287, 293.

51. Halualani uses the term "performative procedures" to explain the extensive proving process that the individual undergoes in order to assert his/her nativeness.

52. Schein, 385.

53. Braun, 14.

54. Benedict Anderson allows that the enumeration of populations is a necessity in legitimizing and enacting state bureaucratic power. The power to name further necessitates clear classifications and lucid categories. "One notices, in addition, the census-makers' passion for completeness and unambiguity. Hence their intolerance of multiple, politically transvestite, blurred, or changing identifications." Benedict Anderson, *Imagined Communities* (New York: Verso, [1983] 1991), 165–66. For Benedict Anderson, together with the map and museum, the state acts as a "totalizing classificatory grid, which could be applied with endless flexibility to anything under the state's real or contemplated control: peoples, regions, religions, languages, products, monuments, and so forth. The effect of the grid was always to be able to say of anything that it was this, not that; it belonged here, not there. It was bounded, determinate, and therefore—in principle—countable" (184).

55. Allaine Cerwonka, *Native to the Nation: Disciplining Landscapes and Bodies in Australia* (Minneapolis: University of Minnesota Press, 2004), 58.

56. Murakami, 45.

57. Noel Kent, *Hawai'i: Islands under the Influence* (1983; Honolulu: University of Hawai'i Press, 1993), 76.

CHAPTER 3. A STORY OF POLITICAL AND EMOTIONAL MANEUVERINGS

1. Cole Harris, "How Did Colonialism Dispossess? Comments from an Edge of Empire," *Annals of the Association of American Geographers* 94 (1) (2004): 172.

2. Yi-Fu Tuan, *Space and Place: The Perspective of Experience* (Minneapolis: University of Minnesota Press, 1977).

3. Prince Kūhiō was someone Queen Lili'uokalani mentioned often when she wrote and spoke about her attempt to receive revenue from the Crown Lands. For example, in a letter to Curtis P. Iaukea on February 10, 1910, the Queen stated that she did not want to "prejudice her claim against U.S. Government and antagonize Kuhio." Iaukea Collection, U-33, Hawai'i State Archives, Honolulu, Hawai'i.

4. Iaukea Collection, U-33, Hawai'i State Archives, Honolulu, Hawai'i; and M-70, Box 1–7.

5. Queen Lili'uokalani told her trustees "*E paa oukou,*" meaning "You hold it," in reference to Prince Kūhiō's fight to break her trust deed. The greater significance of this utterance is explained in chapter 4.

6. Queen Lili'uokalani Collection, M-93, Hawai'i State Archives, Honolulu, Hawai'i.

7. Questions surrounding the signing of a trust deed versus a will are discussed in chapter 4. The primary position of the bill of complaint (1915) put forth by Prince Kūhiō was that Queen Lili'uokalani did not know what she was doing when she signed a nonrevocable trust deed in conjunction with an ordinary will.

8. Queen Lili'uokalani granted power of attorney to Curtis P. Iaukea on May 4, 1909. On May 19, 1909, she revoked this power of attorney. She then granted power of attorney to Joseph K. Aea on May 20, 1909, and revoked the same on October 21, 1909. Curtis P. Iaukea was granted final power of attorney in May 1910. Queen Lili'uokalani Collection, M-93, Hawai'i State Archives, Honolulu, Hawai'i, found at the Bureau of Conveyances, Honolulu, Hawai'i, Book 321, pp. 261–62.

9. Iaukea Collection, U-33, Hawai'i State Archives, Honolulu, Hawai'i.

10. Iaukea Collection, U-33.

11. Iaukea Collection, U-33.

12. Bureau of Conveyances, Honolulu, Hawai'i, *Queen Liliuokalani Trust Deed*, Book 319, pp. 447–59; p. 1. This deed was ratified and confirmed by a "further instrument" on April 20, 1910, and found at Bureau of Conveyances, Honolulu, Hawai'i, Book 335, pp. 8–10. See appendix B.

13. Bureau of Conveyances, Honolulu, Hawai'i, *Queen Liliuokalani Trust Deed*, p. 1. The 1848 Māhele designated that land "interests are divided into two types of Estates, *Freehold* and *less than Freehold*. Estates of *Freehold* are further divided into estates of inheritance, (namely fee-tail and fee-simple), and estates not of inheritance, (namely life estates). Estates *less than freehold* are leasehold or rent." Transcripts for the case

"Lance Paul Larsen vs. the Hawaiian Kingdom," *Permanent Court of Arbitration, The Hague 68*, www.alohaquest.com/arbitration/memorial_government.htm.

14. Bureau of Conveyances, Honolulu, Hawai'i, *Queen Liliuokalani Trust Deed, Amendments*, October 11, 1911, 17.

15. A senior faculty member was given a small portion of Curtis P. Iaukea's diary notes and chapters, from a third party not willing to be cited. Even though I am the one that researched the Iaukea Collection in its entirety and brought these papers to light, the senior faculty member has arranged my *kupuna's* diary notes in a similar way and explains the narrative along the story line I present here in two newspaper articles without citing my dissertation, while he also uses portions of my *kupuna's* diary that were made available to me from the archives from an undocumented collection. I filed a complaint with the University of Hawai'i to conduct an investigation through the Ethics Committee in order to ascertain how much of the professor's work copies my own analysis. After a year of an unofficial investigation, the official investigation was abruptly halted by the university at the moment it was to begin. Of the two deciding parties on the committee, one has resigned from the committee due to the university's unwillingness to investigate my claim, as documented in e-mail correspondence, and the other has retired from academia. I continue to press for a full investigation of the faculty member but to no avail, because the university has declared the query closed.

16. Bureau of Conveyances, Honolulu, Hawai'i, *Queen Liliuokalani Trust Deed, Amendments*, September 2, 1915, 25.

17. In the Circuit Court of the First Judicial Circuit, Territory of Hawaii, E. 2009, *Liliuokalani, et al. vs. Curtis P. Iaukea, et al. For Cancellation of Trust Deed*, 1915.

18. U.S. Court of Claims, *Complaint, Liliuokalani v. the United States of America*, November 20, 1909 (Ref HD243.H3 L55 1909), sec. 12.

19. The U.S. House Committee on Claims was one of the longest standing committees in the House of Representatives. Established on November 13, 1794, and existing until 1946, this committee's function was "to take into consideration all petitions and matters or things touching claims and demands on the United States as shall be presented or shall or may come in question and be referred to them by the House, and to report their opinion thereon, together with such propositions for relief therein as to them shall seem expedient." U.S. National Archives & Records Administration, *Guide to the Records of the U.S. House of Representatives at the National Archives, 1789–1989*, Record Group 223, Chapter 6, Records of the Claims Committees, www.archives. gov/legislative/guide/house/chapter-06-claims.html.

20. *Complaint, Liliuokalani v. the United States of America*, November 20, 1909, secs. 10 and 13: "That portion of the public domain heretofore known as Crown Lands is hereby declared to have been heretofore, and now to be, the property of the Hawaiian Government, and to be now free and clear from any trust of or concerning the same, and from all claim of any nature whatsoever, upon the rents, issues and profits thereof. It shall be subject to alienation and other uses as may be provided by law. All valid leases thereof now in existence are hereby confirmed."

21. *Complaint, Liliuokalani v. the United States of America*, November 20, 1909, sec.

99: "That the portion of the public domain heretofore known as Crown Lands is hereby declared to have been, on the twelfth day of August, eighteen hundred and ninety-eight, and prior thereto, the property of the Hawaiian Government, and to be free and clear from any trust of or concerning the same, and from all claim of any nature whatsoever, upon the rents, issues, and profits thereof. It shall be subject to alienation and other uses as may be provided by law." The wording of secs. 10 and 99 of the complaint mirror one another.

22. *Complaint, Liliuokalani v. the United States of America,* November 20, 1909, sec. 1.

23. *Complaint, Liliuokalani v. the United States of America,* November 20, 1909, sec. 4.

24. Booth delivered the *Opinion of the Court; Supplement to the Complaint Filed by "Ex-Queen" Liliuokalani,* November 20, 1909, 426.

25. *Complaint, Liliuokalani v. the United States of America,* November 20, 1909, sec. 16.

26. Prior to the claim before the United States, Queen Liliʻuokalani wrote to her attorney, J. O. Carter, about Princess Ruth's selling of Crown Lands to Claus Spreckels (Letter from the Queen Liliʻuokalani Children's Center, Archives, Kalihi):

[no date given]

[Hon. J.O. Carter]

The Bill on the Territory of Hawaii is to be brought up next week. It is considered on the whole a very fair one and will please the majority of the population. W. O. Smith and Hartwell are trying their best to deceive the people here. They gave an idea that all the Crown Lands were deeded over to Spreckels by the Princess Ruth and he sold them back to the Hawaiian Government. When asked I told them that Wailuku was the only Crown Land sold by Ruth to S. for $10.000—but it was only her supposed right, but as for actual right she had none. That all the Crown Lands was for the throne its occupant for their lifetime and I am the last occupant and still alive. Ruth was not a Kamehameha but Prince Lot was and she was only a half sister to Lot. By Kekuanaoa, not by Kinau. She had a right to his private property but not to anything pertaining to the Crown because that has been established constitutionally. I understand Archie has returned and is not well. I hope you will go and see him some times. I am told his heart is affected.

With kind aloha to all
Liliuokalani

27. J. Booth, *Opinion of the Court; Supplement to the Complaint Filed by "Ex-Queen" Liliuokalani,* November 20, 1909, 427.

28. J. Booth, *Opinion of the Court; Supplement to the Complaint Filed by "Ex-Queen" Liliʻuokalani,* November 20, 1909, 427.

29. U.S. Court of Claims, *Decision, Liliuokalani v. the United States of America,* May 16, 1910, 419–20.

30. "Hidden in plain view" is a term used by Kathy Ferguson and Phyllis Turnbull in *Oh, Say, Can You See? The Semiotics of the Military in Hawaiʻi* (Minneapolis: University of Minnesota Press, 1999).

31. *Complaint, Liliuokalani v. the United States of America*, November 20, 1909, sec. 17.

32. For a discussion of the territorial government's role in producing public spaces in Hawai'i through "national forests," see Sydney L. Iaukea, "Land Agendas vis à vis Wind Discourse: Deconstructing Space/Place Political Agendas in Hawai'i and the Pacific," *Pacific Studies: A Journal Devoted to the Study of the Pacific Islands* 32 (1) (March 2009): 48–72.

33. "Free Tibet? What About Free Hawai'i?!" http://coconutgirlwireless.wordpress .com/2007/05/06/free-tibet-what-about-free-hawaii/.

34. Timothy Mitchell, *Colonising Egypt* (Berkeley: University of California Press, 1988), 56.

35. For the United States, "the truth of the American dream *is* its landscape"; "The myth of the frontier and of the yeoman farmer marked empty land open and adaptable to human ingenuity." Denis Cosgrove, *Social Formation and Symbolic Landscape* (Madison: University of Wisconsin Press, 1984), 175. Many writers discuss the power to name space and designate usage. James Duncan reflects on a cultural amnesia that takes place in the reordering of imperial spaces through landscape: "It is this forgetting, this 'cultural amnesia,' which allows the landscape to act as such a powerful ideological tool. By becoming part of the everyday, the taken-for-granted, the objective, and the natural, the landscape masks the artifice and ideological nature of its form and content." James Duncan, *The City As Text: The Politics of Landscape Interpretation in the Kandyan Kingdom* (New York: Cambridge University Press, 1990), 19.

36. In his descriptions of the nationalizing of France and the notion of a national identity as evoked by an "equality" of citizenry under the law, James C. Scott explains the simplification of cultural norms, as local customs are made legible to and through a state and national terrain: "They envisioned a series of centralizing and rationalizing reforms that would transform France into a national community where the same codified laws, measures, customs, and beliefs would everywhere prevail. It is worth noting that this project promotes the concept of *national* citizenship—a national French citizen perambulating the kingdom and encountering exactly the same fair, equal conditions as the rest of his compatriots." James C. Scott, *Seeing Like A State* (New Haven, CT: Yale University Press, 1998), 32.

37. *Decision, Liliuokalani v. the United States of America*, May 16, 1910, 420.

38. *Decision, Liliuokalani v. the United States of America*, May 16, 1910, 421.

39. *Complaint, Liliuokalani v. the United States of America*, November 20, 1909, sec. 19.

40. *Complaint, Liliuokalani v. the United States of America*, November 20, 1909, sec. 18.

41. Calculations found in SB 1553, filed in the U.S. Senate in January of 1904—here she asked for $200,000 according to these calculations. Queen Lili'uokalani Collection, M-93, Hawai'i State Archives, Honolulu, Hawai'i, Folder 22.

42. University of Hawai'i, Special Collections Library, *Anti-annexation Protest Documents—Liliuokalani to William McKinley (U.S. President)*, June 17, 1897.

43. Queen Lili'uokalani Collection, M-93, Hawai'i State Archives, Honolulu, Hawai'i, Protest against the Taking of Crown Lands.

44. Queen Lili'uokalani Collection, M-93, Hawai'i State Archives, Honolulu, Hawai'i, Letter from Prince Kūhiō Kalaniana'ole While Serving on the Sixtieth Congress in the House of Representatives in Washington, D.C., to Queen Liliuokalani.

45. Iaukea Collection, M-70, Hawai'i State Archives, Honolulu, Hawai'i, Box 1–1.

46. Queen Lili'uokalani Collection, M-93, Hawai'i State Archives, Honolulu, Hawai'i, Folder 22.

47. Queen Lili'uokalani Collection, M-93, Hawai'i State Archives, Honolulu, Hawai'i, Folder 22.

48. Queen Lili'uokalani Collection, M-93, Hawai'i State Archives, Honolulu, Hawai'i, Folder 1, Petition to President-elect William H. Taft. See appendix C in this book.

49. Petition to President-elect William H. Taft, 6.

50. Petition to President-elect William H. Taft, 8.

51. Territory of Hawaii, *Territorial Pension, Act 43*, "Making Appropriations for the Benefit of Queen Liliuokalani," March 30, 1911:

> Section 1. Be it Enacted by the Legislature of the Territory of Hawaii. The Treasurer of the Territory is hereby authorized and directed to pay, upon warrants issued by the Auditor of the Territory, the sum of twelve hundred and fifty dollars ($1,250.00) each month to Queen Liliuokalani, and to continue so to do for and during the remainder of her life. Section 2. This Act shall take effect on July 1, 1911. Approved this 30th day of March, A.D. 1911. Walter F. Frear, Governor of the Territory of Hawaii.

CHAPTER 4. "E PAA OUKOU" (YOU HOLD IT)

1. "E paa oukou" is a phrase Queen Lili'uokalani used regarding the bill of complaint brought against her by Prince Kūhiō. She commanded her trustees to "hold" and protect the trust from legal attacks.

2. Susan Scheckel looks at the moral and legal arguments intrinsic to a revolutionary past. A new order is legitimized in the juridical realm, even as questions surrounding the indigenous and national past are read within this social context. Susan Scheckel, *The Insistence of the Indian: Race and Nationalism in Nineteenth-Century American Culture* (Princeton, NJ: Princeton University Press, 1998), 15.

3. What follows is Judge Humphreys's statement regarding the deed of trust in 1909. Here Curtis P. Iaukea recounts the judge's words.

4. "Prince Cupid" was a nickname given to Prince Kūhiō by his classmates when he attended university in the United States.

5. Judge Humphreys's statement concludes here. The rest of the chapter notes are in Curtis P. Iaukea's words.

6. "The Late Queen Liliuokalani's Deed of Trust with Her Last Will and Testament— And Revelations behind the Scene." Iaukea Collection, U-33, Hawai'i State Archives, Honolulu, Hawai'i; and Iaukea Collection, M-70, Box 1–8, "Trust Deed of Lili'uokalani, 1897–1915."

7. In the Circuit Court of the First Judicial Circuit, Territory of Hawaii, *Bill of Complaint*, November 15, 1915, sec. XXII, 7.

8. "An Uncommon History-Case Lombardi & Pettit, A Law Corporation-Honolulu, Hawaii," www.caselombardi.com/aboutHistory.aspx.

9. The annual report for the Queen Liliʻuokalani Trust (2008) notes that it directly serves 10,030 orphan and destitute children, and another 50,730 children in group services and community building initiatives. The total expended for 2008 was $12,836,661. The total assets of the trust were $620,718,924. According to the trust: "Queen Liliʻuokalani continues to inspire and light the way for those blessed and honored to be touched by her legacy. Hawaiian values and wisdom of *kūpuna* (ancestors) are the foundation of our *Mōʻī Wahine's* (Queen's) work today. Children's lives are embraced by the best of traditional and modern wisdom, both Hawaiian and Western practices, through their immediate and extended ʻohana (family), as well as their calabash ʻohana (community). The different services we humbly offer to our beneficiary families and their communities are symbolized by each fern or flower that is braided into a *lei haku* (braided lei). The strengths of our children and families is evident in the beautiful colors and intricate design that truly make this labor of love a masterpiece." www.qlcc.org/qlcc2008.pdf.

10. *Bill of Complaint*, November 15, 1915, sec. VIII. The second paragraph refers to the attempted revocation of the trust deed in 1910, as discussed in chapter 3.

11. *Bill of Complaint*, November 15, 1915, sec. XXII. Speaking of isolation and surveillance, the only time Queen Liliʻuokalani refers to these instances directly is in her book, *Hawaii's Story by Hawaii's Queen* (Honolulu: Mutual Publishing, 1990). After serving eight months in jail and then being pardoned by the territorial government for her conviction on charges of "misprison of treason," she nevertheless knew that the acting government kept close watch over her. She remarked, for example: "On the morning following Mr. Wilson informed me that I had been released only on parole, and had been placed in his charge by President Dole. My custodian further notified me that but sixteen servants were allowed to me, and that my retainers (accustomed to maintain a system of watches for my protection ever since the death of my husband) were not to be permitted to come near me again. I was also prohibited from going where there was any concourse of the people, nor could I have any gathering at my own house. In consequence of these regulations I never went to church or to any public place" (296).

12. *Bill of Complaint*, November 15, 1915, sec. VIII.

13. Friends and enemies are a constant concern of Queen Liliʻuokalani, as related in her book and in multiple letters held at the archives of the Queen Liliʻuokalani's Children's Center.

One such instance of pondering who are friends or enemies is noted in *Hawaii's Story by Hawaii's Queen*, in reference to having copies made of the new constitution that was to be promulgated in 1893: "When completed, I was handed by one party a copy of that it proposed, and by Mr. Wilson I was given a copy of the one on which he had been engaged. After reading both over, I employed a young man, simply because he was a very neat penman, to make copies; his name was W. F. Kaae, but he was usually called Kaiu. This is worthy of mention, because I subsequently discovered that, while upon this work for me, he took copies to Mr. A. F. Judd for the examination of that gentleman. It can readily be seen by what kind of persons I was surrounded; it must be remembered that I now write with a knowledge of recent events, but that then I had the fullest confidence in the loyalty of those who professed to be my friends" (230).

14. *Bill of Complaint*, secs. V, VII, XXII. Queen Liliʻuokalani refers to being treated for "nervous prostration" in *Hawaii's Story by Hawaii's Queen*: "On Jan. 6, 1895, came the beginning of a revolt. For three months prior to that date my physician, Dr. Donald McLelan, had been in attendance on me, and, as I was suffering very severely from nervous prostration, prescribed electricity. For two years I had borne the long agony of suspense, a terrible strain, which at last made great inroads on my strength" (263–64).

15. Lilikalā Kameʻeleihiwa, *Nā Wāhine Kapu: Divine Hawaiian Women* (Honolulu: ʻAi Pōhaku Press, 1999), 3.

16. In Hawaiian genealogy, "all the female *akua* come from the lineage of Haumea." Lilikalā Kameʻeleihiwa asserts that "[Haumea] is also reborn in each succeeding generation of her female descendents; she lives in every Hawaiian woman. I am Haumea, too, and she teaches that all Haumea has done, I too can do." Kameʻeleihiwa, 7.

17. Likikalā Kameʻeleihiwa, 7.

18. Kameʻeleihiwa, 6.

19. In the Circuit Court of the First Judicial Circuit, Territory of Hawaii, *Affidavit in Support of Motion to Dismiss, Bill for Cancellation of Deeds*, December 30, 1915.

20. In the Circuit Court of the First Judicial Circuit, Territory of Hawaii, *Discontinuance and Motion to Dismiss, Bill for Cancellation of Deeds*, December 10, 1915.

21. In the Circuit Court of the First Judicial Circuit, Territory of Hawaii, *Assertion of Mental Competency, Bill for Cancellation of Deeds*, February 8, 1916.

22. In the Circuit Court of the First Judicial Circuit, Territory of Hawaii, *Suggestion of Disqualification of Jonah Kuhio Kalanianaole as Next Friend of Liliuokalani, and Motion for His Removal as Next Friend*, January 17, 1916.

23. *Suggestion of Disqualification*, 1.

24. In the Circuit Court of the First Judicial Circuit, Territory of Hawaii, *Memorandum, Re Liliuokalani by Her Next Friend J. K. Kalanianaole, and Kalanianaole versus C. P. Iaukea et al. Trustees*, December 4, 1915.

25. Iaukea Collection, U-33, Hawaiʻi State Archives, Honolulu, Hawaiʻi.

26. For a complete and lengthy discussion by the Queen's lawyers of the role of next friend and the role of an alleged incompetent, see In the Circuit Court of the First Judicial Circuit, *Memorandum of Points and Authorities on Behalf of Liliuokalani, Bill for Cancellation of Deeds*, January 26, 1916.

27. "The action was properly brought, but I think we have arrived at that stage where the Prince should be relieved from acting further as the *Next Friend* of the Queen, and a proper substitute for him should be named, as suggested in the motion of the trustees to relieve him. This substitute will try out the allegations of the complaint, and will

not have any option concerning that proposition. His attorneys will be the attorneys already representing the petitioner. However, they must serve without looking to the substituted next friend or the guardian ad litem herein for compensation. I therefore relieve the Prince as next friend, and appoint in his place Mr. Lorrin Andrews." In the Circuit Court of the First Judicial Circuit, Territory of Hawaii, *Decision, Bill for Cancellation of Deeds*, 1916, 14–15.

28. In the Circuit Court of the First Judicial Circuit, Territory of Hawaii, *Partial Report of Guardian Ad Litem and Next Friend of Liliuokalani, in Chambers*, March 29, 1916.

29. *Bill of Complaint*, sec. IX, 4.

30. *Decision, Bill for Cancellation of Deeds*, 2.

31. First District Court, Territory of Hawaii, W. O. *Smith's Memoranda Re Liliuokalani Trust Deed*, February 23, 1910; Iaukea Collection, M-70, Hawai'i State Archives, Honolulu, Hawai'i, In the Circuit Court of the First Judicial Circuit, Territory of Hawaii, *Testimony of A. S. Humphreys before the Honorable William L. Whitney, Second Judge Thereof, at Chambers*; Iaukea Collection, M-70, "Trust Deed of Liliuokalani, 1897–1915," Box 1-8, 82.

32. In the Circuit Court of the First Judicial Circuit, Territory of Hawaii, W. O. *Smith's Testimony, Before the Honorable Whitney, Honolulu, Hawaii*, July 6, 1916.

33. In the Circuit Court of the First Judicial Circuit, *Statement of C. P. Iaukea*, 1916.

34. Iaukea Collection, M-70, *Testimony of A. S. Humphreys*; "Trust Deed of Liliuokalani, 1897–1915," Box 1-8.

35. W.O. *Smith's Memoranda Re Liliuokalani Trust Deed*, February 23, 1910, 2–4.

36. *Testimony of A. S. Humphreys*, 52–53.

37. See the complete discussion of sanity and the proving of the insanity of an individual In The Circuit Court of the First Judicial Circuit, Territory of Hawaii, *Memorandum of Points and Authorities on Behalf of Liliuokalani, Bill for Cancellation of Deeds*, January 26, 1916.

38. In the Circuit Court of the First Judicial Circuit, Territory of Hawaii, *Bill of Revivor and Supplement*, January 22, 1916, 1.

39. Mary Kawena Pukui, E. W. Haertig, and Catherine Lee, *Nānā I Ke Kumu: Look to the Source*, vol. 1 (Honolulu: Hui Hanai, 1972), 11, 141.

40. Michel Foucault, "About the Concept of the 'Dangerous Individual' in 19th Century Legal Psychiatry," *International Journal of Law and Psychiatry* 1 (1978): 3.

41. "Madness discourse" is articulated by Michel Foucault in *Madness and Civilization: A History of Insanity in the Age of Reason* (New York: Vintage Books, 1988), 10.

42. Foucault, *Madness and Civilization*, 7.

43. Foucault, *Madness and Civilization*, 7, 9.

44. Foucault, *Madness and Civilization*, 11.

45. Foucault, *Madness and Civilization*, 7.

46. Mary Kawena Pukui and Samuel H. Elbert, *Hawaiian Dictionary* (Honolulu: University of Hawai'i Press, [1957] 1986).

47. Foucault, *Madness and Civilization*, 46.

48. Foucault, *Madness and Civilization*, 63.

49. Foucault, *Madness and Civilization*, 270.

50. Hawaii Session Laws, 1862, *Act to Establish an Insane Asylum*, 31–32, KFH25 .A24 1862, c.2, Hawai'i State Archives, Honolulu, Hawai'i.

51. Hawaii Session Laws, 1862, *Act to Establish an Insane Asylum*, 31 (italics mine).

52. *Pacific Commercial Advertiser*, "Insane Asylum," February 4, 1864.

53. *Hawaiian Gazette*, "Establishment at Palama Prepared to Receive Patients," August 25, 1866; and "Lunatic Asylum," August 25, 1866.

54. Hawaiian Kingdom, Interior Department, Book 12, p. 184, April 5, 1873, Hawai'i State Archives, Honolulu, Hawai'i. Also noted at the time were the mundane management capacities of the insane asylum, lumping together the delivery and supply of meat for all inmates of "the Oahu Prison, Insane and Leper Asylum." Hawaiian Kingdom, Interior Department, Book 13, p. 55, August 11, 1875, Hawai'i State Archives, Honolulu, Hawai'i. Vestiges of Foucault's "criminal classes" folded into the insane population with the sick and the lawless, thus duo-compartmentalizing this class of people as both criminal and unhealthy.

55. Hawaiian Kingdom, Interior Department, Book 13, p. 35, July 12, 1875, Hawai'i State Archives, Honolulu, Hawai'i.

56. Hawaiian Kingdom, Interior Department, Book 38, p. 611, May 22, 1889, Hawai'i State Archives, Honolulu, Hawai'i.

57. *Daily Pacific Advertiser*, "The Kalihi Insane Asylum," January 13, 1883.

58. *Daily Pacific Advertiser*, "Kalihi Insane Asylum." The article notes: "There are at present fifty-two patients, of which twenty-two are natives, six Americans, six Englishmen, two East Indians, and fourteen Chinamen."

59. *Daily Pacific Advertiser*, "Kalihi Insane Asylum."

60. *Daily Pacific Advertiser*, "Kalihi Insane Asylum."

61. The commission found possible overworking and neglect of the inmates and offered a plan to change these conditions. The recommendations were as follows: a medical superintendent should be appointed in control and should have a staff; a fireproof building should be built; water should be laid on the grounds of the asylum, and the inmates should not be responsible for transporting water from the nearby stream; a padded room should be added; a Board of Inspectors should be appointed and visit and report on the asylum periodically; and Oahu Prison prisoners should no longer work at the asylum because of their "bad" influence upon the patients. *Hawaiian Gazette*, "The Insane Asylum! A Thorough Investigation, Report of the Commission, Excellent Recommendations!" October 4, 1887.

62. Hawaiian Kingdom, Interior Department, *Letter of Appointment*, Book 32, p. 253, October 25, 1887, Hawai'i State Archives, Honolulu, Hawai'i.

63. Hawaiian Kingdom, Interior Department, *Letter to Appoint*, Book 32, p. 262, October 25, 1887, Hawai'i State Archives, Honolulu, Hawai'i.

64. Hawaiian Kingdom, *Fundamental Law of Hawaii*, 1840–1900, REF 342T4, Hawai'i State Archives, Honolulu, Hawai'i: "No idiot or insane person, and no person who shall be expelled from the Legislature for giving or receiving bribes, or being ac-

cessory thereto; and no person who in due course of law shall have been convicted of larceny, bribery, gross cheat, or of any criminal offense punishable by imprisonment, whether with or without hard labor, for a term exceeding two years, whether with or without fine, shall register to vote or shall vote or hold any office in or under or by authority of the Government, unless the person so convicted shall have been pardoned and restored in his civil rights."

65. Hawaii Session Laws, 1893–1894, KFH 25.A25 1894 c.2, Hawaiʻi State Archives, Honolulu, Hawaiʻi. This act states: "From and after the passage of this Act the Board of Health shall have the management and control of the Insane Asylum; and all the powers and duties heretofore by law vested in the Minister of the Interior in relation to the care of insane persons and the discharge of those who have been insane but have been restored to sound mind shall be vested in and discharged by the Board of Health."

66. Amitav Ghosh, *The Glass Palace: A Novel* (New York: Random House, 2002).

67. The entire area then became part of the British Empire; see Rakesh Sinha, "In Burma, Bahadur Shah Zafar Is an Emperor-Saint," *Indian Express,* www.rebound 88net/sp/ngb/siniall.html.

68. Ghosh, 54.

69. Ghosh, 46.

70. Ghosh, 4.

71. The production of the body through discourse is analyzed by Foucault. Stuart Hall recounts Foucault's analysis and the productive capacities of discourse: "[Foucault] places the body at the centre of the struggles between different formations of power/knowledge. . . . Here, the body has become the site of a new kind of disciplinary regime." Stuart Hall, *Representation: Cultural Representations and Signifying Practices* (London: Sage Publications, [1997] 2003), 78.

CHAPTER 5. THE FINAL INSULTS

1. Mary Kawena Pukui and Samuel H. Elbert, *Hawaiian Dictionary* (Honolulu: University of Hawaiʻi Press, [1957] 1986).

2. Iaukea Collection, M-70, Hawaiʻi State Archives, Honolulu, Hawaiʻi, Box 2–8, "Historical Notes and Articles, n.d., 1845–1888."

3. These points do not, however, mean that Hawaiians thought dreams were transparent: "In two aspects of Hawaiian dreaming we can form no conclusions: We do not know how the Hawaiian dream interpreter of tradition operates today. No *wehewehe moe ʻuhane* would consent to an interview. We cannot classify dream characteristics by the sex or by the age of the dreamer. The total of dreams studied was not large enough to do this. However, we have a definite opinion on how Hawaiians put their dreams to use." Mary Kawena Pukui, E. W. Haertig, and Catherine Lee, *Nānā I Ke Kumu: Look to the Source* (Honolulu: Hui Hanai, 1972), 2: 205–6.

4. Gregory Cajete, *Native Science: Natural Laws of Interdependence* (Santa Fe, NM: Clear Light Publishers, 2000, and Keith Basso, *Wisdom Sits in Places* (Albuquerque: University of New Mexico Press, 1996), reflect on the importance of a co-participation

between self and environment, including the active use of dreams, for native peoples. All facets interact to guide daily life.

5. Pukui, Haertig, and Lee, 2: 206.

6. This letter, addressed to her trustees, directs them to "forthwith convey by deed of conveyance, for the sum of One Dollar ($1.00), the said lands and fishing rights to him [Prince Kuhio] forever, together with the houses and appurtenances and furnishings pertaining to said home; the deed and possession to the lands and fishing rights and appurtenances to take effect immediately upon my death." In the Circuit Court of the First Judicial Circuit, Territory of Hawaii, *Bill of Complaint*, November 15, 1915, Exhibit 11.

7. In the Circuit Court of the First Judicial Circuit, Territory of Hawaii, *Bill of Complaint*, Exhibit 12.

8. "For Joseph Kaiponohea Aea, the premises at Waikiki known as 'Kealohilani,' with the appurtenances and the Fishery of Hamohamo, for his lifetime, and on his death for the lawful heirs of his body for their lifetime (or so long after the death of said Joseph Kaiponohea Aea as the law will permit), with reversion then to the Trustees." Bureau of Conveyances, Honolulu, Hawaii, *Queen Liliuokalani Deed of Trust, December 2, 1909*, Book 319, pp. 447–59, sec. III, no. 2.

9. Hamohamo is the beach area of Waikīkī, from Apuakehau Stream to approximately where Kapahulu Avenue is located today. The fisheries of Hamohamo include the ocean area fronting this *'ili* (smaller land division). The other section of Hamohamo owned by Queen Lili'uokalani is a large area *'ewa* (west) of Kapahulu Avenue at what is today the Ala Wai golf course, part of Date Street, and the area in Waikīkī *mauka* (mountain side) of Kūhiō Avenue.

10. Iaukea Collection, U-33, Hawai'i State Archives, Honolulu, Hawai'i, Letters to and from Castle and Withington, Attorneys and Counsellors at Law, to Trustees, Queen Liliuokalani Estate, May–June 1918, p. 4.

11. www.marriottwaikiki.com.

12. Liliuokalani, *Hawaii's Story by Hawaii's Queen* (1898; Honolulu: Mutual Publishing, 1990), 94–95.

13. Samuel Kamakau, *Tales and Traditions of the People of Old: Nā Mo'olelo a ka Po'e Kahiko* (Honolulu: Bishop Museum Press, 1991), 44–45.

14. Honolulu Board of Water Supply, *O'ahu Water Plan* (Honolulu: Honolulu Board of Water Supply, 1982), 8.

15. George Kanahele, *Waikiki: 100 BC to 1900 AD* (Honolulu: University of Hawai'i Press, 1995), 8.

16. Robert L. Wiegel, *Report UCB/HEL 2002–1*, University of California, Berkeley, CA, Hydraulic Engineering Laboratory, November 15, 2002, 113–15.

17. "February 22, 1848, Mr. Ten Eyck, wishing to honor the name and person Washington, with the consent of Mrs. Dominis, named the mansion 'Washington Place.' He wrote to the Minister of Foreign Affairs Wyllie expressing the wish that it might continue to be so designated in the years to follow. Mr. Wyllie referred the matter to the king, who replied that it was his desire to honor in every possible way

the memory of 'one of the greatest and best men that ever evolved the race of mankind.' The King's order that the name 'Washington Place' be made perpetual was thereupon forwarded to Mrs. Dominis to be recorded along with her title deeds, so that the name should be held in all future transfers of the property." *Pacific Commercial Advertiser*, "Washington Place: Where Hawaii's Queen Has Lived Half a Century," August 25, 1912.

18. *Honolulu Advertiser*, "Washington Place, Former Home of Last Queen of Hawaii, Ready for Governor about March," March 12, 1922.

19. *Queen Liliuokalani's Deed of Trust, December 2, 1909*, Book 319, pp. 447–59, sec. III, no. 1.

20. Queen Lili'uokalani voiced her desire to have Hawaiian language and music taught in her residence after her death when she set up her trust deed in 1909. This idea was then further elaborated on and explained in the testimony of her trustees in the bill of complaint.

21. Queen Lili'uokalani Collection, M-93, Hawai'i State Archives, Honolulu, Hawai'i, "The Trees and Plants of 'Washington Place.'"

22. "The Trees and Plants of 'Washington Place,'" 3–6.

23. Iaukea Collection, U-33, Hawai'i State Archives, Honolulu, Hawai'i, "The Contest over the Queen's Deed of Trust, From My Diary of 1918."

24. Iaukea Collection, U-33, "The Contest over the Queen's Deed of Trust, From My Diary of 1918."

25. Iaukea Collection, U-33, Letters to and from Castle and Withington, 3.

26. Iaukea Collection, U-33, Letters to and from Castle and Withington, 4.

27. Iaukea Collection, U-33, Letters to and from Castle and Withington, 7.

28. Iaukea Collection, U-33, Letters to and from Castle and Withington, 9.

29. Iaukea Collection, U-33, Letter from Trustees to Castle and Withington, May 24, 1918, 8.

30. *Commercial Advertiser*, "Kuhio's Suits Are All Withdrawn: Does Not End Litigation in Connection with Queen's Estate," June 22, 1918.

31. *Honolulu Advertiser*, "History From Our Files," September 18, 1948.

32. *Honolulu Advertiser*, "Washington Place," April 23, 1922.

33. *Honolulu Advertiser*, "Territory Acquires Washington Place; Governor's Residence, Judge Franklin Grants Decree of Condemnation and Sets Value of Property at $55,000," May 12, 1921.

34. *Honolulu Advertiser*, "Territory Acquires Washington Place."

35. The *Honolulu Advertiser* notes this fact in the title of an article that appeared in 1920: "Washington Place Title Secured in Land Court," October 27, 1920.

36. *Star Bulletin*, "Documents on Christening of Royal Home in 1848 Preserved," June 11, 1918.

37. *Pacific Commercial Advertiser*, "Kuhio's Suits Are All Withdrawn," June 22, 1918.

38. *Pacific Commercial Advertiser*, "Kuhio's Suits Are All Withdrawn."

39. The name change was noted on figure 11, entitled "Kūhiō Beach, Waikīkī: Royal Hawaiian Hotel" (Bishop Museum Archives, Honolulu, Hawai'i).

40. The name change was noted on figure 11, entitled "Lili'uokalani's Pier at Waikīkī, now Kūhiō Beach, c. 1920" (Bishop Museum Archives, Honolulu, Hawai'i).

41. Sean Browne sculpted the statue of Prince Kūhiō, which was dedicated on January 12, 2002. *Honolulu Advertiser*, "Kūhiō Beach Park Named for Prince Who Served Hawaii," October 21, 2004.

42. The Lili'uokalani Trust is listed as current owner of this property. Bureau of Conveyances, Honolulu, Hawai'i, Tax Maps Branch History Sheet, Tax Map #2-6-26-3.

43. *Commercial Advertiser*, "Kuhio's Suits Are All Withdrawn."

44. In the Circuit Court of the First Judicial Circuit, Territory of Hawaii, *Probate 5324, In the Matter of the Estate of Lydia K. Dominis, Also Known as Liliuokalani*, June 27, 1918.

45. As mentioned in chapter 3, this will was signed by Queen Lili'uokalani in the name of Leiliuokalani on August 29, 1917, just three months before her death.

46. The fight over the recognition of this particular will resulted in sentencing and jail time for a member of the Wilcox 'ohana for forgery. The trust declared that this new will was forged, even though the signature on this will looks to be the Queen's handwriting. I do know that Curtis P. Iaukea believed that this will was fraudulent—as noted in a letter to his son-in-law in 1918, Mission Houses Museum, Honolulu, Hawai'i.

47. Bureau of Conveyances, Honolulu, Hawai'i, Deed, Curtis P. Iaukea to William Woon, Book 639, pp. 233–34.

48. Bureau of Conveyances, Honolulu, Hawai'i, Deed, William Woon to Charlotte Iaukea, Book 639, p. 235.

49. Bureau of Conveyances, Honolulu, Hawai'i, Trust Deed, Charlotte K. Iaukea to Albert F. Judd et al. Trs., Book 805, pp. 312–17.

50. Trust Deed, Charlotte K. Iaukea, Book 805, pp. 316–17.

51. Bureau of Conveyances, Honolulu, Hawaii, Lien for Improving Insanitary Land in Honolulu to Mrs. Charlotte K. Iaukea by Supt. Pub. Wks., Book 1370, p. 387.

52. In the Circuit Court of the First Judicial Circuit, Territory of Hawaii, *Judgment, Eminent Domain, Territory of Hawaii vs. Albert F. Judd, et al.*, February 27, 1936, Book 1611, p. 4.

53. In the Circuit Court of the First Judicial Circuit, Territory of Hawaii, *Final Order of Condemnation*, August 21, 1940, Book 1611, p. 17.

54. Bureau of Conveyances, Honolulu, Hawai'i, Lien for Improving Insanitary Land in Honolulu, Book 1018, p. 79. This lien reads as follows: "Under and in accordance with Chapter 75 of the Revised Laws of Hawaii 1925, and amendments thereto, notice is hereby given to all whom it may concern, that the Territory of Hawaii claims a lien to the following described lands, to wit: All those certain pieces or parcels of land situated a little Westerly from the junction of Kapahulu Road and Kimo Avenue and on the north side of the Territorial Fair Grounds at Kalualohe, Hamohamo, Hooulu and

Kamookahi, at Waikiki. ... Being a portion of Grant 2615 to Kahaloipua ... the whole of R.P. 5588, L.C.A. 8452, Apana 3, Section 2 to A. Keohokalole...."

55. Bureau of Conveyances, Honolulu, Hawai'i, Deed, Judd & Bishop Trust Company to Territory of Hawaii, March 20, 1935, Book 1273, p. 280.

56. Oral Histories Project, Social Science Research Institute, University of Hawai'i, "Waikiki 1900–1985: Oral Histories, Volume III" (University of Hawai'i, Mānoa, June 1985).

57. Donna Haraway, "The Promises of Monsters: A Regenerative Politics For Inappropriate/d Others," in *Cultural Studies*, ed. Lawrence Grossberg et al. (New York: Routledge, 1992), 295.

58. From Michel Foucault's *The Order of Things* and the analysis of labor and its changing discursive organization, as noted in *Michel Foucault: Beyond Structuralism and Hermeneutics*, ed. Hubert L. Dreyfus and Paul Rabinow (Chicago: University of Chicago Press, 1982), 7.

59. George Chaney, *Aloha! A Hawaiian Salutation* (Boston: Roberts Brothers, 1880), 26, as noted in Barry Nakamura, "The Story of Waikiki and the "Reclamation" Project" (master's thesis, University of Hawai'i, Mānoa, 1979).

60. Historic events as recounted in Kanahele's *Waikiki: 100 BC to 1900 AD*.

61. Nakamura.

62. Kai White and Jim Kraus, *Waikīkī: Images of America* (Chicago: Arcadia Publishing, 2007), 69–71.

63. Hawaii Republic Laws, Statutes, etc., *Laws of the Republic of Hawaii Passed by the Legislature at Its Session*, 1896: 201–4, quoted in Nakamura, 17.

64. Nakamura, 44.

65. Gaye Chan and Andrea Feeser, *Waikīkī: A History of Forgetting and Remembering* (Honolulu: University of Hawai'i Press, 2006), 28–29.

66. Chan and Feeser, 29.

67. Chan and Feeser, 29–30.

68. White and Kraus, 72.

69. The Hawaiian Kingdom adopted laws regarding eminent domain previously in *Principles Adopted by the Board of Commissioners to Quiet Land Titles* in 1846. Specifically, the following three principles support the power of the state to take land: "3rd: To encourage and even enforce the usufruct of lands for the common good. 4th: To provide public thoroughfares and easements, by means of roads, bridges, streets, &c., for the common good. 5th: To resume certain lands upon just compensation assessed, if for any cause the public good or the social safety requires it." hawaiiankingdom.org/land-system. In the United States, the right to own land is protected by the Fourteenth Amendment of the U.S. Constitution, and governed by the legal terms of the Fifth Amendment: "The Fifth Amendment to the United States Constitution states that private land can be taken for 'public use,'" with just compensation, by a governing body. However, every part of the preceding sentence can be challenged and dissected, and every part can be shown to be not factual based on legal precedent. At face value, some basic questions arise with regard to the Fifth Amendment: "What constitutes public

use? Is physical use by the public required or is a public purpose sufficient? Is every physical invasion by the public a taking or can some be excused by public need? How is property defined? Who defines it? Is a regulation that diminishes the value of property a taking? If so, how much diminution is necessary? What is just compensation?" David L. Callies, Robert H. Freilich, and Thomas E. Roberts, *Cases and Materials on Land Use*, 3rd ed. (Minneapolis: West Group Publishing Co., 1999), 255. And, who constitutes the public? The term "the public" is problematized by undoing assumed hegemonic cohesion.

70. Nakamura, 104.

71. Subject/citizen binaries are best addressed by Foucault and others, such as Mitchell, who highlight Foucault: "[Disciplinary power] produces, within such institutions, the modern individual, constructed as an isolated, disciplined, receptive, and industrious political subject." Timothy Mitchell, *Colonising Egypt* (Berkeley: University of California Press, 1988), xi.

72. From *Building a Greater Hawaii*, quoted in Nakamura, 110.

73. Sydney L. Iaukea, "Camera Ready: Narration through Photography in Hawai'i," In *Narratives of Citizenship: Indigenous and Diasporic Peoples Unsettle the Nation-State*, ed. Aloys N. M. Fleischmann and Nancy Van Styvendale (Edmonton: University of Alberta Press, 2011), 292–317.

74. "Feminized, the islands and the people were and continue to be reinscribed with meanings according to the needs of the eighteenth and nineteenth century colonialists and the present day military." Kathy Ferguson and Phyllis Turnbull, *Oh, Say, Can You See? The Semiotics of the Military in Hawai'i* (Minneapolis: University of Minnesota Press, 1999), 15.

75. Chan and Feeser, 25.

EPILOGUE

1. Lilikala Kame'eleihiwa, communication at private gathering, 2010.

BIBLIOGRAPHY

Alexander, W. D. *A Brief History of Land Titles in the Hawaiian Kingdom*. Interior Department, Appendix 1, Surveyor General's Report. Honolulu: P.C. Advertiser Co. Steam Print, 1882.

Ames, Roger T. "The Kumulipo Creation Chant," in Kumulipo: Hawaiian Hymn of Creation, Visual Perspectives by Joseph Feher, An Interpretive Exhibit, Honolulu, Hawai'i, 1988.

Anderson, Benedict. *Imagined Communities: Reflections on the Origin and Spread of Nationalism*. New York: Verso, [1983] 1991.

Basso, Keith. *Wisdom Sits in Places: Landscape and Language Among the Western Apache*. Albuquerque: University of New Mexico Press, 1996.

Beamer, Kamana. "'Na wai ka mana? 'Ōiwi Agency and European Imperialism in the Hawaiian Kingdom." Ph.D. diss., University of Hawai'i, Mānoa, 2008.

Beamer, Kamana Maikalani, and T. Kaeo Duarte. "I palapala no ia aina—Documenting the Hawaiian Kingdom; A Colonial Venture?" *Journal of Historical Geography* 35 (2009): 66–86.

Beckwith, Martha Warren. *The Kumulipo: A Hawaiian Creation Chant*. Honolulu: University of Hawai'i Press, 1984.

Braun, Bruce. *The Intemperate Rainforest: Nature, Culture, and Power on Canada's West Coast*. Minneapolis: University of Minnesota Press, 2002.

Bureau of Conveyances, Honolulu, Hawai'i. Deed, Curtis P. Iaukea to William Woon. Book 639, pp. 233–34.

———. Deed, Judd & Bishop Trust Company to Territory of Hawaii, March 20, 1935. Book 1273, p. 280.

———. Deed, William Woon to Charlotte Iaukea. Book 639, p. 235.

———. Helu 2615, Palapala Sila Nui, Kuleana Helu 128. Land Grant 2615, April 1856.

———. Land Commission Award No. 10364, Apana 2. Recorded in Liber 183, p. 419.

———. Lien for Improving Insanitary Land in Honolulu. Lyman H. Bigelow, Superintendent of Public Works, Territory of Hawaii, July 12, 1929. Book 1018, pp. 79–82.

————. Lien for Improving Insanitary Land in Honolulu to Mrs. Charlotte K. Iaukea by Supt. Pub. Wks. Book 1370, p. 387.

————. *Queen Liliuokalani Trust Deed, 1909.* Book 319, pp. 369–77.

————. *Queen Liliuokalani Trust Deed, April 20, 1910.* Book 335, pp. 8–10.

————. *Queen Liliuokalani Trust Deed, Amendments.* October 11, 1911.

————. *Queen Liliuokalani Trust Deed, Amendments.* September 2, 1915.

————. *Queen Liliuokalani Trust Deed, December 2, 1909.* Book 319, pp. 447–59.

————. Royal Patent Grant 3424, Kamanaiki Valley. No. 93.

————. Tax Maps Branch History Sheet, Tax Map #2-6-26-3.

————. Trust Deed, Charlotte K. Iaukea to Albert F. Judd et al. Trs. Book 805, pp. 312–17.

Cajete, Gregory. *Native Science: Natural Laws of Interdependence.* Santa Fe, NM: Clear Light Publishers, 2000.

Callies, David L., Robert H. Freilich, and Thomas E. Roberts. *Cases and Materials on Land Use.* 3rd ed. Minneapolis: West Group Publishing Co., 1999.

Carmichael, David L., et al. *Sacred Sites, Sacred Places.* New York: Routledge, 1994.

Carter, Paul. *The Road to Botany Bay: An Exploration of Landscape and History.* London: Faber and Faber Limited, 1987.

Cerwonka, Allaine. *Native to the Nation: Disciplining Landscapes and Bodies in Australia.* Minneapolis: University of Minnesota Press, 2004.

Chan, Gaye, and Andrea Feeser. *Waikīkī: A History of Forgetting and Remembering.* Honolulu: University of Hawai'i Press, 2006.

Chaney, George. *Aloha! A Hawaiian Salutation.* Boston: Roberts Brothers, 1880.

Chinen, Jon. *The Great Mahele: Hawaii's Land Division of 1848.* Honolulu: University of Hawai'i Press, 1958.

Cosgrove, Denis. *Social Formation and Symbolic Landscape.* Madison: University of Wisconsin Press, 1984.

Daily Pacific Advertiser. "The Kalihi Insane Asylum." January 13, 1883.

Duncan, James. *The City As Text: The Politics of Landscape Interpretation in the Kandyan Kingdom.* New York: Cambridge University Press, 1990.

Ferguson, Kathy, and Phyllis Turnbull. *Oh, Say, Can You See? The Semiotics of the Military in Hawai'i.* Minneapolis: University of Minnesota Press, 1999.

Foucault, Michel. "About the Concept of the 'Dangerous Individual' in 19th Century Legal Psychiatry." *International Journal of Law and Psychiatry* 1 (1978): 1–18.

————. *Discipline and Punish: The Birth of the Prison.* New York: Pantheon Books, 1977.

————. *Madness and Civilization: A History of Insanity in the Age of Reason.* New York: Vintage Books, 1988.

————. *Michel Foucault: Beyond Structuralism and Hermeneutics.* Edited by Hubert L. Dreyfus and Paul Rabinow. Chicago: University of Chicago Press, 1982.

————. *The Order of Things: An Archaeology of the Human Sciences.* New York: Vintage Books, 1994.

————. *Power/Knowledge: Selected Interviews and Other Writings, 1972–1977.* Edited by Colin Gordon. New York: Pantheon Books, 1981.

————. "Truth and Method." In *The Foucault Reader*, edited by Paul Rabinow, 31–120. New York: Pantheon Books, 1984.

"Free Tibet? What About Free Hawai'i?!" http.//coconutgirlwireless.wordpress.com/2007/05/06/free-tibet-what-about-free-hawaii/.

Geertz, Clifford. "Deep Play: Notes on the Balinese Cockfight." In *Interpretive Social Science: A Second Look*, 195–240. Berkeley: University of California Press, 1979.

Geesaman, Lynn, and Jamaica Kincaid. *Poetics of Place*. New York: Umbrage Editions, 1998.

Ghosh, Amitav. *The Glass Palace: A Novel* New York: Random House, 2002.

Gramsci, Antonio. *Selections from the Prison Notebooks*. Edited by Quentin Hoare and Geoffrey Nowell Smith, India: Orient Longman, 1971

Gregory, Derek. *Geographical Imaginations*. Oxford: Blackwell Publishers, 1994.

Hall, Stuart. *Representation: Cultural Representations and Signifying Practices*. London: Sage Publications, 2003.

Halualani, Rona Tamiko. *In The Name of Hawaiians: Native Identities and Cultural Politics*. Minneapolis: University of Minnesota Press, 2002.

Haraway, Donna. "The Promises of Monsters: A Regenerative Politics for Inappropriate/d Others." In *Cultural Studies*, edited by Lawrence Grossberg, Cary Nelson, and Paula Treichler, 295–337. New York: Routledge, 1992.

Harris, Cole. "How Did Colonialism Dispossess? Comments from an Edge of Empire." *Annals of the Association of American Geographers* 94 (1) (2004): 165–82.

Hawaii Hochi. "A Great Man Passes." March 7, 1940.

"Hawaii Organic Act: Congressional Debates on Hawaii Organic Act." http://libweb.hawaii.edu/digicoll/annexation/organic.html.

Hawaii Republic Laws, Statutes, etc. *Laws of the Republic of Hawaii Passed by the Legislature at Its Session*, 1896: 201–4.

Hawaii Session Laws, 1862. *Act to Establish an Insane Asylum*, 31–32. KFH25 .A24 1862. c.2. Hawai'i State Archives, Honolulu, Hawai'i.

Hawaii Session Laws, 1893–1894. KFH 25.A25 1894 c.2. Hawai'i State Archives, Honolulu, Hawai'i.

Hawaiian Gazette. "Establishment at Palama Prepared to Receive Patients." August 25, 1866.

————. "The Insane Asylum! A Thorough Investigation, Report of the Commission, Excellent Recommendations!" October 4, 1887.

————. "Lunatic Asylum." August 25, 1866.

Hawaiian Kingdom. *Civil Code*, CHAPTER XXXIII.§1463. Hawai'i State Archives, Honolulu, Hawai'i.

————. *Fundamental Law of Hawaii*, 1840–1900, REF 342T4. Hawai'i State Archives, Honolulu, Hawai'i.

Hawaiian Kingdom, Interior Department. Book 12. April 5, 1873. Hawai'i State Archives, Honolulu, Hawai'i.

————. Book 13. August 11, 1875 & July 12, 1875. Hawai'i State Archives, Honolulu, Hawai'i.

————. Book 32. October 25, 1887. Hawaiʻi State Archives, Honolulu, Hawaiʻi.

————. Book 38. May 22, 1889. Hawaiʻi State Archives, Honolulu, Hawaiʻi.

————. *Letter of Appointment.* Book 32, p. 253. October 25, 1887. Hawaiʻi State Archives, Honolulu, Hawaiʻi.

————. *Letter to Appoint.* Book 32, p. 262, October 25, 1887. Hawaiʻi State Archives, Honolulu, Hawaiʻi.

Hawaiian Kingdom, Office of the Regent. *An Historical Overview of the Events Surrounding the Great Māhele.* Vol. 2. Honolulu, Hawaiʻi, Dec. 1998.

Honolulu Advertiser. "History from Our Files." September 18, 1948.

————. "Kuhio Beach Park Named for Prince Who Served Hawaii." October 31, 2004.

————. "Territory Acquires Washington Place; Governors Residence, Judge Franklin Grants Decree of Condemnation and Sets Value of Property at $55,000." May 12, 1921.

————. "Washington Place." April 23, 1922.

————. "Washington Place, Former Home of Last Queen of Hawaii, Ready for Governor about March." March 12, 1922.

————. "Washington Place Title Secured in Land Court." October 27, 1920.

Honolulu Board of Water Supply. *Oʻahu Water Plan.* Honolulu: Honolulu Board of Water Supply, 1982.

Iaukea Collection, M-70. Hawaiʻi State Archives, Honolulu, Hawaiʻi.

————. Box 1–1.

————. Box 1–9, Scrapbook, Campaign Folder.

————. Box 2–7, Historical Notes on Hawaiʻi.

————. Box 2–8, "Historical Notes and Articles, n.d., 1845–1888."

————. C. P. Iaukea. "Col. Iaukea's Letter to the *Advertiser.*" *Honolulu Advertiser,* June 1922, Box 1-9 (l).

————. C. P. Iaukea. "Wise or Jarrett for Delegate? Which? A Reply to Lorrin A. Thurston's Analysis." *Pacific Commercial Advertiser,* June 1922. Box 1–9, Scrapbook, Campaign Folder.

————. "The Colonel on Party Harmony." *Pacific Commercial Advertiser,* June 1922. Box 1–9, Scrapbook, Campaign Folder.

————. "Curtis P. Iaukea 'Runs Amuck' on Lorrin A. Thurston, Challenges Him to a 'Fight to a Finish!'" *Pacific Commercial Advertiser,* October 16, 1922. Box 1–9, Scrapbook, Campaign Folder.

————. "Fantasy and a Dream." Box 2-8, "Historical Notes and Articles, n.d., 1845–1888."

————. Lorrin A. Thurston. "Fight to a Finish: A Reply to C. P. Iaukea's Charges against Wise." *Honolulu Advertiser,* June 1922. Box 1–9 (g).

————. "Wise or Jarrett for Delegate?" *Honolulu Advertiser,* June 1922. Box 1–9 (g).

————. Lorrin Thurston, "Wise or Jarrett for Delegate? Seventh and Final Installment of Reply to Charges by Iaukea against John Wise." *Honolulu Advertiser,* June 1922. Box 1–9 (k).

———. Lorrin A. Thurston. "Wise or Jarrett for Delegate? Which? Sixth Installment of Reply to Charges by Iaukea against John Wise." *Honolulu Advertiser*, June 1922. Box 1–9 (k).

———. "Prince Kalanianaole and the Kealohilani Premises." Box 1–7.

———. "Trust Deed of Liliuokalani, 1897–1915." Box 1–8.

———. "Wise for Big Business." Box 1–9.

Iaukea Collection, U-33. Hawai'i State Archives, Honolulu, Hawai'i.

———. "Believe It or Not, by Ripley (Reg. U.S. Pat. Off.)" *Honolulu Star Bulletin*.

———. "Comments from E. W. Miller to John Balch, President of the Mutual Telephone Company in Hawaii."

———. "The Contest over the Queen's Deed of Trust, From My Diary of 1918."

———. "Iaukea to Speak at Visitors' Club: To Give Reminiscences of Monarchy Days." *Honolulu Advertiser*, March 23, 1937.

———. "The Late Queen Liliuokalani's Deed of Trust with Her Last Will and Testament—And Revelations behind the Scene."

———. "The 'Lele of Hamohamo' and the Attempt to Deprive of It."

———. Letter Diaries. December 30, 1909, to July 26, 1911.

———. Letter from Queen Liliuokalani to Curtis P. Iaukea on 2/10/1910.

———. Letters to and from Castle and Withington, Attorneys and Counsellors at Law to Trustees, Queen Liliuokalani Estate. May–June 1918.

———. Managing Trustee Diary of Letters. December 30, 1909, to July 26, 1911.

———. "Prince Kalanianaole and the Kealohilani Premises."

Iaukea, Curtis P. *Commissioners of Crown Lands, Biennial Report, 1894.* Honolulu: Hawaiian Gazette Company, 1894.

Iaukea, Curtis Piehu, and Lorna Kahilipuaokalani Iaukea Watson. *By Royal Command: Biographical Notes on Curtis Piehu Iaukea.* Edited by Niklaus Schweizer. Honolulu: Hui Hanai, 1988.

Iaukea, Sydney L. "Camera Ready: Narration through Photography in Hawai'i." In *Narratives of Citizenship: Indigenous and Diasporic Peoples Unsettle the Nation-State*, edited by Aloys N. M. Fleischmann and Nancy Van Styvendale, 292–317. Edmonton: University of Alberta Press, 2011.

———. "Land Agendas vis à vis Wind Discourse: Deconstructing Space/Place Political Agendas in Hawai'i and the Pacific." *Pacific Studies: A Journal Devoted to the Study of the Pacific Islands* 32 (1) (March 2009): 48–72.

In the Circuit Court of the First Judicial Circuit, Territory of Hawaii. *Affidavit in Support of Motion to Dismiss, Bill for Cancellation of Deeds.* December 30, 1915.

———. *Assertion of Mental Competency, Bill for Cancellation of Deeds.* February 8, 1916.

———. *Bill for Cancellation of Deeds, Memorandum of Points and Authorities on Behalf of Liliuokalani.* January 25, 1916.

———. *Bill of Complaint.* November 15, 1915.

———. *Bill of Revivor and Supplement.* January 22, 1916.

———. *Decision, Bill for Cancellation of Deeds.* 1916.

————. *Discontinuance and Motion to Dismiss, Bill for Cancellation of Deeds*. December 10, 1915.

————. *E. 2009, Liliuokalani, et al. vs. Curtis P. Iaukea, et al. For Cancellation of Trust Deed*. 1915.

————. *Final Order of Condemnation*. August 21, 1940. Book 1611, p. 17.

————. *Iaukea Court Documents*. January 17, 1916.

————. *Judgment, Eminent Domain, Territory of Hawaii vs. Albert F. Judd, et al*. February 27, 1936. Book 1611, p. 4.

————. *Memorandum of Points and Authorities on Behalf of Liliuokalani, Bill for Cancellation of Deeds*. January 26, 1916.

————. *Memorandum, Re Liliuokalani by Her Next Friend J. K. Kalanianaole, and Kalanianaole versus C. P. Iaukea et al. Trustees*. December 4, 1915.

————. *Partial Report of Guardian Ad Litem and Next Friend of Liliuokalani, in Chambers*. March 29, 1916.

————. *Probate 5324, In the Matter of the Estate of Lydia K. Dominis, Also Known as Liliuokalani*. June 27, 1918.

————. *Statement of C. P. Iaukea*. 1916.

————. *Suggestion of Disqualification of Jonah Kuhio Kalanianaole as Next Friend of Liliuokalani, and Motion for His Removal as Next Friend*. January 17, 1916.

————. *Testimony of A. S. Humphreys before the Honorable William L. Whitney, Second Judge Thereof, at Chambers*.

————. *W. O. Smith's Memoranda Re Liliuokalani Trust Deed*. February 23, 1910.

————. *W. O. Smith's Testimony, Before the Honorable Whitney, Honolulu, Hawaii*. July 6, 1916.

Johnson, Rubellite Kawena. *The Kumulipo: Hawaiian Hymn of Creation*. Honolulu: Topgallant Publishing Co. Ltd., 1981.

Kamakau, Samuel. *Tales and Traditions of the People of Old: Nā Moʻolelo a ka Poʻe Kahiko*. Honolulu: Bishop Museum Press, 1991.

Kameʻeleihiwa, Lilikalā. *Nā Wāhine Kapu: Divine Hawaiian Women*. Honolulu: ʻAi Pōhaku Press, 1999.

Kanahele, George Huʻeu Sanford. *Kū Kanaka Stand Tall: A Search For Hawaiian Values*. Honolulu: University of Hawaiʻi Press, 1986.

————. *Waikiki: 100 BC to 1900 AD*. Honolulu: University of Hawaiʻi Press, 1995.

Kauanui, J. Kēhaulani. *Hawaiian Blood: Colonialism and the Politics of Sovereignty and Indigeneity*. Durham, NC: Duke University Press, 2008.

Kent, Noel. *Hawaiʻi: Islands under the Influence*. 1983. Honolulu: University of Hawaiʻi Press, 1993.

Kincaid, Jamaica. *The Autobiography of My Mother*. New York: Farrar, Straus, Giroux, 1996.

Kundera, Milan. *Ignorance: A Novel*. New York: Harper Collins, 2000.

"Lance Paul Larsen vs. the Hawaiian Kingdom." *Permanent Court of Arbitration, The Hague 68*. www.alohaquest.com/arbitration/memorial_government.htm.

Liliuokalani. *Hawaii's Story by Hawaii's Queen*. Honolulu: Mutual Publishing, [1898] 1990.

———. *The Kumulipo: An Hawaiian Creation Myth.* Kentfield, CA: Pueo Press, 1978.

MacKenzie, Melody Kapilialoha "Historical Background." In *Native Hawaiian Rights Handbook,* edited by Melody Kapilialoha MacKenzie, 3–25. Honolulu: Native Hawaiian Legal Corporation, 1991.

McKinzie, Edith. "The Kumulipo" in Kumulipo: Hawaiian Hymn of Creation, Visual Perspectives by Joseph Feher, An Interpretive Exhibit. Honolulu, Hawaiʻi, 1988.

Mitchell, Timothy. *Colonising Egypt.* Berkeley: University of California Press, 1988.

Murakami, Alan. "The Hawaiian Homes Commission Act." In *Native Hawaiian Rights Handbook,* edited by Melody Kapilialoha Mackenzie, 43–76. Honolulu: Native Hawaiian Legal Corporation, 1991.

Nakamura, Barry. "The Story of Waikiki and the 'Reclamation' Project." Master's thesis, University of Hawaiʻi, 1979.

Nā Kūʻauhau ʻO Kahiwakāneikopōlei. Newsletter for the Grand Convention, Hilo, Hawaiʻi, 2010.

Naughton, Momi. "Introduction" in Kumulipo: Hawaiian Hymn of Creation, Visual Perspectives by Joseph Feher, An Interpretive Exhibit. Honolulu, Hawaiʻi, 1988.

Nora, Pierre. "Between Memory and History: Les Lieux de Memoire." *Representations* 26 (Spring 1989): 7–25.

Oral Histories Project, Social Science Research Institute, University of Hawaiʻi. "Waikiki 1900–1985: Oral Histories, Volume III." University of Hawaiʻi, Mānoa, June 1985.

Pacific Commercial Advertiser. "Insane Asylum." February 4, 1864.

———. "Kuhio's Suits Are All Withdrawn." June 22, 1918.

———. "Washington Place: Where Hawaii's Queen Has Lived Half a Century." August 25, 1912.

Preza, Donovan. "The Empirical Writes Back: Re-examining Hawaiian Dispossession Resulting from the Māhele of 1848." Master's thesis, University of Hawaiʻi, Mānoa, 2010.

Pukui, Mary Kawena, and Samuel H. Elbert. *Hawaiian Dictionary.* Honolulu: University of Hawaiʻi Press, [1957] 1986.

Pukui, Mary Kawena, Samuel H. Elbert, and Ester Mookini. *Place Names of Hawaiʻi.* Honolulu: University of Hawaiʻi Press, 1974.

Pukui, Mary Kawena, E. W. Haertig, and Catherine Lee. *Nānā I Ke Kumu: Look to the Source.* Vols. 1 and 2. Honolulu: Hui Hanai, 1972.

Queen Liliʻuokalani Children's Center, Archives. Kalihi, Hawaiʻi.

———, "Queen Liliʻuokalani Trust, 2008 Annual Report." www.glcc.org/glcc2008.pdf.

Queen Liliʻuokalani Collection, M-93. Hawaiʻi State Archives, Honolulu, Hawaiʻi.

———. *Anti-annexation Protest Documents—Liliuokalani to William McKinley (US President),* June 17, 1897.

———. Folder 22.

———. Letter from Prince Kuhio Kalanianaole While Serving on the Sixtieth Congress in the House of Representatives in Washington, D.C., to Queen Liliuokalani.

———. Petition to President-elect William H. Taft. Folder 1.

————. Power of Attorney. Liber 321, pp. 261–62.

————. Protest against the Taking of Crown Lands.

————. "The Trees and Plants of 'Washington Place.'"

————. Will, 1915.

Sai, Keanu. "The American Occupation of the Hawaiian Kingdom: Beginning the Transition from Occupied to Restored State." Ph.D. diss., University of Hawai'i, Mānoa, 2008.

Scheckel, Susan. *The Insistence of the Indian: Race and Nationalism in Nineteenth-Century American Culture.* Princeton, NJ: Princeton University Press, 1998.

Schein, Richard H. "Teaching 'Race' and the Cultural Landscape." *Journal of Geography* 98 (4) (1998): 188–90.

Schweizer, Niklaus. *Turning Tide: The Ebb and Flow of Hawaiian Nationality.* Bern: Peter Lang, 1999.

Scott, James C. *Seeing Like a State: How Certain Schemes to Improve the Human Condition Have Failed.* New Haven, CT: Yale University Press, 1998.

Singer, Joseph. *Property and Values: Alternatives to Public and Private Ownership.* Washington: Island Press, 2000.

Sinha, Rakesh. "In Burma, Bahadur Shah Zafar Is an Emperor-Saint." *Indian Express.* www.rebound88net/sp/ngb/siniall.html.

Star Bulletin. "Documents Christening of Royal Home in 1848 Preserved." June 11, 1918.

Territorial Government of Hawaii. Senate Bill #68, March 1937, Section 1, regarding "A Territorial Pension for Curtis P. Iaukea."

Territory of Hawaii. *The Organic Act: Legal Periodicals, Historical Note.* April 30, 1900. C339, 31 Stat 141.

————. *Territorial Pension,* Act 43, "Making Appropriations for the Benefit of Queen Liliuokalani." March 30, 1911.

Tuan, Yi-Fu. *Space and Place: The Perspective of Experience.* Minneapolis: University of Minnesota Press, 1977.

Turnbull, David. *Masons, Tricksters, and Cartographers: Comparative Studies in the Sociology of Scientific and Indigenous Knowledge.* New York: Routledge, 2000.

"An Uncommon History-Case Lombardi & Pettit, A Law Corporation-Honolulu, Hawaii." www.caselombardi.com/aboutHistory.aspx.

University of Hawai'i, Special Collections Library. *Anti-annexation Protest Documents—Liliuokalani to William McKinley (U.S. President),* June 17, 1897.

U.S. Congress. *An Act to Provide for a Government for the Territory of Hawaii.* Ch. 339, 31 Stat. 141 (1900).

————. "Hawaiian Homes Commission Act, 1920." Title 2. Hawaiian Homes Commission, Sec. 201 (7).

————. *The Hawaiian Homes Program, 1920–1963.* Legislative Reference Bureau Report, No. 1, 1969.

————. Joint Resolution of Annexation, July 7, 1898. 30 Stat. 750.

U.S. Court of Claims. *Complaint, Liliuokalani v. the United States of America.* November 20, 1909. Ref HD243.H3 L55 1909.

————. *Decision, Liliuokalani v. the United States of America.* May 16, 1910.

————. *Opinion of the Court; Supplement to the Complaint Filed by Ex-Queen Liliuokalani.* November 20, 1909.

U.S. National Archives & Records Administration. *Guide to the Records of the U.S. House of Representatives at the National Archives, 1789–1989.* Record Group 223, Chapter 6, Records of the Claims Committees. www.archives.gov/legislative/guide/house/chapter-06-claims.html.

White, Kai, and Jim Kraus. *Waikīkī: Images of America.* Chicago: Arcadia Publishing, 2007.

Wiegel, Robert L. *Report UCB/HEL 2002–1.* University of California, Berkeley, Hydraulic Engineering Laboratory. November 15, 2002.

INDEX

aboriginal Hawaiians, 56–57, 74, 156. *See also* native Hawaiians

Admission Act (1959), 49

Aea, Joseph Kaiponohea, 64, 72, 75, 90–91, 106, 117, 154–55, 177n8, 187n8

ahupua'a, 16, 24–25

Aimoku, John Dominis. *See* Dominis, John Aimoku

'āina, 1, 7–8, 63, 144. *See also* the land and charges of Queen's mental incompetence, 88, 110, 114; and native Hawaiians, 56–60, 144; ownership of, 14, 17–18, 20–21, 24, 26–27, 41, 131–32, 139–40

akakū, 109

Aki, 155

'aki'aki, 120

akua, 8, 38, 98, 109, 183n16

alahe'e, 120

Ala Wai Canal, 9, 21, 120–21, 132–38, 140, 139*fig.*

Alexander & Baldwin, 50

Alexander III, Czar of Russia, 4, 28, 33–34

ali'i, 1, 4, 8, 27, 114, 144. *See also names of kings, queens, chiefs;* and Iaukea, Curtis Piehu, 19, 36, 44, 58, 97; and Kumulipo, 37; and land legislation, 40, 48–49, 59, 68, 76, 79; and Lele of Hamohamo, 119, 136; in *mo'o kū'auhau*, 38; and Washington Place, 129

Ali'i Nui, 38, 136

American dream, 180n35

American Factors, 50

Americanisation, 56, 176n50

Ames, Roger T., 37

Anaole, 154–55

ancestors, 1, 7–8, 13, 38, 107, 171n4. *See also*

kūpuna; names of ancestors; and land ownership, 15, 17, 26–27, 32–33

Anderson, Benedict, 176n54

Andrews, Lorrin, 97, 102, 183–84n27

Auld, Mary, 155

The Autobiography of My Mother (Kincaid), 27

Awawaloa, 120

Balch, John, 29

Beamer, Kamanamaikalani, 25–26, 48

Beckley, Fred, 70

Bigelow, Lyman H., 129

bill of complaint (1915–1918), 7, 69, 87–89, 93–104, 109, 115–18, 120, 123, 126–27, 130, 177n7, 181n1, 182n11, 183n14, 187nn6,8

Bishop, Charles R., 105

Bishop Museum, 90

Bishop Trust Company, 21, 133

blood quantum, 43, 55–59

body, 14, 39, 61, 173n44, 186n71

boundaries, 24–26, 79

Brown, Cecil, 72, 89, 161

Brown, J. F., 41

Browne, Sean, 189n41

Building a Greater Waikiki, 137–38

Bureau of Conveyances (Honolulu), 14, 18, 23, 26, 92, 134

Burma, 113–14, 186n67

By Royal Command (Watson), 12, 171n4

capitalism, 7, 17, 24–25, 39, 47, 56, 60–61, 110, 114, 139–40, 144; yeoman capitalism, 44, 52–53

Carter, George R., 150

Carter, J. O., 82, 113, 179n26

TEXT
10.5/14 Jenson
DISPLAY
Jenson
COMPOSITOR
Integrated Composition Systems
INDEXER
Sharon Sweeney
CARTOGRAPHER
Bill Nelson
PRINTER AND BINDER
IBT Global